KV-219-276

Poverty and Poor Relief:
Concepts and Reality

SEAN STITT

Centre for Consumer Education and Research
Liverpool John Moores' University

Avebury

Aldershot · Brookfield USA · Hong Kong · Singapore · Sydney

© S. Stitt 1994

All rights reserved. No part of this publication may be reproduced, stored in a retrieval system, or transmitted in any form or by any means, electronic, mechanical, photocopying, recording or otherwise without the prior permission of the publisher.

Published by
Avebury
Ashgate Publishing Company
Gower House
Croft Road
Aldershot
Hants GU11 3HR

Ashgate Publishing Company
Old Post Road
Brookfield
Vermont 05036
USA

British Library Cataloguing in Publication Data
Stitt, Sean
 Poverty and Poor Relief: Concepts and
 Reality
 I. Title
 362.580941
ISBN 1 85628 684 3

Library of Congress Cataloging-in-Publication Data
Stitt, Sean, 1952–
 Poverty and poor relief : concepts and reality / Sean Stitt.
     p. cm
 Includes bibliographical references.
 ISBN 1-85628-684-3 : £35..00 ($59.95 U.S. : est.)
 1. Poverty--Great Britain. 2. Poor--Great Britain. 3. Public
welfare--Great Britain. 4. Economic assistance, Domestic--Great
Britain. I. Title
 HC256.6.Z9P67   1994
 362.5'8'0941--dc20   94-163587
                                                             CIP

Printed and Bound in Great Britain by
Athenaeum Press Ltd, Newcastle upon Tyne.

Contents

Acknowledgements

A vast array of individuals and groups deserve to be acknowledged for their contribution to the production of this book. Unfortunately, I will, of course, fail to mention key figures. To those 'unknown soldiers', I apologise and now pay tribute.

Professor Jennifer Latto and Dr Jenny Peel deserve special illumination because of their support, encouragement and facilitation; as do, Dr Anne Miller, Dr Allan Hackett and Margaret Jepson for allowing me to neglect and covering for my teaching/administrative duties during the preparation of this book. I full appreciate the flexibility awarded to me by the institution of John Moores University and the Centre for Consumer Education & Research at the I M Marsh campus, for carrying out this academic exercise, particularly at a time when economic considerations seem to take primacy over professional academic pursuits. I regard this as an indication of LJMU's commitment to academic professionalism. My special warmth in this respect goes to Elaine Prisk.

Particular mention of commendation is due to Marian Lewis, Denise McKinlay and Mary Harris for their tolerance and hard work in finalising this camera-ready copy.

Diane Grant carried out the research which underpinned the final section of this book and deserves special acknowledgement in her own right as a leading expert in the scientific definition of poverty in Britain in the 1990s. Diane has been financially supported in her research by Kwik Save plc.

For academic, theoretical and practical guidance, it would be preposterous to complete a book which centres on Rowntree's research on poverty without the mention of Professor John Viet Wilson of the University of Newcastle upon Tyne. Thanks again John.

And finally, and most importantly, thanks to all those households on Merseyside who showed courage, principle, self respect, dignity and awareness in participating in the research. The sole motivation for academic activity in social science should be to provide support and advocacy for the most vulnerable people in society. I hope that this book meets that requirement. For this belief, I acknowledge the influence of Bob Holman, David Piachaud and, of course, my friend and colleague, John Veit Wilson.

Introduction

The scene at Lime Street Station, Liverpool, around midnight on a bone-numbing Sunday had the time-warped feel of an old newsreel; a long line of shabbily-dressed men shuffling and stamping against the cold, stirring jerky black-and-white memories of civil upheaval, a stream of refugees. But these people are refugees, refugees from joblessness, making their weekly way to work in a place where they cannot afford to live, London. These people work mostly in London's ever-lively building industry (sic. - own addition); a few work below stairs in the capital's hotels and restaurants. During the week they squat, live in huts on site or sleep in bed and breakfast joints in the East End and the inner suburbs. On Friday night, they take the train back to Liverpool for two days with their families before returning on the cheap fare midnight mail train. (Nevin C, 1987, *'Scousers: Doing the South's Dirty Work'*)

The regionalist flavour to this image of poverty in Britain in the 1990s is no longer valid. Poverty is now not merely synonymous with the North or the inner cities, but is a visible feature of life throughout rural and affluent areas. It is sometimes obvious - 'whether it is the poverty of the beggars in the street, young homeless people bedded down for the night under the arches, or people rummaging in rubbish bins'. It is sometimes hidden - 'inside homes, workplaces and institutions' (Oppenheim, 1933, p.2). No confirmation is required of the biblical diktat: 'The poor always ye have with you' (John 12:8) Throughout each stage of history, in every nation on earth, poverty has existed in some shape or form, however defined, from the slaves of the Roman Empire, to the serfs of the Middle Ages, to the peons of Latin America, to the inmates of Britain's workhouses, to the inner city ghetto-dwellers and the forgotten inhabitants of the wind-swept peripheral estates.

1

A 19th century American Right-Wing sociologist, William Graham Summer (1883, pp. 19-20) held that poverty was an indefinable concept as, because of its perilous elasticity, it could cover a plethora of 'social fallacies'. By May 1989, in a paper entitled 'The End of the Line for Poverty', the then Social Services Secretary John Moore, argued that the poverty lobby and academics had 'manipulated statistics' to portray a grossly exaggerated picture of poverty in Britain. Because standards of living had generally improved, he attempted to argue that 'poverty no longer exists'. But this dismissal of the day-to-day experiences of millions of poor families in Britain cannot cloak the reality of the decades of the 1980s and 1990s going down in the annals of the 20th century as the period in which poverty, by whatever definition or measurement, reached unprecedented depths, both in terms of its nature and its extent.

Poverty is, according to Frank Field, Chairman of the Commons Social Security Committee, 'a social anthrax, a killer mix of deep poverty and a breakdown of the conventional family'. (*Observer*, October 3rd 1993, p. 12) He describes the creation of 'social deserts' in the most deprived areas of Britain, like Everton and Vauxhall on Merseyside - Britain's poorest wards -in which '... the silence, at first reassuring, begins to nag. It is a silence born of lack of industry, jobs, cars; the quiet born of the hopeless passivity of poverty from which even the anger has been leached out.' In such places, long term male unemployment runs at around 50 per cent, while car ownership is the lowest in the country, at 10-15 per cent. According to local GPs and health workers, the health problems and mortality rates are comparable with the Third World. Deaths from coronary heart disease and lung disease are almost twice the national average. Before this Introduction launches into a statistical portrait of the extent of poverty in Britain, for decency's sake, it is necessary to caution that statistics alone hid the real scale of the human tragedy of poverty and unemployment. For example, the *Observer* reported in October 1993:

> Patrick Fitzpatrick was a plumber and maintenance worker from the Vauxhall area whose business folded. Depressed and worried by his mounting debts, he got on to the roof of Liverpool's highest residential block, posing as a council worker. His body was later found at the foot of the twenty-one-storey building.

Statistics from this era emerging from the Department of Social Security's (1993) 'Households Below Average Income' publication show that:

- between 1979 and 1990/91, average income overall increased by 35 per cent, but for the poorest 10 per cent, it fell by 14 per cent;

- the 1988/89 figures show a fall of 6 per cent, so the decline has accelerated;

2

- the share of total national income received by the poorest 10 per cent fell from 4 per cent in 1979 to 2.1 per cent in 1990/91 (2.5 per cent in 1988/89);
- in 1979, 9.3 million individuals (17 per cent of total) lived in families which claimed poor relief (means tested benefits) and by 1990/91, this had risen to 12.7 million (23 per cent of total);
- against this appalling vista, at 1993 prices, in 1979, there were less than one quarter of a million people with incomes above £600 per week, and by 1990/91, this had increased to 2.11 million. These data expose the clinical experience behind the belief that the rich get richer while the poor get poorer (and more numerous).

The Manchester-based Campaign Against Poverty (Action Sheet 54, August 1993) offered statistics which compared incomes among the poorest 10 per cent between 1979 and 1990/91 **standardised at 1993 prices**. These show a decrease for single adults from £40 to £34; for childless couples from £72 to £62; for couples with three children from £120 to £104 and; for all households from £72 to £62. These data starkly show how income levels have fallen for the poorest groups since the beginning of the 'Thatcher era'. However, the current situation, in reality, is even worse than the above figures expose because they have not taken account of the impact on the incomes of the poorest caused by the increase in indirect taxes, such as VAT on fuel and other rises. For example, the average weekly fuel bill for one-adult retired households mainly dependent upon state pensions is £9.25 (couples £11.10) - VAT on fuel will cost another 74p in 1994/95 (couples 89p) and £1.62 in 1995/96 (couples £1.94). The amount of compensation offered by the government is 50p in 1994/95 (couples 70p) and £1 in 1995/96 (couples £1.40), leaving a clear decline in income levels. People on poor relief received an extra 0.4 per cent in April 1994 to reflect the expected impact on the Retail Price Index (RPI) of VAT on fuel. The average unemployed household has a weekly fuel bill of £12.46. VAT at 8 per cent would add £1 a week to this bill. Yet a married couple with a child under 11, relying on Income Support, would receive only 37p per week compensation. There is no compensation for low paid workers. And all of this is taking place in a world of fuel poverty in which Lucie and Natalie Godfrey, aged five and thirteen, in the summer of 1992, were killed in a fire at their homes, caused by a candle in their bedrooms. Their mother, an Income Support claimant, was unable to afford to purchase tokens for the family's electricity meter and instead, used candles; in other words, she had disconnected herself and therefore did not appear on any official records as experiencing fuel deprivation. As CPAG (1993, p.6) concluded: 'Her poverty was invisible, unknown and unrecorded by the Electricity Board; the difficulties she endured were hidden, until the fire created this unbearable havoc in her life.'

And who are the people at the wrong end of the income distribution, the

3

0003938439001

poorest tenth of the population? A full 60 per cent of them are in families with children (families with children constitute 44 per cent of the whole population), compared to 50 per cent in 1979; over 24 per cent are in families with one or more people in full time employment; about 17 per cent are pensioners (14 per cent of the whole population are pensioners). The median income for the poorest decile was £70 in 1979: by 1988/89, this had decreased to £66 (prices constant at 1989). The total number of children in the population fell from 13.8 million in 1979 to 12.5 million in 1988/89, but the numbers in households on less than half average income increased from 1.4 to 1.6 million (a rise of 10-13 per cent). The risk of poverty by family status has been estimated by the Child Poverty Action Group (CPAG 1993, p. 3) according to the proportion of each family type living on incomes below half average income, after housing costs. This suggests: pensioner couples, 33 per cent; single pensioners, 42 per cent; couples with children, 19 per cent; couples, 10 per cent; lone parents, 50 per cent; single people, 16 per cent. Children have been more vulnerable to poverty than society as a whole. On the 50 per cent of average income definition of poverty, over three million children have been living in poverty in recent years, over one in four of all our children. Compare this to 1979, when 1.6 million children, or 12 per cent of all children lived in poverty. These figures represent a significant increase in poverty among children since 1979. A National Children's Bureau's (1993) study indicated how this poverty has affected the lives of children, particularly their health:

- the rate of decline in infant mortality slowed down in the 1980s;
- the ratio of infant mortality (deaths in the first year as a proportion of births within marriage) between social classes V and I increased from 1.8 in 1978-79 to 2.0 in 1990;
- there has been strong social class gradients in child mortality and morbidity, and in height and dental health;
- there has been a significant improvement in the take-up of immunisation, dental and ophthalmic services, but these have been lower in the deprived inner city areas and among children in deprived families;
- the rate of GP consultation has tended to be higher if a child's head of household lived in a council house, did not own a car or was a lone parent. (Kumar, V., 1993)

'Low Income Families', according to the lingo of government data publications, are the new poor; the word 'Poverty' seems to have been banished from the government's vocabulary. The argument, in typical Thatcherite logic, suggests that such a 'label' constitutes a slight on the character of honest citizens. Although the present administration instructed the Department of Social Security to stop publicising these statistics from 1985, the independent Institute for Fiscal Studies (IFS), via the House of Commons Social Security Commission, has continued to present them. In 1993/94, an

4

adult couple with two primary school children in receipt of 'low income' would receive £108.75 after housing costs. In 1990, between 11 and 12 million people - almost one in five of the entire population - were living in this type of poverty. (The comparable figure for 1979 was just over 6 million, or 12 per cent of the population). Of these, almost three million - 5 per cent of the population - were living below this poverty line. (Again, the comparable figure for 1979 was just over two million, or 4 per cent of the population). The IFS studies have concluded that the income of the poorest 10 per cent of the households had risen **less**, not **more** (as government ministers have regularly claimed) in comparison to the population as a whole. The present government's contribution to tackling poverty is clear.

It has been a consistent claim of central government throughout the 1980s and 1990s that the average incomes have substantially increased and that 'everyone is better off' because of the 'trickle-down effect'. For a significant slice of the population, this is simply not true. Average incomes did indeed rise by 30 per cent in the 1980s, but the major contributory factor behind this increase was the high rise obtained by those already on high incomes. Consequently, there has been a significant increase in the proportions of people and different family types on less than half average income in the 1980s. Between 1979 and 1989, the poorest 10 per cent of the population saw their real disposable income decrease by 6 per cent (after housing costs), whilst the average increase in income for the population as a whole was 30 per cent. (Central Statistics Office 1992) The increase in the proportions of various family types on less than half average incomes between 1979 and 1989 has been as follows:
- pensioner couples: 21 per cent to 33 per cent;
- single pensioners: 12 per cent to 42 per cent;
- couples with children: 8 per cent to 19 per cent;
- couples without children: 5 per cent to 10 per cent;
- single with children: 19 per cent to 50 per cent;
- single without children: 7 per cent to 16 per cent.

(*Campaign Against Poverty* 1992, p. 2)

In 1979, 9.4 per cent of the population - five million people - were on incomes below half average incomes. By 1983, this had risen to almost 12 per cent of the population - 6.4 million. By 1990/91, this had risen to 24 per cent - 13.5 million people. The corresponding increase for children was from 10 per cent (1.4 million) to 31 per cent (3.9 million). In 1979, 6 per cent of people with below half average income were in households with one or more full-time workers, and 15 per cent with one or more part time workers. By 1990/91, these figures had risen to 25 per cent and 29 per cent respectively. As the Campaign Against Poverty (August 1993, p. 2) point out, 'Even full time work is not a guarantor of evading poverty.' Mrs. Thatcher in May 1988 in the House of Commons stated that 'everyone in the nation has benefited from the increased prosperity'. She was not telling the truth. A cursory examination of official data shows that one in ten households in the 1980s experienced a substantial cut in their real weekly incomes. The Department of Social Security publish figures annually which show the numbers and proportions of families living on incomes below half average income levels. In 1990, a couple with two children aged three and six were living below such a poverty line if they had less than £134 a week after paying for housing costs. On this measurement, in recent years, 10.5 million have been living in poverty - again almost one in five of the entire population (compared to 1979 when 4.9 million, or 9 per cent of the population were living in such poverty). It is possible to take benchmarks from 1979 and uprate them in line with inflation to measure the extent of 'absolute poverty' during this period. This shows that in 1979, 5 million people (9 per cent) were in households with below half the average income, and by 1990/91, the figures were 5.8 million people (10 per cent). In 1979 1.4 million of these were children, but by 1990/91, this had risen to 1.9 million.

On both definitions of poverty - 'absolute', as in receipt of income support, or 'relative', as in relation to a proportion of average incomes - over 10.5 Million people, around one fifth of the population in Britain, have been living in poverty in the 1980s. Of course, different regions of Britain are characterised by varying degrees of unemployment and poverty. In Liverpool, the City Council's Corporate Policy and Information unit carried out 'the Liverpool quality of life survey' in 1989. With 'poverty' defined as being unable to afford three or more socially determined necessities (Mack & Lansley's 1985 and 1991 'consensual poverty'), 40 per cent of Liverpool's population (173,000 - 186,000 people) were living on or below this standard. But 15 per cent (64,000 - 74,000 people) were living in 'intense poverty', defined as being unable to afford seven or more of these items. This compared to parallel nationwide figures of 21 per cent and 7 per cent, found by Mack & Lansley in their 1991 'Breadline Britain' survey. Some basic necessities many people in Liverpool were forced to go without included: 47 per cent not being able to afford a week's annual holiday; 23 per cent not being able to afford a damp-free home; 34 per cent having had to forego essential heating at times during the previous year. (Liverpool City Council 1991, pp. 5/7)

The largest groups of people in poverty in Britain are:
- the unemployed, the largest single category. It is not possible to give accurate numbers of the unemployed since central government has changed the measurement of unemployment eighteen times since coming to office in 1979 and in every case, bar one, there has been a substantial reduction in the numbers of the unemployed;
- pensioners, almost 2 million live on Income Support, with a further 1 million on an income below that level;

6

- the low paid i.e., under retirement age with earned incomes below the Income Support weekly rates - almost 1 million people;

- sick and disabled, half a million people classified as sick or disabled living on or below the Income Support scale rates.

In the European Community (now European Union) in 1985, almost 52 million people, or 16 per cent of the population, were living in poverty (defined as less than half the national average household expenditure, adjusted for family size). Portugal had the worst poverty levels at almost one-third of its population. Ireland, Spain and Greece followed with levels ranging from 18.4 percent to 19.5 per cent. Of the more prosperous nations, the United Kingdom had easily the highest rate of 18.2 per cent, with France and Italy having poverty rates of 15 per cent, and Belgium, Denmark and the Netherlands with rates of between 6 per cent and 11 per cent. When poverty is defined by 50 percent of average equivalent income, instead of expenditure, Britain has the highest poverty rate in Europe. (Simpson and Walker 1993, p.9) However, the most pertinent trend has been the rate of increase in poverty levels across Europe between 1980 and 1985. The United Kingdom had the sharpest rise in the European Community - from 14.6 per cent to 18.2 per cent. Ireland, Italy and the Netherlands all had rises, but nowhere near the rate in the United Kingdom. Poverty levels remained the same in Portugal and Denmark, while in France, Greece, Germany, Belgium and Spain, the levels of poverty dropped. Using the 50% of national average household expenditure measurement, Britain emerges at the top of the league in terms of the increase in households in poverty in the European Community. (Cross 1993, p.9) Between 1980 and 1988, the extent of poverty in Britain increased from 2.8 million to 3.8 million - a rise of 36 per cent. Only Belgium had an increase factor anywhere near Britains, but on a much smaller scale - 7.5 per cent to 17 per cent. Britain contained 26 per cent of the poor households in the European Community in 1980, but this had risen to 33 per cent towards the end of the 1980s. Malcolm Cross (December 1992) observes: 'The UK unlike the wealthier countries of Europe in having higher rates of poverty, and unlike the poorer ones in seeing this position becoming more entrenched.' (cited in Oppenheim 1933, p. 3). But by 1993, the Low Pay Unit (LPU) reported in a submission to an EC summit in Copenhagen that one in four of Europe's poor were British (12 million of the ECs 50 million). Because of unemployment and low wages, the gap between the rich and the poor widened faster in the United Kingdom than in any other European Community nation. The LPU gave evidence that:

- Britain has a larger proportion earning less than the Council of Europe's 'decency threshold' than any other member state;
- twenty five per cent of British children are living in poverty as defined by

7

the European Community: yet only 6 per cent of Belgians are classed as poor;
- a third of Europe's working children (under 16) are British;
- a fifth of Europe's unemployed are British;
- life expectancy in Britain is lower than in most European Community states;
- maternity leave is a universal right for employed women in all European Community countries except Britain;
- Britons have longer working hours than their European Community Counterparts.

Chris Pond, the LPUs director, stated:

A total of 20 million people in Britain, over one third of the population, have an income which leaves them in poverty or on its margins. Britain's poor feel abandoned by their own government, which has resisted the Social Charter and the Social Chapter of the Maastricht Treaty at every turn. (cited in the *Observer*, May 23rd 1993, p.2)

Trends like these have led to distinguished world commentators such as Geraldine van Beuren, director of the Programme on the International Rights of the Child, describing Britain as the first 'undeveloping' country in the world. She went on to identify the government's failure to finance welfare policy as one of the most important factors leading to the massive increase in child poverty. (cited in CPAG 1993, p.4) Britain's refusal to sign the Social Charter and opt out of the Social Chapter has also led to the charge of 'social dumping', a process in which nations export their unemployment and poverty by reducing wages and benefit levels, and, in doing so, undercutting their international competitors - i.e. employers will move jobs to wherever the cost of labour are cheapest.

Millions and millions of men, women and children live in poverty in Britain as we approach the twenty first century. Michael Meacher, Labour's social security spokesman, commented: 'These figures reveal that British society is now more unequal than at any time since the Edwardian era' (*Guardian*, July 16th 1992), a measure repeated by the poverty findings in this book. That 'poverty' is 'primary' and basic and does not allow for even a stringent, parsimonious lifestyle. It is a major source of concern that clinical data on poverty, overwhelming and conclusive though they may be, do not adequately reflect the experience of poverty - the degradation, powerlessness, want, hungry stomachs, poverty-induced illness and premature death, cold homes, ragged clothing, cheap (and dangerous) furniture, 'paupers' graves etc. The conclusion of this book offers scientific research findings which prove that poverty is not only much more widespread than is generally perceived (or admitted), but also that this poverty is 'plain, old-fashioned and miserable' and represents a 'Third-Worldisation' of poverty in Britain in the 1990s

8

But none of these statistics contain a breakdown of gender or ethnic factors which Chapter Four argues, has led many writers to talk about a 'feminisation' and a 'racialisation' of poverty. Official data publications have always ignored issues of gender and race in their presentations of poverty statistics and academic research has only recently taken these questions on board as worthy of its attention and commitment. Additionally, almost every indicator of poverty demonstrates that black people and other ethnic minorities are at a significantly greater risk of excessive unemployment, low wages, poor working conditions, and suffer from a discriminatory and oppressive welfare benefits system. Chapter Four will argue and offer data which proves that the extent of poverty among ethnic minorities is a manifestation of: racist immigration legislation which excludes people from abroad from the mainstream welfare provision systems; employment practices which have forced workers from ethnic minorities into low paid, low status jobs; discrimination in the social security system; and societal and institutionalised racial prejudice. In much the same way, the nature and depth of poverty among women is a matter of greater significance than merely disparate levels of poverty between the sexes. It involves consideration of : women's access to income and resources from outside the home; intra-household transfer of income and resources; the time spent by women in directly and indirectly generating income and resources for household use. The experience of poverty for women, Chapter Four argues, is a lifetime encounter. Experiences such as inferior rates of wages, careers in employment broken in order to provide unpaid care for dependents, part-time jobs, reductions in welfare benefits rights, all converge to impose poverty on women throughout their life cycle.

Historically, throughout the policy and academic debate on poverty and poor relief, there have been difficulties in classifying the poor and how each 'category' of the poor should be dealt with. In Victorian Britain, the poor were differentiated between the worthy/deserving and the unworthy/ undeserving. The latter were 'social outsiders', denizens of a 'social residuum', or, as Morris (1994 p. 2) has pointed out, the 'dangerous classes'. Like Morris, Chapter Five on 'The Underclass' will argue that the 'danger' surrounding this redundant population, the lumpenproletariat, society's outcasts is twofold: (1) they constitute a threat to social stability and organisation and; (2) these 'outsiders' are perceived as not belonging to the normal societal structures, the threat from them is generated outside normal society and thus they are beyond the responsibility of social citizens. Chapter Five will explain how the 'underclass' has been represented as a threat to the efficient operation of the welfare state, by over-providing for those who accept few responsibilities and make little or no social or economic contribution. A 'culture of dependency' has arisen when endangers the fundamental values and norms of the society to which the 'underclass' notionally belong.

Although the term, the 'underclass', originated in the United States and has been applied to, mainly, single mothers, usually black, who are dependent upon the state for their welfare and young males, again usually black, who are on the margins of the labour market, in Britain, the term has also come to include the long term unemployed, those living on 'welfare estates' which are virtually walled cities where 'social undesirables could be excluded from the more affluent "fortress" areas' (the *Guardian*, September 8th 1993), who are the victims of changing patterns of employment.

Of course, the extent of poverty can only be measured through the application of a poverty line, a cut-off point above which poverty does not exist, below which it does. There have been numerous attempts to establish such a standard of living, mostly in the 1980s, involving an esoteric, phrasemongering struggle between academics who should know better. Chapter Two deals with the main approaches to defining and thus measuring poverty and deprivation and extols their strengths while exposing their weaknesses. 'Absolute' definitions of poverty which offer to measure the extent of poverty by applying a standard minimum subsistence have been challenged recently by 'relative' measurements of deprivation which employ a cut-off point based on the minimum means for social participation. Chapter Three argues that the so-called 'absolutist' studies by Rowntree in 1899, 1936/41 and 1950 have more or less been the determining model for establishing social security benefit levels since the early 1940s, thereby presenting, ostensibly, as the basis for the current Income Support scale rates. But Townsend (1979), Donnison (1982) and Mack and Lansley (1985 and 1991) have argued that poverty essentially constitutes a lifestyle so inferior that it excludes its victims from the life of the community in which they live. Hartley Dean (1992, p. 67) agrees: 'The welfare state must ensure that every citizen is capable, not of subsistence alone, but of participation as a "free" politico-juridical subject within the workings of an advanced capitalist society.' As such, the state must accept responsibility to provide subsistence for the 'failures' and 'casualties' of capitalism, or it must deal with the excessive inequalities inherent in capitalism by guaranteeing the citizenship right to usefully participate in society. The main purpose of this discussion is to provide the reader with an overview of the now subdued debate and to suggest that the clinical objectivity sought by academics simply sanitises the poverty debate and obscures the reality of the experience of poverty for those who suffer from it every hour of every day of every year, many for their entire lives. Haines (1979, p. 123) suggests that poverty can be allowed to adorn 'an apolitical and technical appearance', an image which is far removed from the 'feeling' of poverty and the lifelong experience of all its manifestations. Such a lifestyle is clarified in the Conclusion which provides data which proves beyond doubt that primary, subsistence poverty is extensive in Britain in the 1990s, a poverty virtually taking on, more and more, some of the less savage, but nonetheless unjust, features of Third World poverty.

How poverty is defined and measured is a direct product of beliefs, perceptions and theories of its causation. It is the argument of Chapter One that poverty in economically developed Western nations is caused by the nature of the socio-economic relations within capitalism, relations which alienate the mass of workers from the means of securing their own subsistence. Such an analysis is, of course, not shared by the orthodox policy-making process, which has historically perceived poverty in general pathological terms: the result of irrational decisions by individuals in the labour market, in schools, in shops, in the home; demanding excessive wages leading to unemployment and poverty; bad management of otherwise adequate incomes, leading to deprivation; over generous welfare benefits which create a disincentive to work; and downright laziness. This explanatory model of poverty causation lends itself comfortably to a primary, subsistence definition of poverty, while the inequality approach to conceptualising poverty veers definitely towards the relativist measurements. And similarly, perceptions of poverty causation influence and determine public policy responses towards poor relief. Chapter Three on the history of social security benefits clearly maps a number of trends which largely adhere to a 'blame-the-poor' attitude in the policy-making process since 1834. It is argued that the basic needs of the poor have never been an item on the agenda of those agencies who have established poor relief levels and indeed, such benefits have been purposely provided at an obviously inadequate level in order to compel the poor to 'rationalise their behaviour' and to participate in the economic order and the labour market within the rules structured by the free market economy.

The formal conclusion of this book does not conform to the traditional format of summarising the main points discussed in the text. Rather, the orthodoxy's continuum implied throughout the book can only lead to one conclusion - a life of utter deprivation and absolute want for millions of households in Britain. That dominant continuum suggests that:

- the perception of poverty as a 'social problem' has been dominated by views of the poor as failing or refusing to avail of the opportunities offered to all members of society on an equal basis;
- poor relief has always been inadequate to prevent a disincentive to work, to be fair to the 'honest, hard-working' low income households;
- poverty has only been officially defined and measured on a subsistence model, as a more liberal view would have served to encourage irrational policy responses to the problem;
- those making irrational decisions have included: women - by choosing to interrupt their career to bear and care for children; ethnic minorities -who choose to come to Britain seeking employment and welfare when both are in short supply; and workers - by demanding wages at a level above that determined by the free market economy;

- the lifestyles of the poor in Britain in the 1990s are characterised by all the above and are therefore featured by a lack of healthy dietaries, cold and damp homes, inadequate clothing and footwear, an absence of any social life, barest furniture, little beyond absolute necessities and sacrifices required to attain a brief respite, even for an evening, from a dreary, hopeless, drudge towards an early grave.

The data presented in the conclusion to this book are evidence of the return to 19th century poverty levels as Britain approaches the 21st century and the 'back-to-basics' march of the Conservative government is revealed in some of its human suffering and exclusion from society of Britain's poor.

> The effort and ingenuity that have gone into ensuring the survival of poverty are one of the wonders of the modern world; of a piece, in their way, with splitting the atom or walking on the moon. (Seabrook 1985, p. 12)

1 Theories of poverty causation

Introduction

It is apparent that: (a) social policies to deal with various social phenomena are influenced by the theorization and conceptualization of relevant ideas and; (b) consequently, the construction of concepts pervades the policy response to the problem. In other words, how the state responds to the problem of poverty, mainly in terms of income maintenance/poor relief will be determined by its perception of the causes of poverty. An administration, such as that which has governed Britain since 1979, drawn towards believing that poverty is the result of personal inadequacy and lack of motivation, is unlikely to provide generous financial services for the poor. There is constant reciprocal dependence between perceptions of causation and policy responses. By striving to offer an account of existing explanatory models of poverty, this chapter will discuss individualist accounts, involving orthodox economic, minority group and sub-cultural theories, labour market theories, both dual and segmented, the structuralist/functionalist explanation and the Marxist school. The task at hand is to discuss the beliefs of the causation of poverty and to identify, either through stated assumptions or through extrapolating the implications inherent in the various ideas presented, the policy prescriptions in terms of the level and nature of poor relief/social security and the underpinning model of measurement and definition of poverty.

Individualist theories

This section will deal with those explanations which identify the causes of the phenomenon of poverty within the traits, characteristics and motivations of individuals. It will be contended that these hypotheses prescribe policy responses which target the individual and his/her own value systems for change and imply that treatment of and provision for the poor must be functional to adapting their personal attributes to enhance their employment prospects - in other words, the means by which they can escape poverty. As such, the nature and level of provision of poor relief will be determined by this schematic process.

Orthodox economic theory

Orthodox economics is founded upon very general assumptions and progresses along its theoretical path by analyzing, discussing and predicting various issues 'as if' certain situations are given or taken for granted. For instance, poverty can be explained by reference to the worker's productivity, 'as if' all other factors can be held constant - that is, employers act primarily to maximize profits in a rational way and the market functions in an equilibrating direction. The poor are thus poor because they are unemployed and they are unemployed because they expect and demand too high a price for their productivity - i.e., wages. This approach depends upon 'rational' arguments and solutions and this, in such problematic situations, the rationally calculated answer would be to, for example, reduce the worker's standard of living during unemployment, through the level of cash welfare benefits paid, to such an inferior standard, that it becomes 'rational' to seek and accept paid employment. Thus, during unemployment, benefit levels would act as a strategy of cogent economic processes be being set at a standard so low as to encourage (or coerce) the unemployed back into the labour market. For the market to operate in its essence, unemployment benefit levels should afford the claimant a standard of living which is inadequate and which deters acceptance of and complacency with the lifestyle of the unemployed.

The production process is made up of many constituent factors. Orthodox economics contains a particular view of human nature which assumes that labour is the only 'irrational', problematic factor of production (beside capital and land) and thus attention is centred upon the worker's role, with specific focus on the skills of the poor, the level and quality of which are largely determined by freely-exercised choices - for example, in the areas of education, training, employment constancy etc. Poverty is thereby caused through choices exercised in such a way as to reduce the potential skills of workers. An example might be, which giving birth, a woman causes an interruption in her skills development programme. She has therefore expressed a rationally-arrived at preference, with the possible outcome being poverty - i.e., through a lack of necessary skills, leading to unemployment. The orthodox view does not take account of the sexist nature of responsibility

14

and the sexual division of labour - the patriarchal perception of the various roles that women play in society.

The orthodoxy's central proposition in its explanation of poverty suggests that, in a particular industry, workers' wage levels in normal circumstances are equal to the value of the extra contribution made to output by the last member of that section of workers. This is the orthodox economists' 'income/marginal productivity hypothesis'. Where wages exceed this value, unemployment must necessarily occur and the standard of living provided via poor relief benefit to the unemployed must necessarily push the labourer back into the market at the level determined by the above rational process. Poverty is imposed, in such circumstances, through the provision of an inadequate lifestyle in unemployment; not that the policy makers who adhere to this model would label the situation of the unemployed as constituting 'poverty', but the hidden agenda of such lifestyles centres on the coercive nature of such approaches, encouraging a return to the labour market at a level determined by market forces. A poverty line income is thus the means of such coercion. Where no employment prospects exist for the foreseeable future and the unemployed are likely to be surplus to the requirements of the labour market for a long period of time, then the level of poor relief is determined by economic health. As long term unemployment is generally regarded as an indication of economic recession, then relatively little cash is made available for benefits for the unemployed, reflecting the 'top-down' approach to policy making. Potential complications, such as public opinion and moral judgements are relatively unproblematic, as the ideological climate generated by this economic philosophy is generally unsympathetic to the poor.

The orthodox economic models 'explain' poverty in their own terms and these are based on three major assumptions:
- perfect competition and market equilibrium;
- workers' sovereignty and;
- harmony of interest.
Through these assumptions, the political, social and economic undercurrents of the theorists in relation to poverty are laid open.

Perfect competition

Gordon describes this assumption in terms of the 'as if' theory - in this case, the orthodoxy proceed 'as if markets were perfectly competitive'. (Gordon D, 1972, p. 34). In a situation where this prevailed, the Orthodox Economic Theory (OET) argues that the wages of workers would be equivalent to their marginal productivity, a concept upon which, much of its discussion on poverty centres. The productivity of the labour force can best be measured by the value of the last singular addition to the workforce. A numerical example might be a case in which labour produces £100,000 of manufactured goods in a year. If, with the addition of one worker, that value rises to £110,000 per year, then marginal productivity equals £10,000 and thus annual wages should equate with this. Any imbalance in favour of higher wages would cause the employer, compelled by market forces of competition, to rectify the disequilibrium in this process by shedding labour costs, resulting in unemployment (and poverty). The latter conditions thus are caused by the irrationality of labour in demanding too high wages, (or 'pricing themselves out of a job', in current Right Wing rhetoric) and the consequences must therefore be borne by the labourers - a poverty lifestyle. However, given that this situation of utopian rationality does not uniformly and permanently prevail in the market economy and deviations occur frequently (and inevitably, according to Friedman and Thrurow, two important orthodox economists - both cited in Gordon 1972, p. 28), at this stage of the debate, poverty will occur when an imbalance of significant proportions develops in the relationship between income and marginal productivity. One of two things can happen:

(a) firstly, workers can be paid at less than the value of their marginal product. The consequent reduction in wage payments will relegate the underpaid workers into a state of poverty;

(b) secondly, the labour force can be renumerated at a level greater than the value of their marginal productivity. However, the dynamic competitiveness of the market economy will soon demonstrate to the recalcitrant employer, the folly of his/her actions and will force an equilibrating of the process. Since direct wage cuts would be difficult to impose a reduction in the workforce is necessary, coupled with an increase in the productivity levels of the remaining labour. Thus, many workers find themselves unemployed and in poverty as a result.

In the first case, where wages are paid at less than their marginal product, the employer is to blame, whilst the employees are the culprits when wages exceed marginal product. It is assumed that: (a) employers act rationally in a profit-maximizing way and; (b) labour (and thus wages) is the least 'controllable' of the factors of production, and therefore will usually be the unbalancing or disequilibrating interest.

In the majority of cases, thus, poverty will be caused by the labour force, particularly in demanding too high wages, in which case, the employer will be forced to reduce labour costs through unemployment and therefore generating deprived standards of living for the unemployed. The workers are therefore to blame for unemployment and the poor for poverty. Undoubtedly, of greater interest to the debate on poverty management and definition (see Chapter Two), is one of the main conclusions of the works of the orthodox economists on perfect competition - i.e., that the 'poverty line' can be drawn

16

at the level of the value of workers' productivity. Provided wages are paid at this level, poverty can be avoided, but any deviation either above or below this standard would cause unemployment and poverty. In this context, policies to prevent poverty are located in the field of the labour market and employment. Outside this arena, the factors and players change radically, as does the terminology. The area outside the labour market - in unemployment, poverty alleviation - is not an important issue and is superseded by the objective of returning the unemployed labourer back to the market at the level decided by the equilibrium, via the provision of a poverty standard of living. Thus, these theorists are only concerned with **poverty in relation to wages at a 'perfect' level and as a necessary strategy for teaching the labour force a lesson in market economics.**

Workers' sovereignty

A central theme of the OET assumes that employees and employers operate to maximise their own benefits: (a) through training, education, conditions of employment etc., for the worker and; (b) through productivity and profitability levels for the owner. Thus workers appear to have a wide scope of choices which basically constitutes a form of workers' sovereignty. The implied hypothesis is that individuals have a virtually open ended range of opportunities through their careers and that choices are expressed and are freely selected. The similarity between 'workers' sovereignty' in income theories and 'consumers' sovereignty' in consumption theories is apparent. According to OET in consumption and demand theory, consumers have a virtually unlimited choice among a basket of goods and services, each of which, theoretically, has a different price. However, scant discussion is focused on how economic and political institutions determine the availability of commodities for choice. Similarly, orthodox theories of income focus on the means by which workers express choices among a basket of goods including education, training, experience and mobility opportunities but tend to shun discussion of the limitations placed upon such choices by the same institutions - the class/gender/racial structure of privilege.

Naturally, workers' sovereignty does not dogmatically dictate that all workers have the same opportunities, nor indeed the capacity to avail themselves equally of these opportunities. Productivity levels in given work situations are greatly influenced by skills, abilities, talents etc., of which individual workers have differential levels. The orthodoxy concedes that these attributes, these productivity components, have an unequal distribution and, accordingly to Townsend (1979, pp. 31/32), there is significant agreement on the five main sources of these capacities: inherent ability; education; vocational education; on-the-job training; and on-the-job experience. This explanation of poverty which concentrates on the quality of the supply of

17

labour (supply-side economics) would identify its causes in the inferior nature of the levels of these productivity attributes among the poor as evidenced in the educational attainment differentials among the poor and non-poor, the variations in the benefits obtained from vocational training etc., as statistical justification for their explanation. In short, the problem of poverty resides in the poor and thus, rationally, policy responses to it should include measures aimed at the poor as the target group of individuals for change, to encourage the enhancement of these attributes. In practical terms, this would mean a social security system with two interacting objectives: firstly, to provide merely a poverty line income; and secondly, through this experience, to encourage the under-privileged to attain the necessary productivity attributes in order to make them a more attractive proposition to employers and to strengthen their bargaining stance in the labour market.

Orthodox economists would tend to clinically categorize all income as solely a return on 'human capital investment' - i.e., through the freely chosen opportunities of education, training, mobility etc., workers can invest in their own capital realization potential and income is allocated on a human capital basis - the greater the investment, the greater the value of the human capital, the greater the return - i.e., wages/income. The continuum is thus: study hard at school = advance into vocational training = well paid employment. According to US economist, Becker (1967), all earnings can be primarily attributed to differential levels of investment, mainly by the individual with support and encouragement from his/her family, with 'ability' being more accurately reflected in terms of 'an endogenously determined component of human capital, attributable to parental investment' (cited in Gordon 1972, p. 30). And, logically, the reverse should apply - i.e., where there is no real investment at the required levels, or an inadequate investment in human capital, then the return will be of a similarly inadequate nature. In other words, where an individual declines, through his/her own choice, to attain the necessary skills for sale in the labour market, then that worker can expect little or no reward in the form of income and lifestyle. During periods of unemployment, social security benefit levels will thus be under no pressure to provide anything other than relief of a similarly inadequate quality. Thus poverty ensues either through low wages in a low status job or through unemployment benefits.

In this view, individuals cause their own poverty by failing to invest sufficiently in their own worth of human capital in the labour market and marginal productivity (their contribution as individuals to increasing the productivity levels in their area of employment) - through under achieving at school, low take up of training opportunities etc. As Gordon (1972, p 42) put it, 'The presence of poverty...can be seen, through this approach, as a simple aggregation of individual income maximizing decisions among workers.' Irrational decisions, freely arrived at, bear consequences aimed at 'rationalizing' the individual's behaviour and choices - i.e. a poverty lifestyle. Such rational pursuit of self interest itself presupposes a degree of passivity and tolerance among individuals and groups with conflicting interests. The third major assumption in an orthodox economics view of poverty relates to the roles played by all the different players in the economy as it proceeds along the path to equilibrium.

Harmony of interests

This supposition regards the outcomes of perfect competition and workers' sovereignty as situations in which the ultimate economic good emerges from a harmony of or consensus among various interests. Any movement towards upsetting natural arrangements reduce living standards and create poverty because all individuals have their own economic and social interests invested in the equilibrium of the economy, which while maintained, will improve the lifestyles of everyone. Michael Zweig (1972) encapsulated this assumption succinctly by explaining

> ...in market exchanges, both parties gain from trade, establishing a supposed harmony of interests among all, in the perpetuation of exchange through markets organized on a private capitalist basis. Each actor, whatever his position, is a co-operative and committed member of capitalist society, in which he does the best he can. (cited in Gordon, 1972, pp. 33-34)

Such an approach recognizes no other divisions in society, other than individually based ones, (buyer/seller) and identifies no other conflict of interests except between individual actors, whether employees or employers. These focuses, seen through explanations of poverty, reflect the individualistic causal and contributory factors and, consequently, regard solutions to poverty and poverty alleviated policies on a correspondingly individualist level. Townsend (1979, pp. 74-75) summarizes the conceptual ideologies whereby explanations are sought which transcend institutional and historical variations within or among societies, and therefore favour simplicity '...., take institutional structures as constant and therefore shift attention to individual choices in relation to education, training and mobility.'

Minority Group Theory (MGT)

Townsend (1979, pp. 64-65) first coined this phrase in 1979 in reference to an explanation of poverty which identifies causal factors in the characteristics of groups of poor people (as opposed to individuals, as in the OET). The first piece of established research to be labelled as representing the MGT was that by Charles Booth in 1897 (p. 70). Although he conceded that the majority of poor people lived in a state of, at least, semi-permanent poverty through no fault of their own, there were, he added, widespread vices such as drink, fecklessness, lack of motivation, bad company etc. generally among the '... lower class which consists of some occasional labourers, street sellers, criminals and semi-criminals.' These individuals lived in poverty because of their own inadequate qualities and through choice. Booth's pursuit was then taken up by Rowntree in 1899 during his 'scientific investigation of poverty' in York. (Rowntree, B.S., 1901).

For Rowntree, a form of extreme poverty ('primary poverty') could be defined and explained partly in terms of nutritional inadequacy which, in turn, was measured from expert opinion and existing medical knowledge of the subsistence needs for physical efficiency. Rowntree held that people existed in 'primary poverty' if their income failed to meet the costs of this subsistence diet and other necessary expenditure (fuel, housing, clothing etc.). The causes of such a poverty were investigated and listed by Rowntree as a catalogue of characteristics of individual households: the absence of a breadwinner in the household through death, unemployment or illness; low pay in employment; or the large size of families where the number of dependent children was excessive relative to their income. Rowntree also introduced tow other concepts in his discussion of poverty. Firstly, he suggested that 'secondary poverty' was a condition suffered by those whose incomes were actually sufficient, or more than sufficient, to meet the costs of subsistence living, but who, through wasteful expenditure and an absence of planned budgeting and financial management, failed to acquire the frugal necessities of life. Thus a person could be 'poor' but still have an 'adequate income', although such income would be subject to stringent inflexibility and would have to be applied in strict weekly budgeting and economizing. Secondly, Rowntree hypothesized that the poor experienced a 'cycle of poverty', that at some stage(s) in the lives of the working class, individuals would fall below the poverty line and rise above it at other stages. Experiences of life below the poverty line occurred during early childhood, early adulthood, married with dependent children and old age. By blaming poverty on the traits of a minority of individuals, Rowntree's and Booth's approach to poverty and to its relief has been highly influential in social policy and social research.

Holman (1978, p. 54) succinctly provides a brief understanding of the MGT of poverty:

> The explanation is based on the belief - deeply rooted in our society - that individuals are self-determining beings, able to control their own environments and destinies. It follows that they are individuals who are wholly responsible for their behaviour, morals and conditions. Consequently, their poverty is explained in terms of individual failure.

If society sees the poor as a group, set aside from normal social interaction and structures, who are unwilling through free choice or incapable through pathological weakness to avoid poverty by availing of the opportunities offered by a meritocratic market system, then the implication that follows is that the provision made by the state in such a set-up, in terms of poor relief, need not be, and, indeed, should not be, more than a poverty line existence. Rather, state intervention should aim to discourage idleness, apathy and fecklessness and to encourage self help and self reliance, and these can best be achieved by generating dissatisfaction among the poor with their living standards through a system of poverty alleviation which provides only an unacceptable standard of living.

MGT constructs its hypothesis around very simplified observations of the features of the poor - for example, death of a breadwinner, old age, low pay etc. Its explanatory strength is somewhat weakened by Rowntree's almost total evasion of, what he called, the 'ultimate causes of poverty' Rowntree, in fact, only skirted the issues, by making a huge and largely contrived leap from an 'individualist' to a 'social' explanation when he said: 'It is no part of the object of this (study) to discuss the ultimate causes of poverty. To attempt this would be to raise the whole social question.' (Rowntree, 1901, p. 152). He did present himself as being aware of and convinced by 'the social question' by linking poverty to issues such as land tenure, the State, the aggregation and distribution of wealth, (Rowntree 1901, p. 180) and, indeed, even the causes of secondary poverty, Rowntree claimed, could only be identified as part of the wider social problem. Drink, gambling, wasteful expenditure etc. were themselves the product of adverse conditions, sordid housing, overcrowded and unhealthy accommodation, monotonous and laborious work, limited education, lack of intellectual stimulation etc. '... what wonder that many of these people fall a ready prey to the publican and bookmaker?' (Rowntree 1901, p. 179). It is clear that Rowntree understood that the causes of poverty were to be found, as Rose (1972 p. 20) put it '... in the ill-organized labour market or the ill-drained slum'. However, this cannot be laid down as a criticism of Rowntree's work. He was aware of the deterrent nature of the Poor Law (this will be discussed in Chapter Three on the history of the poor relief) and set about generating concern about poverty in a hostile ideological environment. He attempted this by trying to convince policy makers and the community at large that the income of many of the poor were so inadequate as to render them incapable of meeting the most basic, subsistence needs.

MGT, and particularly the content and dynamics of Rowntree's discussion of poverty, quite comfortably accommodates current welfare intervention. Within this concept, welfare policies concentrate upon and attempt to reform the inadequacies of their 'targets' - individuals and groups - by providing income levels so low as to deter settlement with the lifestyles of the

21

unemployed. It is therefore suggested that the poor relief policies of successive governments, in reality, culminating in the current Income Support System, bear more resemblance to the approaches of MGT than to any of the other explanations of poverty.

Culture/sub culture of poverty theory

Various forms of explanatory research have speculated on the location of the causes of poverty within the personality characteristics of individuals and the impact of the poor's immediate social environment on their behavioural patterns and interactions by focusing attention mainly on 'problem families', 'problem communities', "inner cities" and, most recently, the 'underclass' see Chapter Five) - that is, approaches which strive to explain a culture or a sub-culture of poverty. Most of the investigations which uphold the sub-culture hypothesis have been founded in investigations which uphold the sub-culture hypothesis have been founded in a wide range of studies in the fields of sociology, anthropology and eugenics. Such an understanding was founded initially within the vociferous expression in two modern authors' works - Oscar Lewis and David Matza. Lewis (1965) argued that a sub-culture of poverty existed among the most economically and socially deprived members of society and that this represented an institution which was characteristically distinct from the predominant culture of wider society and one which possessed its own perennial impetus, its own self - perpetuating cycle. Matza (1966) referred to the 'disreputable poor' who were a virtual sub-layer of all the poor and remained unemployed or casually employed even during economic booms when vacancies were plentiful and, because of their constant distancing of themselves from even the norms that other disadvantaged people lived under, they placed themselves in statuses and positions of disrepute.

The sub-culture theory was originally aired and nurtured in the U.S., with its theoretical cousin, he concept of cultural deprivation, 'arriving' in the U.K. towards the beginning of the 1970's when the political climate was experiencing a major shift away from collectivist, social understanding and policies and towards more individualist approaches. The cultural deprivation thesis, the intellectual product of Right-wing analysts in Britain like Keith Joseph, describes those living in poverty as being there, not solely, or even mainly, because of income deprivation, but because they are imbued with and accustomed to poverty and such acclimatization encourages them to develop and construct a sub-culture or secondary value system which, in turn, is handed down through family interaction to children. (This approach underpins the usage of the relatively contemporary term, the 'underclass', and will be discussed in more detail in Chapter Five).

As an explanation of poverty, the sub-culture approach is, of course, heavily

22

inter-twined with the cultural analysis, but both possess distinctive explanatory angles. The sub-culture theory sets the poor within a value system which is not only different from the societal culture, but which is also adrift and divorced from dominant social institutions. Whereas the culture of deprivation hypothesis argues that people in poverty are integral entities within the macro framework - full members of society - but find themselves poor because of, during their formative years, inappropriate participation in societal interaction. They are thus incapable of taking advantage of the opportunities which society provides. They are viewed as being deprived of those attributes of the culture which permit the non-poor to keep themselves out of poverty. The implied policy response of both, in the form of state-provided social security, would logically aim to encourage and facilitate the individual or group to break out of their value-ghetto and to adapt to the systems, structures and opportunities of the 'normal' wider society. As a catalyst to this process, the state would offer social security at such a level as to make living standards unpleasant enough to prompt rectitude by the poor person/group. The function of social security therefore, would not be to provide the means of attaining a reasonable standard of living, as poverty is either self-inflicted or avoidable, but to offer a subsistence income which would deter complacency about the lifestyles of the poor and force them to look beyond their immediate group into institutionalized society for the means by which they can escape from poverty.

That the poor are much more modest, ambiguous and self critical in their perceptions and aspirations than the non-poor, is beyond doubt. To claim these characteristics are the result of a distinctive cultural framework is a gross over-simplification. In Coates and Silburn's (1970, pp. 166-7) research, they found that their poor sample in Nottingham responded to the same values and central perceptions as the rest of the community. They concluded that, 'Far from the lower pitch of their stated aspirations being evidence of a detachment from the accepted value system, it could simply be an expression of a "realistic" appraisal of their possibilities, given that they had so little power at their disposal to change them.' Such a materialist observation destroys the validity of the subjective judgements which are at the core of the culture of poverty thesis. And the *Observer* (3 October 1993) offers a derisory dismissal of the sub-culture explanation in reporting on levels of poverty and unemployment in Liverpool. The report argued that the lack of opportunities for full time work and shrinking benefits has indeed generated a sub-culture of local people 'working on the side to make ends meet'. 'Benefit fraud' has become synonymous with sub-culture notions of poverty, but what this means in reality is a new pair of shoes for a child or an evening out. The 'wages' on 'the side' are meagre and those taking the risk face serious consequences; a part time cleaning job five mornings a week attracts £20 (or legitimately, £60), while detection would result in three months loss of benefits. 'Take the case of one Everton man who was working as a porter -

£5 for a full night's work. When his wife suddenly fell ill and was taken to hospital, he asked if he could take the night off. "Sure," came the reply, "but if you do, don't bother coming back". He worked his shift'.

Labour market theories

Both the theories presented below (dual and segmented labour market) concentrate on the labour market as the main arena of poverty-causation and, in particular, the needs and demands of the market for differential qualities in the labour force, different levels of workers and the interaction of these requirements with the motivations of workers. They imply that, due to the nature and dynamics of the existing system of production, those outside the labour market must exist in such conditions as to encourage and prepare them to accept employment at the wage-level and time required by employers.

Dual labour market theory

This explanation of poverty proposes that the labour market has become divided over a period of time with two distinct and separate entities developing, one being the 'primary' and the other, the 'secondary' markets. In both sectors, there are clearly identifiable behavioural norms, expectations and rules by which both employees and employers function and fulfil their roles. Both the Dual Labour Market Theory (D.L.M.T.) and O.E.T. assume that competition plays a central role in the development of poverty; but the main aim of the D.L.M.T. hypothesis is to refine and rationalize, to a limited degree, the orthodox approach which identifies a single, competitive labour market. The duality theory is sometimes described as a response to the insubstantial tunnel-view of the orthodoxy which maintains that open competition is available to all workers in the labour market. Both theories, however, imply similar characteristics and functions for poor relief levels.

Primary labour markets

Doeringer (1980, pp. 211-231) describes an internal labour market as an administrative unit which concerns itself with the market functions of pricing, training and allocating labour. Identifiable and enforceable regulations control entry by external workers, usually those from the secondary sector, into the primary units and these rules are designed to protect the maintenance of the dual structure. The level of access to the primary market is governed by these rules and it is the existence of them in the primary sector and the absence of them in the secondary sphere which define the different nature and structure

24

of both markets and contribute to a theoretical, explanatory discussion on poverty. In explaining the need for a primary market, Amsden (1980, pp. 21-22) argues that improved technology requires and provides for high levels of in-service training and 'firm specific skills'. Employers offer workers, in whom they have invested substantial finance, time and resources, training, higher wages, security, comfortable and amenable work conditions etc., to ensure that such workers will remain in their employment and 'repay' the employer. The separateness of the primary market is then perpetuated through socialization and acceptance of behavioural characteristics towards work, traits which correspond to the needs of the market - e.g., primary sector workers are 'reliable', while secondary workers are unreliable'. Another vehicle through which the dualism is maintained and consolidated is the organized and strong trade union movement which is much more effective among primary workers. Currently, the electricians' and the engineers' unions (whose members are usually highly trained) are regarded as much more 'loyal' to their employers than, say, the National Union of Public Employees (whose membership consists largely of untrained workers).

Secondary labour markets

The relatively high wages, employment tenure and good working conditions for the primary workers are in stark contrast with the poor wages, poor working conditions, considerable variability in employment, harsh and often arbitrary discipline and little opportunity to advance of the secondary market, to which the poor are often confined. Mainly due to a belief that certain classes of workers are incapable of working at a highly skilled level and that their labour is inferior and due, in some cases, to subjective bigotry, identifiable categories of workers are much more likely to be employed in the secondary market. For example, Black people in Britain and in the U.S. would be unequally allocated to secondary jobs. (And Cormack, Osborne and Miller (1983, Chapter 3) found that Catholics in the North of Ireland are not only more likely to be unemployed than Protestants, but those in employment are much more likely to be secondary workers, than their Protestant counterparts). This explanation has also been applied to account for unemployment and poverty among women. (Glendenning and Millar, 1987 & 1991). (These issues of race and poverty and the 'feminisation of poverty' thesis will be debated in more detail in Chapter Four).
The experiences of working in the secondary market, in much the same way as in the primary sphere, reinforce the behavioural traits expected of secondary workers and living alongside the socializing with cohort workers also contributes to the predominance of such characteristics, forming a virtual self-fulfilling prophecy. According to Doeringer and Piore (1971, p. 92), 'This grows both from work patterns on the job and from lifestyles in the ghetto or

in the family'. The explanatory direction of the D.L.M.T. of poverty therefore shifts the focus of attention partially (but only partially) away from individual inadequacies, to create an approach which allocates much more emphasis to the negative traits of the secondary labour market than upon the characteristics of the individual employees in such occupations. Another element concerns the concentration in the previous economic and social theories of inadequate wages and poverty on supply side analysis - i.e., they emphasize the individual attributes of workers, such as intelligence, skills, motivation, health, age, etc. The D.L.M.T., at least, locates explanations of low wages and poverty in the demand side of the labour market (the requirements of employers for specific levels of workers), as well as the supply side. Discussing the entity of a secondary labour market facilitates a more comprehensive understanding of the problems of the unemployed and poor, who, at this stage, can be perceived as constituting a 'reserve' platoon for the market, sitting on the substitutes' bench waiting for a vacancy to materialize on the team. And, individual and structural theories of poverty and it clarifies many of the main differences as a type of half-way stage between the two 'opposing' perspectives (individualists/structuralist). However, the D.L.M.T. of poverty may, in fact, be no more than a rather haphazard or ad hoc attempt to describe the material form of the occupational class structure in a given industry, and in essence, the hypothesis is more a practical, observational investigation of one element of structuralist accounts of poverty, rather than an independent school of thought in social theory.

As an explanation of poverty, its consequential implications, in terms of theoretical prescriptions and policy responses, the D.L.M.T. suggests that the labour market has developed to such an extent that it demands two distinct sectors, for which there must be a steady and appropriate supply of labour. To ensure that such a supply is readily available for the primary market, employment conditions in the secondary sector are so unfavourable that, given the opportunity through training etc., most secondary workers would sacrifice short term benefits (lower wages) in order to enhance their promotion chances. Thus they would be prepared to endure short term poverty for the sake of an opportunity to advance to the secondary sector. And, to guarantee a steady supply of labour for the secondary market - i.e., to ensure that there will be sufficient quantities of workers to fulfil the most unpleasant, menial and unsatisfactory jobs with the worst working conditions and renumeration, ti can be deduced that the standards of living of those outside either labour market - i.e., the unemployed - must be of an even more oppressive and coercive nature in order to instill a sense of urgency and primacy to escape. The escape is, of course, from dire poverty into less dire poverty and such a path in facilitated by the provision of unemployment welfare payments of, merely, a subsistence nature, in terms of meeting life's needs. Thus, once again, the primary function of the level of poor relief can be seen in relation to creating an appropriate and readily available supply of labour o meet the demands of the free market by infusing dissatisfaction with their standards of living into the unemployed through the state provision of an income which is not acceptably adequate to provide for the primary necessities of life.

Segmentation theory

The segmented labour market theory (S.L.M.T.) may be regarded an as extension of the D.L.M.T. The major differences lie in the argument that the labour market is subjected to much more complex segmentation than a simple, solitary scission. Segmentation theory also adds that class interests are a determinative factor in the construction of such a partitioned labour market. Writing on the U.S. labour structure, Reich (1980, pp. 233-234) suggests that it is segmented, fundamentally into primary and secondary sectors (as in D.L.M.T.), but also, the primary market is sub-divided into a 'subordinate' or 'routinized' layer, and an 'independent' or 'creative' strata. Further divisions relate to variables such as race and gender (as discussed above). This introduction of additional divisions within the labour market is a much more realistic approach than that of a simple duality but its inclusion of the important role of class interests will be seen as superficial. The policy responses implied in this explanatory model of poverty are largely the same as the D.L.M.T., with a number of minor refinements.

Origins

The theory accepts as its starting point, the changes brought about by the transition from competitive to monopoly capitalism. It is argued that this transition united and organised, not just capital, but also the labour force and encouraged them to press political and economic demands, which, of course, posed a threat to the system of monopoly capitalism. And, to confront this challenge, employers omnisciently, in a mass consciour contrivance, created labour market segmentation in pursuance of the 'divide and conquer' objective. Thus, employers, acting in their own interests and controlling powers, planned and developed a rigidly partitioned labour market, characterized mainly by a non-manual and manual division, with further concretely defined economic and occupational classes within each layer. Different job clusters were defined, each with their own qualifications, methods of recruitment, working conditions and renumeration. These objectives were achieved by a variety of strategies: structuring internal labour markets; attracting female labour (this was viewed as a means b y which anti-trade union forces could be encouraged); absorbing workers from different ethnic and racial backgrounds (this was also seen as a strategy to combat unionization); establishing the importance of educational achievements for 'skilled' workers etc.   The theory is thus founded on a suggestion that monopoly capitalists were unhindered in, and beyond the influence of, their relations with other class interests and forces - i.e., that their ability to determine their total rule (hegemony) was unimpeded.

In order to secure the power and control hierarchy and the division of the workers, monopoly capitalism may conceded benefits to certain segments of workers.   The dynamic nature of this segmentation process suggests that, rather than actively creating some sort of occupational class hierarchy, most employers simply adapt to the process, forced to do so by competition, government and the development of social classes.   As Townsend (1979, pp. 78-79) put it, 'The formation of monopoly capitalism and of multi-national corporations ... widen as well as further institutionalized social inequality'. Such a process is offered by segmentation theorists as an explanation of the manifestation of poverty in terms of those employees in the inferior jobs and those unemployed.   The most positive contribution made by the S.L.M.T. is its exposition of the basic flaw in the orthodox explanations which accept as given, a perfectly competitive and smooth running labour market which fail to explain the roles of workers' organizations, the hegemony of monopoly capitalism and state regulation.   But the composition and organization of the labour market as a product of compromise and resolution between classes is beyond the scope of the S.L.M.T. model which merely recognizes the process by which one class, the 'bourgeoisie', unhindered by opposing interests and forces, imposing its needs on the other class, the 'proletariat'.   As with the D.L.M.T., segmentation theory would logically imply that the need for appropriate workers for different layers of the market can best be met by dangling the carrot of the sectors above in front of the noses of the lower status employees.   And, of course, those outside the labour market can be held in a state of readiness and availability for the lower, inferior stations in the labour market hierarchy by their poverty income levels and lifestyles.

Structuralist theories

By emphasizing the roles and conditions of the non-poor, as well as the poor, structuralist approaches refuse to isolate from the rest of society, individual traits, group sub-cultures or labour market developments.   This general approach suggests that poverty can be understood by identifying distinct and separate strata of various natures within society and by discussing the means by which the very existence of poverty is functional to the maintenance of this societal hierarchy.   These means include various social mechanisms which operate to perpetuate poverty which itself, in turn, encourages the 'victims' to respond in such a way as to serve to consolidate its existence.   And if the causal factors of poverty are located within the constituents of society, then the solutions should confront major societal obstacles. However, even though poverty may be accepted as a social problem, attempts to relieve it or to abolish it may become stifled because its existence serves the interests of politically and economically powerful groups of 'elites'.

Structuralism suggests that, 'The implication is obvious. Without some kind of fundamental change, the problem (of poverty) is not going to be solved. Any claim to solve it within the present system is self-contradictory'. (Taylor-Gooby & Dale 1981, pp. 43-44). If the causal base of poverty is located within the unequal structures in society, then the solution to the phenomenon must address this inequality and thereby reform social and economic systems, such as the distribution of income and resources and the values which consolidate the inequality of deprivation and privilege. The fate for those at the bottom of the societal structures. As Kincaid (1973, p. 23) put it, 'Poverty cannot be considered as a residual, historically determined effect of an otherwise fair society, but as an integral element that helps support a competitive social order'.

Functionalism

The idea that poverty is functional to reinforce the foundations upon which social structures of inequality are built bears contrived, theoretical relationships with underlying suppositions within the O.E.T.'s explanation of poverty. Functionalism's central hypothesis focuses attention on the importance of the various types of employment and unemployment and thus, corresponds, in limited terms, with those economic theories which explain inequality in terms of the distribution of individual ability, education, skills and training. However, the structuralist approach blames societal institutions for these inequalities while the orthodoxy lay responsibility with the individual. Given that there are differing levels of the occupational hierarchy which have their own layers of functional importance and attraction, then social systems operate to ensure that all positions are taken up by offering incentives which become accepted as the conditions of employment. The greater the material inducements, the higher the social or occupational status, the stronger the induced motivations to endeavour to fill specific occupations. And, the lower the standard of living, the greater the dissatisfaction and the greater the desire to elevate oneself out of such base positions. Thus, the function of financial provision for the poor would be to coerce them into offering their labour power to meet the demands of the market and the needs of employers and the market economy. This 'coercion' takes the form of imposing lifestyles which are parsimonious, stressful, uncomfortable and 'poor'. Thus the conditions of unemployment involve disincentives as opposed to the conditions of employment which include incentives. Therefore, poverty is not merely a dysfunction of society; if it were, pressure could be instigated to rectify the maladjustment and abolish it. Holman (1978) suggests that there are three main examples of the way in which poverty functions in a structured, hierarchical society:

1 *The justification of poverty and wealth* - because of the refusal of the poor to save and invest in the future, because of their fecklessness, idleness, neglect of their children and exploitation of the social security system (scroungers, doing the double etc.), then a hierarchical and stratified social system, with top and bottom layers, is justified;

2 *Lessening prospects of change* - if society is clearly categorized into two unified and opposing forces, the disadvantaged and the advantaged, a large mass of poor people and a small minority of capitalists, then revolutionary movement by the deprived to alter or overturn the hierarchy would be, more or less, inevitable. But, the poor in Britain are a minority, albeit a sizeable and growing minority, and the categorization of society involves far more than two groups - it consists of various sub-classes which frequently intermingle. Based on the Dickensian adage that 'tuppence ha'penny looks down on tuppence farthing', then poverty can function to reduce the prospects of alterations to the nature of society. Social class identify their structurally immediate neighbours, directly above or below, as their point of reference. Those groups just above the poor can compare their position favourably with those below them and feel relatively well off and thus, any movement for social change among them is lessened. Thus, the conditions of the unemployed and poor would not receive significant attention or sympathy and those marginally above them can feel relatively superior, thereby diluting any potential for unrest. In this sense, the lower the level of poor relief, then the lower the chances of growing dissatisfaction and friction among those just above the poverty line. As employers act, in the main, to maximize profits and as one of the main ways this can be achieved is through depressing labour costs (cutting wages), then the function of poor relief in this respect is to instill some element of superiority among the low paid, thereby banishing any real risk of radical demands for wage rises. This process multiplies up the social hierarchy so that the positions of the rich and poor are virtually guaranteed and invulnerable;

3 *Dirty workers* - A stratified society, by its very nature, contains a number of unpleasant employment roles and tasks. Historically, Middleton (1971,

p. 34) explained that the 19th century Poor Law systems not only degraded the poor recipients, but also ensured a steady flow of base workers, '...fitted to undertake tasks essential to the more affluent classes, but which they would not do themselves'. The poor thus help to ensure that 'dirty, dangerous, menial and undignified work' gets done. And the most effective way of ensuring that there are individuals willing to accept these posts is to make the alternative as unpleasant and unacceptable as possible - i.e., to confront them with an income in unemployment which is the epitome of poverty. Another function of the poor, in a similar vein, is to accept unemployment when the economy wishes to reduce the size of the labour force, in the sense that a pool of unemployed with poverty incomes can function to depress wage levels by discouraging wage claims and thereby expand the profitability of industry (the Tory idea of workers 'pricing themselves out of a job').

Herbert Gans (1972) pointed to the focus of society's attention on the 'problem' and 'costs' of poverty and the failure/refusal of this focus to recognize the functional benefits of poverty to society, or to be more accurate, to those groups (and their value systems) who are not poor and who do not attach much importance to the conditions of the poor. He listed a whole catalogue of the poor's and poverty's functions which benefit the non-poor and help maintain the social hierarchy. These include: subsidizing the affluent by saving them money (paying regressive taxes); creating a number of highly paid professions (social workers, police, etc.); helping to uphold the legitimacy of dominant norms by providing examples of deviance (laziness, dishonest, promiscuity); providing emotional satisfaction, evoking compassion, pity and charity, so that the affluent may seem righteous; assisting in the upward mobility of the non-poor (by being denied educational opportunities or being stereotyped as stupid or unteachable, the poor enable others to obtain better jobs); absorbing the economic and political costs of change and growth in society (reconstruction of city centres and 'inner cities', industrialization etc.); and playing a relatively small part in the political process and indirectly allowing the interests of others to become dominant and distort the system. (Cited in Stitt & McWilliams 1986, p. 9). Gans emphasized that, because of its beneficial nature to the advantaged classes, poverty persists, but he rather ambiguously suggests that it is not clear whether the functions outweigh the dysfunctions or vice-versa. He concludes that poverty's functionalism ensures its persistence, as does the fact that, 'the functional alternatives to poverty (equality) would be quite dysfunctional for the more affluent members of society' (cited in Townsend, 1979, p. 86).

Conflict view

A structural approach to poverty identifies an 'elite' social group at the apex of the societal pyramid who can manipulate the lower classes in such a way as to ensure their supportive participation in the mechanisms and the agencies that serve the material interests of that elite. The social hierarchy is presented by this elite as a necessity to upward mobility, which is both desirable and obtainable. But by being preoccupied with increasing capital accumulation, this elite does not have the necessary requirements to govern as a class and so they ensure the election of governments to rule in their interests and they determine the statutory policies which prevent any redistribution of income or wealth. These policies can be seen to operate in the level of welfare payments to the poor.

Mechanisms of a stratified society

How are these differences between the various social classes in the structure of society maintained and perpetuated? The structuralist view explains that major societal institutions and agencies contribute to the reinforcement of the privilege/poverty relationship, the major ones being: the education system; the mass media; the social services, all of which function to support the elite. This occurs in the welfare services in three main ways: (1) the level of the services and benefits they provide are so low that the problem of poverty is contained but not improved; (2) by doing this, they reinforce the lowly status of the poor, a position designated to them by society; (3) they present and provide services in such a way as to attribute blame to the poor for poverty by offering them, for example, income levels which make it impossible to make ends meet and to budget properly, in view of the non-poor in society. As a result, the response of the poor consists of even less 'acceptable' behaviour and the perception that poverty is deserved is consolidated and the need for a stratified system is unavoidable and indeed, morally valid.

Structuralist conclude their arguments by suggesting that, although social services do operate together to insulate recipients from the even more dreadful poverty that would exist if no services were provided, and thus, the poor would be in a much worse position without state provision, it must be recognized that poverty and deprivation have not been eliminated - only a slowing down of the rate of deterioration has occurred. Services, having characteristics which uphold poverty and consolidate the structural inequalities and hierarchical divisions in society, are presented as a series of well regulated compromises that offer short term assistance to the working class and much longer term advantages to the upper classes. Thus they operate, not just to relieve misery, but to perpetuate inequality. Poverty is viewed as the greatest incentive to work and social security has always been dominated by the requirement of the capitalist system to maintain work incentives intact. The lower the poor relief scale rates, the heavier the incentive, the more beneficial to the employer and the powerful elites

Marxism and poverty

A Marxist/materialist explanation of poverty gathers its impetus from the social relations of production. From such a broad base, Marxists present their explanations as being totally polarized from, not only orthodox economic analysis, but all non-Marxist theories. The orthodoxy proceeds with arguing on the basis of the permanent nature of the status quo in social and economic arrangements. The other non-Marxist approaches accept as given, the fundamental mechanisms of capitalism and explain poverty in terms of malfunctions in its administration. For Marxists, the 'cause' of poverty is the very existence of capitalism and thus the 'solution' to poverty can only be found in the complete overthrow of the capitalist system.

In the mid 19th century, Marx and the traditional empiricists of English social investigations were vigorously gathering data on the social and economic conditions which prevailed in the most prosperous nation on earth. While similar data were collected, they were analyzed differently and utilized for two opposing purposes. The empiricists employed their findings to argue for a reform of the capitalist system, whilst Marx presented the data as conclusive proof that capitalism was beyond reforming the required replacement. As Pinker (1971, p. 32) put it, 'The normative orientations of Marxist theory were ... alien to the ends of practical social administrators and reformers...'. The three main sources of this fundamental distaste between Marxist social theory on poverty and what has become known as social administration are outlined as: (1) Marx's explanation of the nature of the state in the capitalist system and its institutionalized objectives; (2) Marx's understanding of social policies (such as poor relief) as designed to prevent materialist class consciousness and revolutionary development; (3) Marx's own stated perceptions of the nature and characteristics of certain layers of the poor.

Another point of departure from the analysis of orthodox economists and even functionalists, centres on their view of poverty and the unequal distribution of wealth as an objective necessity to motivate the poor to strive for social and economic improvement by equipping themselves with the necessary qualities for responsible employment with high wages, which would help them avoid poverty. Marx rejected such a dubious and narrow approach while proposing a sequential process which involved the necessity of low paid employment for capital to expand and the lowering of the living standards of the unemployed to such an extent that they would be willing to accept these low paid jobs, again in the interests of capital. This is the central point in all Marxists' explanations of poverty. Because capitalism places the ownership and control of the means of production and distribution in the hands of private individuals and groups, Marx argued that poverty is the natural outcome of such a system. Whilst capitalists invest their capital to create private wealth, workers try to barter their labour power in the market in order to earn an income which is capable of providing them with the means for subsistence and, if possible, for an acceptable standard of living. In such an arrangement, the level of wages (i.e. what the capitalist pays to purchase the labour power of the workers) will largely influence and determine, to a certain extent: (a) the level of profitability; and (b) the satisfaction of the needs or the worker and his/her family. But because the capitalist system gives primacy to the interests of capital accumulation, then, without doubt, many workers' wages will be at a level whereby their needs will not and cannot be met. In such a structurally-determined conflict situation, poverty is the 'natural outcome' of capitalist production relationships.

In order to obtain the means of living, the worker has little of the freedom of choice espoused by the orthodox economist - he/she either sells his/her labour power at a price largely determined by the capitalist, or lives in, generally, the lowest levels of poverty. The workers therefore must accept the wage levels dictated by the capitalists' terms and conditions in the labour market. In other words, the price of labour power (wages), for many workers, is set at a level which is barely sufficient to purchase the commodities which satisfy contemporary needs, themselves determined by the dynamic need of the capitalist system for profit. And, by implication, the level of financial assistance to the unemployed must be set below this standard - i.e., inadequate to provide an acceptable lifestyle - so that there are in-built disincentives to unemployment and to demanding too high wages within the poor relief systems and an in-built incentive to accept low paid posts in the labour market. In this sense, an objective is to reduce the wage level down to a minimum subsistence amount. Of course, such a process is not such a one sided affair, as workers struggle to continually increase the level of wages by including more and more new basic needs, as society develops economically and socially. The degree of success in such a struggle is influenced by the level of organization, the depth of cohesion and the solidarity and class consciousness of the workforce. However, Marx believed that a historical tendency towards the 'relative pauperization' of the working class was clearly identifiable - i.e., only a part of the increase in productivity and profitability went to the labour force (in pay rises) and this part tended to decline. This downward tendency can, of course, be accompanied by an increase in real wages. However, the gap tended to increase between: (a) the new needs created by the development and growth of capitalist production and; (b) the ability to satisfy these needs with the earned wages of the labourer and, to an even greater extent, the incomes of the unemployed.

Marx characterized capitalist society in the following terms:

The modern bourgeois society that has sprouted from the ruins of feudal society has not done away with class antagonisms. It has but established new classes, new conditions of oppression, new forms of struggle in the place of old ones. Our epoch, the epoch of the bourgeoisie, possesses however, this distinctive feature: It has simplified the class antagonisms. Society as a whole, is more and more splitting up into two great hostile camps, two great classes directly facing each other: Bourgeoisie and Proletariat. (Marx Engels, 1962, pp. 34/5)

For Marx, a class was a collective of workers or capitalists who shared a common relationship with the means of production, who either owned or did not own the primary material essentials for production. Marx argued that the fundamental cause of the antagonisms between these two classes is that the bourgeoisie have the means to exploit the proletariat by extracting 'surplus labour' from them. This involves the production by the workers' labour of a 'social product'. However, this product is not retained as a whole by the workers - they receive only a fraction of it, in the form of 'consumption goods' such as food, fuel, clothing, accommodation etc., while the remainder is appropriated by the bourgeoisie. Ian Gough (1979, p. 18) defines this process:

The total labour time devoted to providing the necessary consumption goods for the producers - the subordinate class - is termed necessary labour; the remainder is termed surplus labour, and the goods and services it provides for the dominant class is termed the surplus product.

Against this background of class antagonism, division of labour and exploitation, Marx refused to identify poverty merely as a social problem, as the result of group conflict, of industrialization or urbanization, or of a lack of skills or motivation. Such views are designed to confuse and cover, ' ... structural issues of inequality, oppression and alienation with an individualist cloak'. George and Wiling (1985, pp. 95/119) concluded that Marx perceived, '... the capitalist mode of production and the forms of social relationships which it fosters ... as the causal base of poverty', and that this explanation is 'direct and obvious'.

Marx (1967) clearly identifies his point of departure from all other models of social science and explanations of poverty by saying,

Insofar as Political Economy remains within that (bourgeois) horizon, insofar, i.e., as the capitalist regime is looked upon as the absolute final form of social production, instead of a passing historical phase of its evolution, Political Economy can remain a science, only as long as the class struggle is latent or manifests itself only in isolated or sporadic phenomena.

In other words, whilst causal models of poverty are explained within the confines of the existing social and economic system, i.e., capitalism, whilst the very existence of this system is beyond the critical analysis of theories of causation of poverty, then such paradigms will continue to be accepted as valid and applicable only insofar as the working class struggle is too weak, disorganized and lacking in consciousness and cohesion to theoretically and practically challenge them. And as long as social analysis confines itself to these limitations, then the solutions to poverty and other natural manifestations of capitalism are over looked in favour of palliatives which, in the short term might marginally improve the standards of living of the poor, but which will, in the long term, benefit the non-poor proportionately more. In essence, Marx provided an explanatory framework which allows contemporary analysts to define the reasons why, for example, the current poor relief system, as a 'social palliative' is not, and indeed, could not be adequate to cover all the fundamental requirements of the unemployed and poor.

Historical materialism

A crucial concept in Marxist explanations of poverty is historical materialism. Through this, Marx compared previous socio-economic patterns with those of 'modern industry' under capitalism. He was particularly interested in the role of the state in all areas under various systems of production. Unlike previous social formations, Marx argued that under capitalism, individuals arrange economic relations which are not associated with the societal structure as a whole but are carried out on an individual/private basis.

Poverty and exploitation of one class by another are not, of course, unique to capitalism - indeed, in both the slave and feudal areas, exploitation and subsequent poverty formed the basis of economic relations. The peculiarities of them lie in the form that they take under capitalism. Under previous epochs, the political, social and economic relations between slaves and slave-owners, barons and serfs, were closely affiliated. Slaves were forced to labour for specific periods of time for their lords by political and legal subjection. In both areas, the stratified class nature of society was clearly identifiable and accepted by various political, social and religious institutions. However, during the transformation from feudalism to capitalism, the labour power of the sub-ordinate classes became a commodity to be freely bought and sold in the labour market. The essential character, thereafter, of labour, was that unlike previous arrangements, the workers were afforded to sell their labour power to the highest and most suitable bidder, or indeed, not to sell it at all. This was the theoretical point of departure for the relationship between labour and capital; economic relations were freed from their feudalistic constraints and the identification of commodities as private property to be exploited to accumulate and deploy wealth, completely altered the relationship which

36

existed previously between people and the material necessities of life. Freedom, as a prerequisite right, banished an individual's obligations to anyone but him/herself and his/her family and comfortably facilitated the choices in-built in the wage-labour system. This logihanism for escaping poverty through the pursuit of self-interest among either individuals, or, increasingly, among groups with mutual interests, such as trade unions. Within these groups, the common-denominated has been self-interest.

However, Marx explained that this transformation brought with it a corresponding detachment of politics from commercial activities and financial and economic relations. Feudalistic forms of political rule gave way to democratic processes, whereby individuals could enter the decision-making world of government and could begin to critically question the role of the political state, in relation, of course, to their own self-interest. However, Marx's analysis would describe a more basic division in society, one characterized by a holistic, unconscious collective, rather than so many independent units. Society continues to be based on exploitation, but the worker is not owned by the employer, nor is he/she politically inferior to the capitalist (each, in theory, has only one vote each). The distinction between them is that the latter owns and controls the means of production, whereas the worker has no access to these. He/she therefore has no means of leading a socially acceptable lifestyle or of escaping poverty other than by entering a contract of exchange with the capitalist. In the same way as the slave-owner appropriated the surplus produced by the serf, so the capitalist appropriates the surplus produced by the worker or wage-labourer. The difference is that, under capitalism, exploitation takes place on the basis of formal relations of apparent equality. As the Conference of Socialist Economists (C.S.E.) (1979, p. 55) argued:

> In pre-capitalist class societies, class distinctions openly permeated every aspect of social life. Under capitalism, exploitation is concealed under a formal veil, a veil of freedom and equality in exchange. Workers are "free" to exchange their labour power with any capitalist they choose. This is an "equal" exchange, in the sense that the workers receive the value of their labour power (as defined only by the money needed to ensure survival and reproduction). But the "equal" exchange conceals exploitation because they do not receive the full value of what is produced by their labour power in action.

This process forms a theoretical foundation for explaining, not just poverty, but the relative nature of such deprivation. Thus Marx explained the exploitation process of wage-labourers and exposed the reality of the 'freedom' of workers in the labour market and the 'equality' of exchanges in the market. To elaborate on these conditions, Marx compared the contradiction between: (a) the 'freedom and equality' in the exchange arrangements and; (b) the 'coercion and inequality' in the production process. In the latter, the relations between capital and labour, employer and employee, manifest themselves starkly, as the worker as a paid employee must accept control by the employer. Whilst in the former, the worker is forced to market his/her labour power to the capitalist by economic necessity - the alternative: starvation, the workhouse, social security. And these alternatives have to be as unpleasant as possible in order to force the worker to sell his/her labour power. It is this contradictory 'freedom' and illusory 'liberty', and the alternatives to it which are at the core of Marx's explanations of poverty.

Industrial reserve army

Marx was adamant in his analysis that the working class would have to constitute an adequate supply of labour power in order that the capitalist economy may grow continuously. In order that this may occur, there must be '... a development of all the circumstances which produce a relative surplus population among the working-class'. This surplus would reflect ' ... the varying proportions in which the working class is divided into active and reserve armies'. Marx claimed that ' ... every special historic mode of production has its own special laws of population, historically valid within its limits only ', and he had identified '... a law of population peculiar to the capitalist mode of production'. (Marx 1967, pp. 518 & 632). This surplus population is relative by nature because lab our power is measured against capital's demand for it. In reality, this reserve army consists of ' ... workers needed by capitalism for the potential expansion of enterprises, but who can never be regularly employed ... The surplus population ... is an indispensable attribute to the capitalist economy, which could never exist nor develop without it.' (Lenin 1963, pp. 180-81).

During periods of economic expansion, such as the post-war era, the surplus population functions to maximize profits by keeping down wage levels when the reserve army is occasionally returned to employment. Their periods of dependence on state or charity welfare support render them amenable to working for relatively low wages. In this process, the reserve army is 'repelled' during times of economic recession or technological advances and 'attracted' during periods of economic expansion, to coincide with the needs of production. The means of replenishing the reserve army include the introduction of intuitive technology which saves labour costs. As real wages continue to rise, the motivation and need for capitalists is to hold down the costs of labour and maximise capital. It can do this through the introduction and development of technological advances which usually result in substantial unemployment (and thus absolute poverty), the generation of a relatively few highly skilled workers and the consolidation and expansion of inequality (and therefore relative poverty). In this way, science becomes subordinate to capital accumulation. The Industrial Revolution bears witness to this dynamic. The unprecedented development of technology is evidence of this but, ' ... its origins and its raison d'etre is the need continually to recreate the industrial reserve army in order to preserve and extend surplus value and hence permit capital to accumulate.' (Gough 1979, p. 26).

The Marxist economist Robert Freedman (1961, p. 148) suggested that over-work of the employed sector of the population expands the reserve army and as a consequence, the employed must submit to this more intensive exploitation because of the ever-present competitive threat from the reserve army, the unemployed living in poverty. Workers either subject themselves to more intensive labour or face the consequence of unemployment and poverty, this threat being even more real because of the millions of unemployed only too willing and ready to accept a job, even one which requires them to work unjustly hard. A related and very important reason why the employed sectors concedes to more work and lower real wages is the standard of living provided for the unemployed by the state, a standard which they would sacrifice much to avoid descending into because of the totally inadequate and unacceptable nature of it. This is one of the most relevant concepts of Marx's approach to poverty. What is being said is that the financial assistance offered by the state to the poor, or the reserve army, must be characterized by subtle (or explicit, as in the social policies and stated assumptions which underpin them, introduced by central Government throughout the 1980s and early 1990s) coercive force - i.e., poor relief/social security must be of an inadequate and unpleasant nature in order to produce a system of coercive attraction, whereby the wage-labourer has little alternative but to accept employment, on conditions dictated by the employer, or suffer the consequences - for example, subsisting on welfare benefits which are incapable of affording basic needs. As Marx stated, 'Taking them as a whole, the general movement of wages (and thus poor relief levels) are exclusively regulated by the expansion and contraction of the industrial reserve army.' (Marx 1967, p. 637). The centrality and primacy of the 'free market economy' based on economic inequality, in determining wage levels and welfare benefit levels is clarified.

A central objective of capitalism is to de-militate the labour force, to reduce their enthusiasm for resisting greater demands put upon it by: (a) increasing the threat of unemployment; and (b) making the deprived conditions in which the unemployed live highly unacceptable. It seems a logical reaction for workers not to complain or pressurize too strongly on work and pay issues if acceding to their demands increases the possibility of bankruptcy for the employer and unemployment and dependence upon poverty line welfare benefits for them, especially with labour in such a flexible and available form, as in the mass unemployment of the 1980s and early 1990s. Individuals become intimidated and subdued and labour groups, such as Trade Unions, see their powers diminished and their resources reduced, faced with high unemployment levels. The threat of bankruptcy prompts employers to resist wage claims and the threat of unemployment and the consequences of that for individual workers dissuades any opposition to lower money wages and thus, workers accept poorly-paid employment with low safety controls etc. In this way, money wages are depressed, consequently improving the profit margin for firms, while reducing the level of inflation by decreasing the amount of cash in circulation.

The evidence of industrial changes in Britain during the early part of the last century, the global restructuring of manufacturing in the 1950s to the 1970s, the increased participation of women in the workforce and even the collapse of manufacturing in the U.K. in the 1980s and 1990s and the consequent expansion of the labour force employed in the service sector, all provide reinforcement for Marx's theory of the process of attraction and repulsion of the reserve army of labour as a substantive explanatory model of poverty. Marx summarized the role of the reserve army this way:

> The greater the social wealth, the functioning capital, the extent and energy of its growth and therefore, also, the absolute mass of the proletariat and the productiveness of labour, the greater is the industrial reserve army. The same causes which develop the expansive powers of capital, develop also the labour power at its disposal. The relative mass of the industrial reserve army increases therefore with the potential energy of wealth. But the greater this reserve army, in proportion to the active labour army, the grater is the mass of a consolidated surplus population, whose misery is in inverse ratio to its torment of labour. The more extensive finally, the lazorous-layers of the working class and the industrial reserve army, the greater is official pauperism. This is the absolute general law of capitalist accumulation ... It establishes an accumulation of misery corresponding with the accumulation of capital. (Marx 1967, p. 604).

In this paradoxical, if inevitable, process, the richer society becomes, the deeper the extent and nature of relative poverty.

Wealth and poverty:

In other words, Marx explained that the very nature of capitalism and its dynamics for survival by continually expanding must essentially cause poverty among one section of the population and generate wealth among another. This fundamental law of capitalist motion has never been addressed. far less disputed by bourgeois economists who recognize only a permanent, if less than perfect capitalist economy. But, as Marx argued, the core element of capitalist poverty consists of unemployment and underemployment - the industrial reserve army - which deprives the poor of adequate income and undermines

40

the bargaining power of those who compete with the poor for scarce work - thus the nature of the plea of Right wing economists and the Tories for workers not to 'price themselves out of a job' in Britain in the 1980s and 1990s is explained.

Baran and Sweezy (1966, pp. 252-53) argued that standards of living, not least for those at the bottom of the economic ladder, improved significantly all over the advanced capitalist world after the second world war. However, this was perceived by 'bourgeois ideologists, wearing the blinkers provided by the orthodox economic theory' as evidence of 'normal' capitalism operating in its true form. The widespread poverty of the 1920s and 1930s was merely a brief malfunction in the economy and unfettered capitalism would soon eliminate it, totally and permanently. But Marxism sees the development in inverse. While bourgeois economists see poverty as a malfunction and its absence as normal behaviour for capitalism, all Marxists would argue that the apparent improvement in living standards was a temporary malfunction for capitalism, widespread poverty being the norm. It was not long before the levels of unemployment began to gradually increase, as the progress of technical development in the 1950s and 1960s took its toll on the unskilled and semi-skilled workers and aggravated the gap between the poor and the rest of society. The impact on the disadvantaged was double-edged. Relatively, they had benefitted more from the postwar full employment era, but soon, unemployment and poverty began to emerge again and evidence suggested that it was spreading and deepening. Baron and Sweezy concluded, 'Affluence began to appear for what it was - not the cure for poverty, but its Siamese twin.' The 'discovery' of mass poverty by Booth and Rowntree in the 1890s, the Great Depression of the 1930s, the extensive poverty exposed by Rowntree in the 1940s and 1950s, the 're-discovery' of poverty by Townsend and Abel-Smith, Coates and Silburn in the 1960s, and the unchallengeable poverty research of the 1980s and 1990s provide empirical reinforcement of this explanation.

The state:

In order to comprehensively understand Marx's approach to poverty, it is necessary to analyze his views on the role of the state and its policies under capitalism. (There is, of course, a significant degree of diversity among commentators describing themselves as Marxists, about the nature and role of the state. To avoid being drawn into this lengthy and complex deb ate which would require a lengthy book on its own, only those issues which are not contended and which find consensus among the various Marxist factions have been discussed).

Generally, Marx perceived the state as action ' ... as an organizing committee on behalf of the bourgeoisie', (cited in Corrigan 1980, p. 15) to deal mainly with the economic, political and social crises of capitalism by developing into an 'institution' which has the scope to arrange and maintain a suitable and flexible labour market on a national scale. It is a task which the state alone is capable of carrying out and, in doing so, it has come to provide an essential prerequisite for modern capitalist production. Marxists such as Corrigan (1980) view the state as going beyond an institution and see it as ' ... a form of social relations, a class practice ... a process which projects certain forms of organization upon our every day activity, forms of organization which do not pose any threat to the reproduction of capitalist social relations.' (Corrigan 1990, p. 15). In times, such as the present era, when the nature of the capitalist system in Britain is, as the C.S.E. (1979, p. 57) put it, 'particularly oppressive', with unemployment increasing, social security and other services cut, the function of the state is to ask individuals, both wage-labourers and capital-owners, to vote in elections in order to influence the policies which the successful party will implement in governing the capitalist system. Voters are asked to participate, not as a class or classes, but as individuals. When poverty emerges inevitably under capitalism, the role of the state is to direct claimants of welfare benefits to fill in forms as individual poor persons, to discourage the poor from unifying as a collective of 'the victims of class domination'. The C.S.E. conclude, 'At every step, our relations to the state breaks us up, pushes us into certain moulds, removes from sight all mention of class or exploitation, or anything which might raise the question of the interrelation between our fragmented ills ... exploitation is presupposed before bourgeois politics even begin. 'The predictable disputes within the limitations of bourgeois politics are related merely to the form of social relations which emerge from exploitation and while these may be crucial to individuals, such conflicts fail to address the primary issue of class exploitation. Thus, when differences of opinion manifest themselves in Parliament over, say, the level of financial assistance to welfare claimants, the discussions at best, attempt to concern themselves with tampering with the standard of living of various families or categories, not the overall causes of poverty and the fundamental reasons why so many millions of people live in poverty.

Of course, there may well be powerful social and economic interests which exert pressure on the state in its efforts to ameliorate social problems such as poverty. As evidence of this explanation, it is worth considering the contents of a memorandum from the Department of Industry to the Ministry of Social Security in September 1979, which argued that the payment of state welfare benefits to strikers involved in disputes enables them to avoid actual deprivation and suggests that policies should be implemented to neutralize this 'fundamental imbalance in industrial relations ... it is contrary to all reason that the Government should add to industrial difficulties ... we are tilting the balance against employers and allowing strikes to be held on the cheap.'

(cited in Taylor-Gooby and Dale 1981, p. 96). The government went on in the mid 1980s to disentitle employees involved in strikes from claiming welfare benefits, a strategy largely regarded at the time as being targeted at defeating the miners' strike. Conceptually, what was being said was that the state's role in alleviating poverty should succumb to the primacy of its function of upholding the power of capital in the class struggle, and more precisely, the concept of profit accumulation may not essentially parallel with the objectives of social and welfare policies aimed at, not only eliminating, but also, merely alleviating poverty. Thus, where capital accumulation requires it, the level of state assistance to the poor will be reduced, without any reference to the impact on the lifestyles of poor households. Such a policy would be generally unhindered by the state or by class pressure which is fragmented and decimated by the dominant ideology of individualism.

The very idea of a governing, representative, democratic state under capitalism, Marx argued, is a contradiction in theoretical terms. The free market economy thrives on individualism, self interest and self help. Taylor-Gooby and Dale (1981, pp. 131-32) ask, 'How could a centralized structure of power, dictated to only be common interests, operate in a society motivated by private interest, and inevitably and naturally, beset by the struggle and conflict of such interests?A In a similar, more practical and relevant vein, how could the state, dictated to by the requirement of the poor to receive an income adequate to meet socially determined or even their basic needs, operate in a system which requires the reserve army, or the unemployed, to subsist in conditions so unpalatable, that they are permanently ready to be coercively attracted into the low wage, low status sectors of the labour market, to cater for the changing needs of capital? In a normative sense, the function of the state under a free market economy, whose essential dynamic is the pursuit of self interest, would be to facilitate the smooth operation of the mechanisms of such pursuits. And the main way in which it can achieve this arrangement on a basis of non - or minimal intervention in the free market economy. Specifically, it therefore maintains and operates a poor relief system which holds the reserve army of the unemployed in readiness for the changing labour market by reducing their standards of living to an inferior anti-social level.

The individualistic nature of capitalism, the notion that all participants in the market are ostensibly free and equal to protect their own self interests and to escape poverty, Marx argued, would necessitate the existence of a distinct and unrelated structure to represent the common good. Thus, what should develop would be separate institutions of the state to achieve this framework and their superficial divorce from the process of exploitation. Through this analysis, Marx demonstrated that before exploitation can succeed, this image of political freedom must be presented to and accepted by the masses, with the state being the visible manifestation of this innate - therefore the state in its abstract form in capitalist society plays a vital role in the generation of poverty - by legitimising the system which produced it. So that exploitation can occur and labour power can be bought and sold as a commodity on the market, capitalists and workers alike should be free and equal partners before the law, with equal access to justice and freedom. But the dilemma ultimately lies in this set of arrangements because Marx believed that the control and exploitation of one class by another rests on force and repression, requiring distinct apparatuses of coercion, e.g. the armed forces, the judiciary, the police and, more subtly, the legislature, including the rules and nature of the social security system. The employed are coerced into obedience to the capitalists and the unemployed are coerced into accepting low paid and menial employment, if and when it becomes necessary for the profit margin, and all this is facilitated by the inferior nature of the poor relief system. This form of coercion has been a common characteristic of all class based societies but, Marx explained, coercion only divorces itself from the ruling class and consolidates itself in the separate agencies of the state, under capitalism.

With this view of the state and its organs, Marx argued and administration and administrators were the executive arm of the ruling class. For him, the essential character of social democracy was as follows: 'Democratic, republican institutions are demanded as a means, not for the abolition of the two extremes, Capital and Wage Labour, but for the mitigation of their opposition and for the transformation of their discord into harmony.' (cited in Pinker 1971, p. 33). And to exemplify this theory, Marx concentrated upon the phenomenon of 'pauperism' and argued that the actions of governments to tackle pauperism have constituted merely 'administrative and charitable measures', because the state itself presents as a crucial contributory factor to this problem. As Pinker (1971, p. 34) put it, 'The central point for Marx was that, under capitalism, the efforts of even the best administrators would be negated by factors beyond their control.' Any attempt thus, by the Department of Social Security to improve the level of benefits to the unemployed would meet with resistance from other economically and politically powerful interests - such as the Confederation of British Industry.

To summarize and generalize Marx's conceptualization of the causes of poverty, the following can be identified as the major explanatory components:

1 Low real wages in employment caused by: (a) the expansion of the commodities which are socially, morally and historically determined and which are required to achieve an acceptable standard of living, but without a corespondent increase in the workers' ability to purchase and obtain these commodities; (b) the depression of wage level increases by constant competition, particularly in times of high unemployment, from the industrial reserve army of labour, the unemployed;

2   A standard of living among the reserve army, so low and unacceptable, and so incapable of achieving socially-determined lifestyles, that unemployed labour will be coercively attracted into low paid sectors of the labour market, which themselves, as the last point explains, are not adequate enough to provide the means to escape poverty, but rather facilitate a move from dire deprivation into merely a less harsh lifestyle;

3   The imbalance of class forces allows capital to do this without fear of serious political instability during areas when it is organized, strong and untied and to raise the exploitation rate of labour and to lower the income levels of labourers and the unemployed when the latter is divided, weak and lacking in class consciousness and principled leadership, as in the Thatcherite 1980s and the Majorite (sic) 1990s.

Conclusion

If the explanatory models of poverty presented here can be crudely and semi arbitrarily categorized into three major approaches, it is clear that each classification: (a) perceives 'the poor' in different ways and; (b) normatively demonstrates he treatment of the poor - either as a corrective remedy or by way of explaining the relationship between inadequate incomes for the unemployed and wider socio-economic objectives - under each of the paradigms. It has been a consequence of this chapter to suggest that each and every one of the theories discussed openly states or logically implies that the standard of living afforded by the financial provision made by the state to the poor is/should/must necessarily be of an unpleasant, unacceptable, coercive and inadequate nature.   Some theories actually prescribe low assistance standards, while others explain why poverty and deprivation exist and are necessary within the prevailing social and economic order.
    The individualist vision sees the poor as that group of single beings who are characterized by maladaptive traits (O.E.T., M.G.T., culture/sub culture theory); the labour market and structuralist theories (which crudely lump together dual and segmented labour market theories and structuralist approaches) view the poor, in general, as groups of people in a relatively vulnerable state in relation to their ability to negotiate improvements in their standards of living because their occupational status, or lack of it, attracts little concern from the dominant ideologies which govern society; and the Marxist explanation identifies the poor as components in the capitalist mode of production who function to depress wage levels and who are at the beck and call of the needs of capitalist industry, to be drawn in and pushed out of employment and unemployment as the requirement arises.   And, by rational intrinsically, obvious in all cases, each hypothesis involves quite varied

programmes for tackling poverty and the poor: the individualist school would direct policy towards encouraging and facilitating change in individual beings, targeting the person for change; the labour market and structuralist models, in locating the causal factors of poverty in social arrangements and the organization of society and the economy would tend, to varying degrees towards social reform of the institutions of the state; and the Marxist analysis would advocate socialist revolution and the establishment of a communist state on the grounds that the capitalist system cannot survive or function without poverty and the poor and is therefore beyond reform.

But it is in the understanding of each of the paradigms as to the nature and level of the provision made for the poor by the state that is of crucial importance to the sequential arguments of this book and which dictates the direction of the discussion. Thus, it is accepted that as all the major schools of thought on poverty hold common perceptions, albeit from widely differing approaches, (either prescriptive or analytical) that the poor, normatively under present arrangements, must, for one reason or another, receive a poverty income, then the poor relief system in Britain, must reflect this philosophy. The O.E.T. 'rationally' argues that those who live in poverty are unemployed and they are in this situation because they demand wage levels which are 'irrational' - i.e., they are too high in terms of the worth of the productivity. Such a 'rational' understanding of the poverty problem begs a similarly 'rational' solution, in this case, the deterioration of the standards of living of the unemployed. Thus, it becomes 'rational' to search for and accept renumerative employment, but at a level determined by the market. In this sense, for example, the level of welfare benefits operate as a catalyst in a 'rational' economic formula - low and inadequate benefits encourage the unemployed to return to the labour market at a 'rational' stage and on 'rational' conditions.

The explanation offered by the M.G.T. similarly perceives individuals as self determining entities and thus the poor are regarded as being apart from normal society, unwilling or incapable of benefiting from the opportunities afforded to every member of the community. Financial provision by the state should thus fall well short of the common living standards of the employed and should function to banish idleness and fecklessness and to imbue the recalcitrant with the necessary virtues of self help and self reliance. The most appropriate mechanism for achieving this is to spawn distaste among the poor with the lifestyles imposed on them by self inflicted unemployment, via offering them a deterrent system of poor relief. The implied policy response to the S.C.P.T's suggestions would target the value systems of the poor for change and put on offer, the various fruits of personality-reform and conformity. To instigate such a process and to provoke the poor to turn their backs on their murky pasts, the provision of assistance must ensure that the poor consciously feel deprived, so that they may strive for the alternative which society has to offer.

The D.L.M.T. and S.L.M.T. hypothesize that the existing mode of production requires a supply of labour for the lower labour markets which must be immediately available and that this can be achieved by rendering the standard of living of those outside any of the labour markets, the unemployed, unacceptable and coercive, in the sense that the poor will have little choice but to acquiesce to the demands of employers for low paid, low status workers when the need arises. This escape involves, of course, mainly a passage from the dire poverty of poor relief into the less dire poverty of the low wage sector of the labour market. Structuralism examines the question of the actual existence of poverty as functional and vital to the maintenance of the societal hierarchy and thus, policies to protect against it or to eliminate it will be confronted with the interests of powerful forces in the economy and in the political sphere. The different layers of he employment market are consolidated by differential material inducements leading to more materially-beneficial social or occupational statuses. On the other hand, however, the more inferior the material inducements, the lower the lifestyles, then the deeper the resentment leading to a more concentrated effort to rise out of poverty. In this light, social security operates to coerce recipients into selling their labour power when and how the production system demands it. The benefit levels are the conditions of unemployment involving mainly disincentives as opposed to the conditions of employment which seek to promote incentives. The levels of public assistance also function to prevent dissatisfaction and non cooperation among those just above the poverty line and to ensure that dirty and menial jobs are done by rendering the alternative as unpleasant and as unacceptable as possible.

Similarly, Marxism analyses that low paid employment is necessary for capital to have the scope to expand and to help to provide this, the living standards of the unemployed have to be lowered to such an extent that they would be willing to accept these low paid jobs. Capitalism allocates the ownership and control of the means of production and distribution to private individuals and groups and the underlying aim of capitalists is to increase their rate of capital accumulation. This situation impels the workers either to barter their labour power in conditions dictated by the laws of capitalism or live in a state of deprivation. To 'encourage' the wage labourers to pursue the former alternative, the latter conditions must be generated by a system of state provided income maintenance which is regarded as a poverty existence. Thus, in reality, the freedom and democracy of the capitalist system is mystificatory - there is no real freedom in the choice between accepting the capitalist terms of employment or, for example, subsisting on welfare benefits. The social security system must also contribute to the smooth operation of the attraction and repulsion process for the reserve army of labour, by strengthening the attraction operation through coercing the unemployed into allowing themselves to be absorbed into the low wage sector of industry, having been subjected to subsistence on the poverty line. Another one of the terms of reference of the poor relief system is to reduce the proneness of the working class to resist growing demands placed upon it to increase their productivity without a proportionate rise in their wages. Highly unacceptable social security rates would act as a disincentive to those who perhaps were contemplating action which would place their employment and source of livelihood in some danger.

Throughout this chapter, all the theories discussed have stressed, either overtly or by logical implication, that the level of poor relief in times of unemployment should be, or necessarily is, functional to the changing demands of the production system and the needs of the economy and the labour market. They all similarly imply, or indeed, recommend, that benefit levels should be incapable of affording basic needs so that some degree of deprivation is experienced, in order that the demands and need of the market are met. And there is consensus that this can be achieved by encouraging or coercing the recipients of such benefits to enter or return to the arena of paid employment to wage labour on the conditions dictated by the rationality of the market or the requirements of capital accumulation. , This is not to suggest that the condition of poverty is left behind once employment is accepted. There is little doubt that the level of wages in some sectors of the labour market are not much above, and in many cases below, the poverty line as determined by welfare benefit levels. What this chapter has suggested is that, among the plethora of theories on the causation of poverty, there is concordance as to the requirement of modern capitalist society, particularly during economic recession, for a system of public financial assistance to the poor, which is inadequate in terms of meeting the basic needs of claimants. Only the individualist theories would actually recommend this (prescriptive) - the other see it as inevitable, given the existing arrangements (analytical/observed).

2 Measurements and definition of poverty

Introduction

A number of issues need to be clarified at this stage. It must be stated at the very outset of this chapter that what follows is an account of what can only be described as an academic battle of scholarly semantics and fanciful phrasemongering ('a stale and tedious dispute' - Silburn, 1988, p. 6) which characterised the poverty debate in the 1960s, 1970s and climaxing in the mid 1980s and which involved the commitment of many intellectual gladiators such as Townsend, Piachaud, Veit Wilson, Sen Desai, Walker, Mack and Lansley. Thankfully, a ceasefire appears to have grounded itself in an atmosphere of agreeing to disagree and the theoretical framework within which various academics have taken sides appears to have carved the schools of thought, or camps, into three main approaches to defining and measuring poverty: (1) absolute/budget standards; (2) relative deprivation/observational/behavioural; (3) consensual. This chapter will offer a description of each of these approaches followed by a critical, conceptual and practical discussion, outlining the major criticisms. Some critics may point to the absence of the 'inequality' model of poverty from this chapter. For example, Alcock (1987, Chapter 1) includes inequality as a way of defining poverty. It is held in this book that inequality - as in the hierarchical structures of privilege and disadvantage in capitalism - is more a causative explanation than a measurement of poverty and thus has been widely discussed in Chapter One.

It should also be clarified at this stage that all measurements and definitions of poverty require value judgements from whatever source. Mollie Orshansky (1969, pp. 37-41), for example, argued:

Poverty, like beauty, lies in the eye of the beholder. Poverty is a value judgement; it is not something one can verify or demonstrate, except by inference or suggestion, even with a measure of error. To say who is poor is to use all sorts of value judgements.

The 'like beauty' simile may be dubious, but the message is clear and valid, as the OECD (1976, p. 62) agrees: 'There cannot be any definition of "poverty" which is free from value judgements'. Acceptance of this argument does not in any way imply that all endeavours to establish measurements of poverty are totally subjective, meaningless exercises. Rather, by introducing and permeating this message throughout this chapter, it is hoped that the result will be a more open and honest discussion on the extent of poverty, leading to a greater awareness of its causes and thus solutions.

The core aim of most poverty studies is quite straightforward: to establish how many people in a given country/region/city are currently considered to be 'poor' as opposed to 'non-poor'. In pursuit of this, the most common approach is to identify a 'poverty line', a weekly monetary amount, in order to calculate the number of people living below this standard. A broad range of various methods for establishing such a poverty line income has been, and continues to be employed, with the differences between them in some cases referring back to the concept of poverty being used, but sometimes reflecting different methods of operationalizing the same concepts. To broaden the horizon for study, many investigations have employed indicators of poverty and deprivation other than cash income to identify the poor - e.g., lacking 'necessities' or other indicators of the standard of living, health standards, mortality etc. Within the confines of official records and premises, poverty does not exist in Britain - because Britain does not have an official poverty line. The theme of governmental resistance to defining and measuring poverty seems to be that a 'scientific', neutral, objective definition would be implausible and thus any exercise to 'count the poor' would inevitably fail in essence because it would involve 'experts' (to whom governments appear to hold an unhealthy antipathy) making subjective judgements about the criteria for poverty.

The sociologist who has contributed to an influenced the poverty definition debate more than any other in the 1980s, John Veit Wilson (October 1989, pp. 74-95), catalogues the prime purposes of measuring and defining poverty as follows:

1   to count the numbers defined as poor in the population;

2   to explain why people are poor;

3   to prescribe a poverty line - a minimum level of money income on which people ought to be able to live and avoid deprivation (as defined by the prescriber) if they spend their money as prescribed;

4   to report a poverty line - a minimum level of money income on which the population in general thinks it would be able to live and avoid deprivation as it defines it;

5   to discover a poverty line - a minimum level of money income on which empirical research shows that the population in general manages to avoid what is defined as deprivation. This comprehensive framework provides the structure within which most recent poverty debates on measurement and definition have taken place.

The argument that poverty is a relative concept and needs to be defined and measured in such a context is widely acknowledged and accepted among academics, policy makers and most politicians. Does this mean that the absolute/relative poverty debate has been settled and that all developments forthwith will be in terms of refining the relative concept: are we all relativists now? It should be noted that the concept of absolute poverty has not been entirely rejected nor universally abandoned. The poverty line still employed in official circles in the US is founded on subsistence nutrition standards for various family compositions, with a built-in element of relativity in the application of a multiple to arrive at a poverty line. Theoretically, Sen (1979, p. 289) holds that there is 'an irreducible core of absolute deprivation' within the poverty definition debate and that relativist measurements supplement rather than supplant poverty as defined in terms of absolute depossession. He argues that absolute deprivation keeps issues of starvation and hunger central to the concept of poverty. 'If there is starvation and hunger, then - no matter what the relative picture looks like - there clearly is poverty.' The names of the relativists spring easily to mind - Townsend, Mack and Lansley, Piachaud, Veit, Wilson etc. The names of recent absolutists are, however, more difficult to recall (other than Sen). Certainly, no major academic pieces of work in post war Britain have sought to defend the absolute definition of poverty. Political economists of a Right-wing persuasion have addressed poverty in the latter's terms, not by way of carrying out the 'versus' debate, but to: (a) argue that absolute poverty no longer exists in Britain, in that no one lives in or below a state of bare subsistence; (b) make a case for enshrining the work incentive in social welfare, in order to maintain a standard of living for the workforce which is more than starvation prevention and which will hold it ready and willing to enter the labour market, if, when and at what level it is required.

Indeed the 'versus' debate seems to have been initiated and sustained as much by non-academics as by academic researchers and theorists. The former arena has been largely the domain of those state agencies responsible for social security provision and by anti-poverty lobbies such as the CPAG and Campaign Against Poverty, groups which have sought to expose the inadequacy of the poverty line welfare benefit levels. The other non-academic scene has centred on notional attitudes among the population towards poverty and the poor. This is addressed by Richard Silburn (1988, p. 5)

> Here the debate was an indirect response, on the one hand to the tone of the discussion of poverty issues, and the nature of the evidence presented in the more brutish sections of the popular press, which periodically panics about alleged welfare scroungers; and on the other hand, was a reaction to an apparently deeply-seated set of widespread public prejudices, fanned no doubt by the tabloids, but rooted much more deeply in British popular culture, in folk-memories of the stigma attached to the Workhouse and the Poor Law, and asserted either as categorical denial of the possibility of there being poor people, or more equivocally expressed in such ambivalent and defensive cliches as "poor but proud", "poor but honest" etc.

In search of the source of an absolute measurement of poverty, the social policy literature has honed in on the classic studies of B.S. Rowntree as the traditional example of subsistence poverty measurement. But, thanks to the work of John Veit Wilson (1986), this fundamentally erroneous assumption has been rectified. As a result of Veit Wilson's work, Townsend (1987, (a) p. 497) commented that, 'all those who quote Rowntree will do so in future with greater care'. Indeed earlier, Veit Wilson (1981) summed up the interwoven relationship involved in the absolute poverty versus relative deprivation paradigms as:

> the **condition** of DEPRIVATION means unmet need;
> unmet need is **caused** by lack of resources of all kinds (tangible, intangible, interpersonal, intrapersonal);
> the **condition** of POVERTY means lack of money resources;
> the lack of resources, including money resources, is **caused** by the **condition** of POWERLESSNESS in social, economic or social systems.

Absolute/Budget standard approach

A comparison often made by those who prefer to condone the current state of inequality and poverty in Britain is that of contrasting the UK poor with the hundreds of millions of people in the Third World, whose life expectancy can be lower than thirty years, who can look forward to only a life of physical hunger and even starvation. Compared to these people, the poor of Britain are well-off, we are told, and should count their blessings. Rhodes Boyson MP, as Minister for Social Security, contributed to this debate in the Commons in June 1984:

> Those on the poverty line in the United States earn more than fifty times the average income of someone in India. This is what relative poverty is all about ... Apparently, the more people earn, the more they believe poverty exists, presumably so that they can be pleased about the fact that it is not themselves who are poor. (cited in Mack & Lansley 1985, p. 28)

In cold, clinical, Thatcherite logic, this is a valid statement. Although the parallel development of affluent countries who suffer more from problems associated with over consumption and poor nations whose people live a life of daily survival is ethically reprehensible and repulsive, it does not automatically follow that there exists some convenient, readily calculated, absolute poverty cut off point. It does not imply that we can construct a UK minimum income level which is based purely on scientific, 'factual' and clinical criteria - without have to make political, social, moral and economic decisions. The absolute approach is the definition which most clearly corresponds with the current level of welfare benefits payable to the poor in Britain in the 1990s. The main thrust of this approach involves: the construction of a list of necessities; the costing, usually on a weekly basis, of these items; and the determination of a poverty standard/line based on these estimates. Budget standards are defined for various areas of expenditure by experts who arrive at informed judgements on the required amounts of money for food, clothing, fuel etc. This poverty line can be drawn, firstly by using the estimates of dieticians on the nutritional requirements of a family and determining a minimum weekly amount to purchase these. Secondly, additional amounts to cater for housing costs, fuel costs, clothing and footwear, personal and household sundries etc. are added. For example, the task Rowntree set himself was to measure the numbers of people living in poverty, as defined by appearance, and to identify the reasons why people led such a lifestyle. In order to ascertain explanations, Rowntree was bound to establish whether such deprivation was the result of: (a) financial mismanagement and wastage of an otherwise adequate income or; (b) incomes inadequate to purchase a lifestyle free from the visible traits of poverty.

So that he could pre-empt the expected attacks on his message from predictable quarters, Rowntree opted to construct a poverty standard based on the absolute minimum weekly amount of case necessary to cater for what he identified as the four main, conventional components of working class needs: food; fuel and personal and household sundries; clothing; and housing. No other requirements were to be considered but those which were absolutely necessary for 'physical efficiency' and this standard was an irreducible lifestyle called 'primary poverty'. Rowntree went to great lengths to clarify the nature of this device by differentiating between: (a) what he believed was an income level upon which no one in Britain could be expected to live and; (b) a hypothetical measurement calculated for the sake of heuristic argument, to prove a point. On this basis, Rowntree discovered substantial numbers of households living in a state of primary poverty as a result of having incomes insufficient to afford even these basic, subsistence needs, even if they spent their incomes in exactly the asocial and apsychological way which Rowntree had implied. In exposing the depth of subsistence deprivation in prosperous Britain, Rowntree developed a measurement of what became misunderstood as 'absolute' poverty which was to become the yardstick adopted and employed by statutory agencies in the 20th century. As it seemed possible to measure basic requirements and thus establish whether these were or were not being met, then the objective of welfare systems was obviously to eradicate such poverty by offering financial assistance to provide for these subsistence requirements. All of the notable state policy responses to poverty have pursued the subsistence/absolute poverty model. The Poor Law compelled the Guardians to evaluate the 'needs' of the poor when assessing entitlement to support. Its replacement, the Unemployment Assistance Act 1934 offered benefit only after a probing and degrading inquiry (the means-test) was carried out to make sure that only a 'safety net' income level was provided to allow minimum provision for claimants. During Beveridge's 1942 establishment of a social security system, his main advisor was Rowntree who interwove his subsistence model into the benefit levels calculations. When Supplementary Benefit was introduced in 1966, the means test to ensure that minimum subsistence was the ceiling above which the poor could not rise (rather than the floor below which they could not fall), remained the central plank of the provision. No major changes occurred to the nature and level of Income Support when it replaced Supplementary Benefit in 1988. Contemporary Right-wing political commentators have adopted the absolutist view with enthusiasm. The then Secretary of State for Education and a guru of the New Right, Keith Joseph (and John Sumption, 1979, pp. 27-8) suggested that: 'An absolute standard means one defined by reference to the actual needs of the poor and not by reference to the expenditure of those who are not poor. A family is poor if it cannot afford to eat. It is not poor if it cannot afford endless smokes and it does not become poor by the mere fact that other people can afford them'.

But it is this total emphasis on physiological needs and complete ignorance of social and psychological needs which dominates the measurement of absolute poverty and which leads to the consensus: 'In short, the concept of absolute poverty is literally an absolute nonsense. Its use in debate always means no more than a decision by some non poor people to allow the poor only certain shared human needs and not others'. (Veit Wilson 1989, p. 14). Measures of absolute poverty are thus, inherently non sociological by failing to take account of the social environment in which poverty is generated and thrives. Ideas of the constituents and nature of a certain, specific standard of living are, as Peter Worsley (1984) points out,

> Cultural specific norms, defined by people in specific societies, according to their criteria of what constitutes want or plenty, not standards deemed appropriate for them - often arbitrarily - by social workers, statisticians or nutritionists and measured against some universal biological yardstick (WHO calorific guidelines). Social want, not asocial, biological needs, define health and wealth.

As far back as 1954, Peter Townsend was complaining that the sufficiency of these subsistence, minimum standards was wholly dependent upon efficient and provident spending, this being equated with the manner in which the architects deemed proper. Explaining that many factors militated against such efficiency, Townsend (1954, p. 131) suggested that:

> It may be that people do not know what goods are 'necessary' and where they can be obtained cheaply. Or it may be that spending habits are determined by the conventions of the lowest stratum of society and by economic and social measures ... currently adopted by the community as a whole. All this is quite apart from individual habits and inclinations.

What can be considered 'necessary' as opposed to 'unnecessary' For example, Rowntree deemed clothing, travel expenses, newspapers as 'necessities': why not coffee, cosmetics, hairdressing, house contents insurance, contraceptive etc? Townsend was thus arguing that the definition of 'necessities' goes beyond mere physical subsistence and stretches into the realm of socially determined conventions.

Although Townsend was making these statements in the early post war period, criticisms of subsistence poverty standard and references to the relativist nature of deprivation were made in the works of the classical political economists. For example, in 'The Wealth of Nations', Adam Smith (1776) said: 'By necessaries, I understand, not only the commodities which are indispensably necessary for the support of life, but whatever the custom of the country renders it indecent for creditable people, even of the lowest order, to be without'. And Marx wrote in 'Capital' that the workers' 'natural wants, such as food, clothing, fuel, housing, vary according to climatic and other physical conditions of his country. On the other hand, the number and extent of his so called physical wants ... are themselves the product of historical development and depend therefore to a great extent on the degree of civilisation of a country'. (cited in Coates & Silburn 1970, p. 36).

The traditional criticisms levelled against this method are threefold: one descends upon the expert centred nature of the estimates; the second notes the absence of analysis of actual expenditure trends; and lastly, it deprives poor people of any flexibility or discretion to decide how much they should spend on food, how much on clothing etc. As Silburn (1988, p. 9) states: 'In short, it is thought to be arrogantly prescriptive and elitist.' But, need this always be so? Are budget standards always characterised purely by assumptions of absolute minima? No so, according to John Veit Wilson. The works of Rowntree, for an unforgivably long time, were regarded as presenting the epitome of the subsistence approach. But Veit Wilson (1986) has exposed the non prescriptive intention of Rowntree's works and thus, in principle, the relative and useful character of weekly budget standards. For example, Rowntree's use of the concept of secondary poverty (see Chapter 3 on the History of Poor Relief) was based on a recognition that actual spending patterns would not simply adhere to a predetermined design of shopping and consumption. And it is inherently logical in this model that the construction of a poverty standard can be animated by the dynamic framework of developing socially determined needs and by the broad range of expenditure practices among different groups in the population.

In reply to the criticism that this approach is 'arrogantly prescriptive', it needs not be pointed out that absolute budget standards have been used by a number of social researchers in a non minimalist and non prescriptive manner. The work of the Family Budget Unit, has centred on the use of budget standards as a means of indicating basic needs which policy makers require to consider, and for international comparisons (Family Budge Unit, 1990). Before this, Stitt (1989 & 1991) employed weekly budget standards to expose the serious inadequacy of Supplementary Benefit Income Support scale rates. And in 193, Stitt and Grant used minimalist budget standards in the non prescriptive manner employed by Rowntree to demonstrate the radical growth in primary poverty throughout the 20th century. None of these sets of work were offered as prescriptive statements in terms of instructing households on their shopping or consumption. Research of this nature is prescriptive only in the sense of providing policy makers with persuasive evidence of the depth of poverty endured by benefit recipients. The at6traction of this approach is that the level of the budget standards drawn can be increased or decreased in accordance with the audience and with the arena of debate. In this way, the budget standard approach is capable of contributing to definitions and measurements of even relative deprivation.

As Stitt (1989) showed, this issue was paramount in the social security reforms 1986-88, when government agencies for the first time this side of the introduction of the Welfare State, began to discuss claimants' budgeting patterns. The majority of single payment grants were abolished and replaced by 'budgeting loans' available for recipients who are experiencing difficulty in making ends meet. Notwithstanding the significant financial saving that this change has generated for central government, the move can only be perceived as pertinent if it is assumed that basic benefit levels are demonstrably adequate to meet the needs of claimants. Governments have never engaged in research to establish whether this has been the case. The crucial role of the research of the GPAG, the Family Budget Unit, Piachaud, Stitt etc., is apparent in this light. Stitt (1989) describes how it necessitated three years of constant investigation to get the DHSS to admit to the assumptions upon which poor relief has been constructed since 1948 and how reluctant the Department was to enter into the debate of recommending or expecting claimants to spend their benefits in any specified way. Official sentiments have always argued that claimants are at liberty to determine the manner in which they use their income. Such a stance has led to a complete absence of any official definition, measurement or defence of minimum income levels, of safety net standards, or of adequacy for subsistence. Yet, Stitt concludes, although the Department may hold this viewpoint, this should not be used to resist attempts to address the inadequacy of benefit levels.

Many attempts have been made to dress up absolute poverty perceptions in relativist clothes. As chairman of the Supplementary Benefit Commission (SBC), David Donnison (1982, pp. 7-8) claimed that his and the Commission's view of poverty was basically a relativist one: 'I believe that poverty means a standard of living so low that it excludes people from the community in which they live'. But when Donnison went on to elucidate what his view of poverty meant in practice, there is little difference between the lifestyle proposed and that of many subsistence poverty lifestyles, such as Rowntree's primary poverty line. Donnison asserted:

> They must be able ... to keep themselves reasonably fed and well enough dressed to maintain their self respect and to attend interviews for jobs with confidence. Their homes must be reasonably warm; their children should not feel shamed by the quality of their clothing; the family must be able to visit relatives and give them something on their birthdays or at Xmas time; they must be able to read newspapers and retain their TV sets and their memberships of Trade Unions and churches. And they must be able to live in a way which ensures, so far as possible, that public officials, doctors, teachers, landlords and others treat them with the courtesy due to every member of the community.

The above reads like an extract from Rowntree's primary poverty work of 1899. Donnison claims that his view and that of the SBC was relativist inspired. It would be immensely illuminating if Donnison were to give his account of what subsistence or absolute poverty meant if the above is a manifest example of relative deprivation. For Watts (1987), budget standards have four different uses, other than that of developing a poverty line:

1 They can provide standards of living norms for a given family type.

2   They can be used to derive standardised comparisons of living standards. (equivalence scales) for different family types.

3   They can be used to compare living standards over time.

4   They can be used to compare living standards between areas.

However, strong arguments still abound that the budget standard approach can generally be equated with absolute subsistence characteristics. Although such commentators as Bradshaw et al (1987) hold that, 'Social needs can be represented in budgets' even the 'social' side of subsistence measurements - for example, the same involved in being recognised in public as poor - is perceived in absolute terms. Put illustratively by Adam Smith (1776, p. 161), the test is 'not so much having equal shame as others, but just not being ashamed, absolutely'. Michael Harrington (1962, pp. 39-40) provides an interesting, novel, yet socially important interpretation of the meaning of absolute poverty: 'To have one bowl of rice in a society where all other people have half a bowl may well be a sign of intelligence and achievement ... to have five bowls of rice in a society where the majority have a decent, balanced diet, is a tragedy'. Thus, it is as unacceptable to compare an 1899 subsistence poverty line in Britain (concerts, chapels, dolls, marbles etc.) with a 1990s standard (televisions, telephones etc.), as it is to compare subsistence poverty in a Third World society with similar deprivation in Britain. Poor people in Britain are not starving but their standard of living is socially intolerable: they are thus absolutely poor. Third World people are starving: but subsistence poverty is so rampant that the quality of their life is the norm. Whilst clearly exhibiting an affinity with the relativist notion of poverty in the above statement, Harrington asserts that: 'Poverty should be defined absolutely', not in the sense discussed above, but in terms of 'what man and society could be'. Whilst entire nations and individual citizens are operating at less than their full potential, then not only are people impoverished absolutely; but so to are nations: BAR 4,27As long as there is the other America, we are, all of us, poorer because of it'.

Converted into the terms of reference of this chapter, this implies that the sole, rational absolute measurement should not be a minimum one, but rather one based on optimal criteria or one founded in maximum possible social achievement. Coates and Silburn argue (1970, p. 40): '... the stringently calculated subsistence level poverty line is seen as an aberration on the part of those whose yearning for precision and parsimony exceeds not only their common humanity, but also their desire for sociological sophistication'. (Sociologists take note!). Generally, absolute measures of subsistence poverty standards have also been the option preferred by upper income people, concerned at being forced to hand over part of their substantial income, either

58

through higher taxes or prices, in order to fund improved welfare benefits for those less fortunate than themselves. Walker (1987) goes further by arguing that, in the absence of this consideration, all measurement and definitions of poverty are incomplete, because they are purely hypothetical.

Within the historical context of changing ideas about poverty, Veit Wilson (September 1992, p. 2) identifies three stages in the use made of the minimum subsistence model of poverty:

1   Rowntree used its apparent scientific objectivity as a heuristic device in 1899;

2   it was then used by other social scientists as a survey instrument (e.g. Bowlby);

3   it has been used to rationalise 'less eligibility' (see discussion on Poor Law in Chapter 3 on The History of Poor Relief) in social security benefits.

As Veit Wilson has rightly implied, the language of the Labour movement, of Beveridge, of the Welfare State's national minimum - an income floor below which no one in society should fall - was steeped in the acceptance of the state's responsibility to calculate and provide a tolerable minimum standard of living. This idea of what poverty is - subsistence poverty - has survived largely intact, mainly because it corresponds with the liberal conscience to help the poor, but not at the unacceptable cost of imposing any restrictions upon the wealth-accumulation activities and privileges of others. By adhering to this definition of poverty within a system of relative economic development such as in Britain, the standard of living of all citizens could be increased to the extent of eradicating this type of subsistence poverty, whilst escaping any significant redistribution of wealth and income and any restructuring of the balance of class forces in capitalist society. Similarly, on an international level, poor nations can leave poverty behind them by aping the industrial path of the developed countries. But David Donnison (1982, pp. 5-7) asks: ' ... what should we do not that we are (in) ... a period when the nation's living standards are not going up and indeed ... (are) falling ... ? Do we abandon altogether the attempt to reduce poverty?'

Behavioural/Observational or relative approach:

The most traditional way of identifying poverty was steeped in observing behaviour and ways of life in order to acknowledge evidence of 'obvious want and squalor' or to look for 'the pinched faces of the ragged children' (Rowntree 1901, pp. 115-16). This view investigates the relationship between behavioural patterns and income levels and endeavours to define a poverty cut-off point parallel with an alternation(s) in social behaviour. It is argued that as a household reaches a specific poverty threshold, deprivation increases radically as income drops: however for households above this standard, deprivation increases much more slowly and indeed, declines.

Such an approach encountered little challenge since its introduction to the public eye by Booth and Rowntree until the 1940s and indeed, it regularly emerges in accounts of poverty based on superficial judgements of people's lifestyles. There is, quite clearly, within this approach, no determinative role for money or income measurements. Veit Wilson (1989a, p. 12) explains that this paradigm:

> involves non poor people making a prescriptive judgement about what sort of visible lifestyle is to be defined as deprived and called poor. In itself, it carried no power of explanation why people defined as poor in this way, live the lives they appear to live ... Nor does the appearance of the lifestyle to an observer necessarily indicate anything about the life experience of the poor subject. People may be deprived and unobserved; they may also be deprived in many more ways that the observer sees.

This approach fits neatly into the subculture of poverty thesis, discussed earlier. Taking visible human behaviour as a way of defining poverty is clearly, for sociologists, permeated with class-ridden, personal, subjective judgements and has no contribution to make to the explanation of poverty debate. It has been referred to as the 'social coping' paradigm. (George & Howards 1991, p. 6). There is the danger of this becoming a label slapped on those who cannot cope with everyday life and the natural trials and tribulations of capitalist, competitive interaction, therefore emphasising the weaknesses of he poor rather than the injustices of the system. B ut George and Howards (1991, p. 7) continue: 'he emphasis in this definition is on the fact that people who are poor do not merely fall behind the rest of society but they do so in a marked way. They are not just unequal; rather they do not have enough income to copy with the basic needs and the basic social expectations of their community and society.'

However, such minor obstacles have never stood in the way of those individuals and groups who would deny the existence of 'real' poverty and deprivation and who would refuse to acknowledge the validity of any other less subjective approach to identifying poverty. A contemporary defender of this approach has been Desai (1986). But undoubtedly, the major proponent of this approach, somewhat more refined and democratised, has been Townsend in his 'elative deprivation' model. Poverty 'disappeared from the public view' and went underground in the late 1940s and 1950s and when it saw the light of day again in the 1960s, it inhabited a different conceptualisation - relative deprivation. The current debate on definitions and

60

measurements of poverty and deprivation can be identified as stemming from a 1965 publication by Abel-Smith and Townsend, particularly int he context of the Galbraith (1958, p. 252) were referring to the relative nature of poverty in the 1950s: 'People are poverty - stricken when their income, even if it is adequate for survival, falls markedly below that of the community. Then they cannot have what the larger community regards as the minimum necessary for decency; and they cannot wholly escape therefore the judgement of the larger community that they are indecent. They are degraded for, in the literal sense, they live outside the grades or categories which the community regards as acceptable.'

The core theme is the proposition that any exercise to define poverty within narrow, absolute, subsistence confined is unsuitable and sociologically incomplete. Instead, these two authors asserted that, 'n any objective sense, the word has no absolute meaning which can be applied in all societies at all time. Poverty is a relative concept.' (Abel-Smith & Townsend 1965, p. 63) (Townsend 1970 said elsewhere: 'The subsistence concept seemed too static, somehow locked up in the distant youth of the grand parental generation.' p.x) However, in pursuit of practical convenience, they selected as their measurement of relative poverty at the time, the National Assistance weekly scale rates, on the grounds that it provided a semi official definition which could be operationalized as a measurement of 'he minimum level of living'. (p. 17). The National Assistance benefit levels were, of course, as Supplementary Benefits and Income Support have bene, based on an absolutist, subsistence concept of poverty line needs. In the 1970s, Townsend carried out an extensive research exercise into the definition and measurement of 'relative deprivation', which culminated in the publication of the classic 'Poverty in the UK' in 1979 in which he introduced the relative concept of poverty in these terms:

> Individuals, families and groups in the population can be said to be in poverty when they lack the resources of obtain the kind of diet, participate in the activities and have the living conditions and amenities which are customary, or are at least widely encouraged or approved in the societies to which they belong. Their resources are so seriously below those commanded by the average individual or family that they are, in effect, excluded from ordinary living patterns, customs and activities.' (p. 31)

Put more succinctly by Fitzgerald (1981, p. 13), 'We recognise as poor, not only those who can barely feed and clothe themselves, but also the many whose incomes and living conditions fall below the accepted minimum norms of our society.' The EC has accepted this wider view of poverty through its establishment of the Third Poverty Programme (and the 1995 Social Exclusion initiative), explicitly designed for the 'integration of the excluded': ' ... the poor shall be taken to mean persons, families and groups whose resources (material, social and cultural) are so limited as to exclude them from the minimum acceptable way of life in the member states in which they live.' (cited in Cohen 1992, p. 5). Implicit in this notion thus is the idea that being poor is relative to the standards of living of others and about being incapable of affording the commodities and services that have become generally accepted as components of a socially normal lifestyle. For example, the single parent with a five year old son complained of relative poverty be recounting (Mack & Lansley 1985): 'Now that he is at school, and tells me about other children's bikes, and the toys they take, and holidays, and days out with parents, and it breaks my heart for there is nothing for him; if he has food and clothes, then he can have nothing else.

A bicycle is not an absolute necessity; nor are toys, holidays, days out etc., for all can survive without them. But when friends, neighbours, the community in which one lives all enjoy ownership of such items, then the quality of life of those who cannot afford them is depreciated somewhat, to the extent of stigma, degradation, shame, isolation, worthlessness. As a harsh example of the inability to socially participate in traditional customs because of a lack of adequate income, the mother of two children living in London said (McEvaddy & Oppenheim 1987):

> Christmas is not a time for celebrating for our family as we can only manage to buy the bare basic things to tide us over the holiday period. We do manage to buy a chicken for Christmas Day, that's all. After that it's back to basic meals - eggs and chips, sausage and mash etc. We cannot even afford trivial things like jellies, mince pies, crackers etc. to brighten up the festive season.

The concept of relative poverty is based upon, centrally, a critical weakness in the absolute measurement of poverty - that the latter is impractical and inappropriate to operationalize. The core argument of the relativists is that value judgements and social assumptions inevitably underpin even the most basic of human needs - nutrition. For example, perceptions of food requirements develop with the advance of scientific nutrition, dietary needs constantly change and customs, preferences, practices, styles of eating etc. all call for premises which are moulded by social influences. As Townsend (1979, pp. 59) argued, 'People's needs, even for food, are conditioned by the society in which they live and to which they belong'. Thus poverty can be perceived as 'relative' in three ways: firstly, in historical terms; secondly, in international terms; thirdly, in intra-national terms (one group in Britain - e.g. black people compared to the native white Brits). This view thus argues that poverty in Britain in the 1990s is defined only in terms relative to the prevailing living standards, whilst subsistence poverty claims that specific requirements are central to physical efficiency. On this latter rationale, these needs would form the constituents of a primary poverty line, whether or not they were affordable by the majority of the citizens of that country. Consequently, relative deprivation is employable only in developed, advanced countries because in poor, Third World nations, since the prevailing standards of living are dominated by malnutrition, slum housing, ragged clothing, practically non-existent education, then the majority of the population cannot be living in poverty.

The deprivation standard measurement of poverty is operationalized through a catalogue of lifestyle indicators, including nutrition, household commodities and activities and socialising. These 'necessities' are established through surveys of attitudes among the population and also from the expert opinions of scientists on socially defined standards of living. A list of sixty indicators was constructed by Townsend as reflecting the main components of personal, household and social life. This covered diet, clothing, fuel and light, domestic amenities, housing and housing facilities, domestic environment, security, welfare benefits or work, family support, recreation, education, health and social relations etc. In operation, only twelve of these were employed and Townsend gave no indication of how these were short listed. The following is Townsend's (1979) 'provisional' list of deprivation indicators:

1   Has not had a week's holiday away from home in last twelve months.

2   (Adults only) Has not had a relative or friend to the home for a meal or snack in the last four weeks.

3   (Adults only) Has not been out in the last four weeks to a relative or friend for a meal or snack.

4   (Children under fifteen only) Has not had a friend to play or to tea in the last four weeks.

5   (Children only) Did not have a party on last birthday.

6   Has not had an afternoon or evening out for entertainment in the last two weeks.

7   Does not have fresh meat (including meals out) as many as four days a week.

8   Has gone through one or more days in the past fortnight without a cooked meal.

9   Has not had a cooked breakfast most days of the week.

10 Household does not have a refrigerator.

11 Household does not usually have a Sunday joint (three in four times).

12 Household does not have sole use of four amenities indoors (flush WC; sink or washbasin and cold water tap; fixed bath or shower; and gas or electric cooker.

Allocating a score of one to each of these indicators, a rating of five, six or more on the summary deprivation index in 'highly suggestive of deprivation', and again, the author does not offer a rationale for this cut off point. Townsend explains that the deprivation rating is not the instrument by which the poor are to be identified, but is rather the foundation for establishing a poverty line income. The population is then investigated to measure the numbers lacking one or more of the deprivation indicators. Townsend's conclusion was that, 'in descending the income scale ... a significantly large number of families reduce more than proportionately their participation in the community's style of living. They drop out or are excluded.' (p. 249). Although his findings were conceded to be inconclusive, they did, V4,27
suggest that such a threshold may exist' (p. 255). Consequently, within the downward income spiral, each individual or family approaches a stage or 'threshold' at which non participation in social/community lifestyles (relative deprivation) accelerates significantly. Townsend concluded that 'resources for a sudden withdrawal from participation in the customs and activities sanctioned by the culture. The point at which withdrawal 'escalates' disproportionately to falling resources could be defined as the poverty line.' (p. 57).

Townsend involved himself again in a more elaborate exercise to define and operationalize this multiple deprivation index in the Greater London area in 1987. (Townsend, Corrigan & Kowarzik 1987). The researchers attempted to represent as many aspects as possible of both the material and social conditions of life. Thus Townsend went from his 1979 general deprivation index of:

Material Deprivation
    Dietary
    Physical & mental health
    Clothing
    Housing
    Home facilities
    Environment
    Work (conditions, securities, amenities)

Social Deprivation
   Family activity
   Social support & integration
   Recreation
   Education   (Townsend 1979, pp. 1173/6)

to his much more comprehensive and detailed index in 1987:

Material Deprivation
   Dietary
   Clothing
   Housing
   Home facilities
   Environment
   Location
   Work

Social Deprivation
   Rights in employment
   Family activity
   Integration into community
   Formal participation in social institutions
   Recreation
   Education   (Townsend et al 1987, pp. 91-94)

There are two main criticisms of Townsend's methodology:

1 the income threshold/poverty line derived:- Townsend related deprivation
   scores with income and established a threshold 'below which people are
   disproportionately deprived' which was then presented as the poverty line.
   The identification of a discrete break or poverty cut off point on this basis
   is clearly fraught with ambivalence.   This threshold in the
   income/deprivation relationship in Townsend's study, as with any comment
   on the measurement of poverty, is of crucial importance as this forms the
   basis of the presentation of an 'objective' poverty line income. Piachaud
   (1981, pp. 419-21) argues that such a solitary cut off point between the
   poor and the rest of society is essentially impractical given that: (a) poverty
   is relative and; (b) there is such a diversity in styles of living. What is
   preferable is a continuum from abundant wealth to chronic poverty, with
   a wide range of living standards and life experiences within that spread;

2 the selection of deprivation indicators:- it would appear that the short
   listing of the twelve 'illustrative'indicators by Townsend was quite an ad

hoc procedure. Again Piachaud (1981, p. 420) argues that there is an absence of logic in relating many of the indicators to poverty. Broadly speaking, it is not tractable to disentangle differences in taste from differences in income and thus, much of the variation in deprivation scores can be explained with reference to diversity in styles of living, which can be and often are, unrelated to poverty. Households may choose to forego some of the commodities included as deprivation indicators in Townsend's list, rather than be compelled to sacrifice them because of poverty or income restraint. A number of the indicators may indeed have an identifiable relationship with poverty - holidays, entertainments, refrigerators, household amenities. However, other articles such as fresh meat, cooked meals, Sunday joint, may be indicators of taste rather than poverty. Piachaud wittingly and diplomatically suggest that, ' Not having a cooked breakfast ... is often a remedy for overindulgence on other occasions. (p. 420). Opting to stay at home, eating salads and uncooked food is not a valid indication of deprivation: but Townsend's deprivation index would regard it as so. More important to the debate on poverty is the range of choices individuals have and the limitation on those choices. Opting not to go on holidays or eat meat may be stimulating material for academic sociologists or social psychologists, but is of no concern or relevance to the problem of poverty. On the other hand, having no holiday or not purchasing meat because one cannot afford to is crucial to those concerned with poverty. Piachaud believes that the relative deprivation index is of no plausible value as an indicator of deprivation. He unambiguously concludes:

> If all the components of the deprivation index were unambiguous indicators of some form of deprivation, then you might argue that those on high incomes with high deprivation scores are, despite their incomes, deprived. But this is not the case. A large part of the variation in deprivation scores is merely due to diversity in styles of living wholly unrelated to poverty. There can be no doubt that Townsend's provisional deprivation index is of no practical value whatsoever as an indicator of deprivation.' (p. 420).

However, even if one agrees that, by any of the approaches discussed in this chapter, it is not possible to define a poverty threshold, at least Townsend's measurements isolate certain social and personal activities from which the poor, however defined, are generally excluded. The crucial question in defining poverty is, of course, whether such exclusion is due to inadequacy of income or personal choice but the very least that Townsend achieved was a measurement of the extent of exclusion which the poor encounter - surely a worthwhile exercise, even if it was not the one which he set out to achieve. The basic conception of Townsend's relative deprivation thesis itself, however, does not escape criticism. Townsend theorises that those living in poverty 're deprived of the conditions of life which ordinarily define membership of society' The implication of this standpoint is that the poor constitute a distinct and separate body - almost an 'underclass' even though such a term was not in vogue when Townsend publicised his research. Rather than a view of social inequality based on a simple scission of 'normal' society and the poor, a more accurate and just perception involves a pendulum swing from excessive sets of circumstances and styles of life. The poor in Britain in the 1990s, as in other eras, are at the most disadvantaged point on this societal continuum, but are nonetheless members of that class-based society.

Any academic research is most appropriately evaluated in terms of its contribution towards changing and improving attitudes and policies. It is undoubtedly true that Townsend's conceptualisation of relative deprivation altered the value judgements of many commentators and researchers. However, his mammoth exercise did not provoke any identifiable response from central government in terms of either converting it to relativism or persuading it to re-evaluate social policies for the poor. Townsend, in other words, had engaged the policy making process in a conceptual arena which was/is alien to it. Tory philosophy, ,as personified by the individualist theories of poverty causation in Chapter 1, regards poverty/deprivation as the result of failure to avail of the opportunities offered to all citizens and consequently, its definition is perceived in individualistic terms, not Rowntree's work; he talked about primary poverty, subsistence, minimum standards, all of which were concordant with the dominant ideology towards poverty in 1899. His original study is largely regarded as one of the main influences provoking the Liberal Reforms which began in 1906. (see Chapter 3).

Broadly speaking, relativist definitions of poverty are popular among those who hold the view that standards of living should be as universal as possible across society and who believe that this commitment should be operationalized by social policies designed to redistribute wealth to avoid anyone experiencing deprivation int he affluent society that we live in. Although support for relativist notions does come from unpredictable quarters, such as the then Conservative social security minister, Lynda Chalker MP (November 1979): 'It is not sufficient to assess poverty by absolute standards; nowadays it must be judged on relative criteria by comparison with the standard of living of other groups in the community ... beneficiaries must have an income which enables them to participate in the life of the community.' However, under a relative notion of poverty, the problem cannot be eradicated short of altering the relative standards of society in general, involving, as it necessarily would, a redistribution of wealth from the better offs to the poor. The social consensus for this to happen has never been a feature of public opinion in Britain, especially in the Thatcherite years and thus the notion is formed that poverty will always be with us. As Alcock (1987, p. 7) argues: 'Recognising a relative notion of poverty therefore raises a fundamental question about the relative distribution of resources within society between the poor and the rich. Within any society, the problem of poverty is thus also the problem of inequality, with the poor merely being those receiving the smallest share.' For obvious reasons, this social participation index raises more questions than it answers and certainly involves more queries than the other models of measurement and this has inevitably led to a degree of ambiguity and a tendency among its proponents towards being non specific. This is why many relativists have turned their attention and research in the direction of measuring poverty via average income levels.

Statistical inequality approach:

The core feature of this approach is the view that the social participation poverty line should equate with a specified percentage of, usually, the net disposable income per capita or median household income. Thus the central task of this method is to stipulate a percentile or a proportion of the income distribution as a measurement of poverty line or minimum income.   For example, the Low Pay Unit (1988, pp. 7-9) defined 'low pay' as the income level of the lowest decile (bottom 10 per cent) of specified earners.   The European Union 'decency threshold' relates to a proportion of weekly earnings levels among a specified group in the labour force. Fuchs (1967, pp. 88-96) suggested that poverty could be defined at the level of any family whose income is less than one half the median family income. Fuchs argued that this approach accepts that poverty lines reflect prevailing living standards and therefore change over time. But he added, it also 'represents a tentative groping toward a national policy with respect to the distribution of income' The main methodological problem with Fuchs' idea was that it was a universal measure applied across all family compositions and would in all likelihood over-estimate the cause of relatively small households and under estimate that of larger families. Thus we have the move towards drawing the poverty line by using disposable per capita income - e.g. 40, 50, 60 per cent of median disposable per capita income.

Now it may be that these statistical measurements are useful in offering a device for enumerating those living in this form of relative poverty. It may be that they facilitate informative comparative analyses between different income groups. What they do not, of course, do is: (a) to provide policy prescriptions for eradicating poverty; (b) to forward calculations of the minimum income necessary to attain adequate lifestyles and; (c) to comment upon the quality of life pertaining for those deemed living in poverty.

Consensual approach:

A more refined approach with a somewhat different emphasis to measuring poverty has been developed by Mack & Lansley for the two London weekend television series 'Breadline Britain'. Although this model is firmly rooted in the relativist school and on lifestyle indicators, in that their aim is to, 'measure the extent of poverty not in terms of some arbitrary income level but in terms of the extent to which poor people are excluded from the way of living that is customary in society today', (Mack & Lansley 1985, p. 9), these two authors reject Townsend's indicator method in favour of, 'aims to identify a minimum acceptable way of life not be reference to the views of experts, nor by reference to observed patterns of expenditure or observed living standards, but by reference to the views of society as a whole.' (p. 42). In other words, this approach, in general, attempts to establish what the public perceived to be the poverty line, either:

1   the 'desired' poverty line - i.e. what should be provided at the minimum standard (this can involve: (a) asking people to specify a list of necessary items - the 'deprivation indicator method' or; (b) requiring the public to estimate an adequate minimum income - the 'income proxy method' or;

2   the 'financeable' poverty line - i.e. what poverty income level society is prepared to pay for through taxation.

Just because experts hold certain credentials, such as in nutrition, health etc., this does not qualify them as voices of authority in human social experience. Thus, the proffered attribute of this approach is that it attempts to by pass self appointed and opinionated experts and allows vox populi to dictate the measurement. Mack & Lansley proudly proclaim: 'For the first time ever, the poor in Britain have been identified on the basis of those who fall below the minimum standard of living laid down by society.' (1985, p. 10). Instead of talking about 'poverty', they asked respondents questions about things which no one should have to go without. By interviewing a large sample from the community in general, the researchers constructed a catalogue of foods, services and lifestyle elements which the substantial majority (51 per cent - plus) regarded as 'socially perceived necessities', things 'which every household should have, and no one should have to do without.' (p. 45). Poverty was thus to be measured and defined by a consensus of 'public opinion', not by experts or by observed behaviour. This method thus departs from Townsend's approach in a number of very significant ways:

1   conceptually, Townsend's measurement of poverty concentrates upon the exclusion from normal lifestyle, while Mack & Lansley appear more

interested in poverty as 'an enforced lack of socially defined necessities' which, in turn, deprives individuals and households of a minimal, socially acceptable standard of living. Acknowledging that income based approaches such as Townsend's emphasise the important and practical issue of an inability to afford a socially defined minimal standard of living, they prefer a more direct method of simply inquiring of individuals if they 'would like, but can't afford' these items: If so, then this is regarded as a 'lack'; if they do not have an item, but do not want it anyway, this is labelled 'going without' an item and is the result of low expectations. Townsend used simple possession or none possession of articles as indicators of deprivation and in the process left his findings open to the 'taste versus enforced deprivation' criticism, while Mack & Lansley controlled for taste differences by including only those articles which individuals 'would like, but can't afford' as indicators of deprivation;

2   Townsend opted for the use of customary behaviour to select items for his deprivation index, while Mack & Lansley sought public opinion to represent socially defined necessities.

The strength of the consensual approach lies in its recognition that poverty is not just a sociological, moral and economic phenomenon, but also a political issue and in this sense, it acknowledges the vulnerability of policy makers to the voice of the public on sensitive issues. It involves the contribution of public attitudes towards defining problems and therefore needs, which the other models lack. Without fairly widespread consensus on what constitutes a necessity, there would be little point in attempting to influence the policy making process into accepting the feasibility of a socially approved minimum standard of living. Taking account of the core nature of this approach, it is arguable that the concepts of citizenship and democracy are central values permeating the consensual model because the public are, in theory, integrally involved in informing the policy making process and this compels policy makers to evaluate their stated or actual commitment to such priorities. Mack & Lansley discovered a significant homogeneity of opinions across the population and consequently argue that the model of a minimum standard acceptable to all social groups is a viable paradigm. But if relative deprivation is a refinement of absolute approaches, and if consensual methods are an improvement on relativist paradigms, then is the consensual model theoretically and methodologically ideal? Not according to David Piachaud (1987, pp. 151-2):

the social consensus approach still requires expert involvement in defining questions and interpreting answers, if fails to resolve the problem when

70

the practices of the poor do not correspond with the priorities prescribed by the majority ("desired" poverty line), and it does not necessarily produce a poverty line which taxpayers will pay for ("financeable" poverty line) ... finally, and perhaps most importantly, there may be no real social consensus - the opinions of those who are poor, of the majority, of taxpayers and of those who are rich may be at odds; which opinions prevail depends on the distribution of power in society.

Piachaud's main contribution to the debate lies in his sociological argument that problems, needs and public opinion are social constructs and heavily influenced and moulded by broader ideological forces. As such, the attitudes of the public can be more subjective than objective, influenced as they are by dominant values and prevailing norms. Townsend (1985, p. 44) makes this point:

> Certain needs of a community may not be perceived by any members of that community, or may not be perceived by more than a few, or may be underestimated universally by a population. These statements are hardly contentious. But they oblige us to look for criteria of need other then in social perceptions - whatever might be said about the valuable legitimating functions of mass endorsement of particular standards in a political democracy ... For good reasons therefore, the social scientist cannot be satisfied with the consensual judgement of society at large.

Robert Walker (1987) also clarifies this problem by explaining that budget standard exercises to draw a poverty line can involve years of work, whereas survey methods require the respondents to provide immediate answers to rigidly structured questions about 'complex and sensitive' issues, without the luxury of forethought. 'The danger is that the "people" will mouth back what they think the "experts
" want to hear, or, perhaps more correctly, what they think the experts "ought" to hear.' Walker goes on to feed into the social forces debate by arguing that the consensual survey does not tune into the 'interactive process' which is the vehicle for constituting informed consensus. Thus the crucial issue for critics questions whether these surveys of public opinion actually reflect the true extent of poverty or whether they represent 'that kind and that degree of poverty which the dominant ideology enables respondents to express'. (George & Howards 1991, p. 18). Of course, the power of ideology issue suggests that both respondents and researchers possess opinions which clash with those of the policy making process.

In exposing the significant conceptual chasm between a consensual poverty line based on 'desired' criteria and one based on 'financeable' grounds, Veit Wilson (1987) forcefully suggests that the two are very different exercises and that the determination of a poverty line is, in sub stance and in practice, at

71

odds with decisions taken by the policy making process on the level of public expenditure which central government is willing to distribute to the poor. Indeed, the record of successive governments demonstrates that they are largely impervious and even hostile to overwhelming and conclusive research findings which clearly expose the inadequacy of benefit levels payable to the poor. (See, for example, the debate in the House of Lords, 21 March 1991 on the research findings of Stitt 1991). Clearly, the rationale adopted by statutory agencies in ignoring research data, particularly those of a consensual nature, is that public acknowledgements of such survey findings would inevitably generate a reaction from the electorate demanding the redistribution of state resources and finance towards the poor and away from private profit making enterprises. This, in turn, would involve creating the potential for a backlash from the tax payers who would be expected to make sacrifices in order to finance the redistribution of income.

Mack & Lansley investigated what the public regarded as 'necessities', constructed a list of fourteen items on which a substantial majority reached consensus and then isolated the poor as those lacking three or more of those items. How come these researchers equated the lack of three or more items with poverty? If there was consensus that the fourteen items were 'necessitiesA why does the lack of even one item not define poverty? Ashton (1984) points out that a large number of respondents in the survey, although they lacked 'necessities', they did not, at the same time, lack 'non necessities'. How can it be concluded that a family is poor if it cannot afford necessities, but is able to obtain non-necessities? Ashton argues in a singularly Thatcherite logic:

> The lack of three or more items has to be because the household cannot afford them in order for it to be counted among those in poverty. But the reason for lacking them is self assessed. Many people who say they cannot afford an essential may have, or may have had, the resources to purchase it but allocate their resources instead for an apparent non essential. To give an example, a household might lack the items "carpets in the living room and bedroom" because they claim they cannot afford the, but may possess, say, an expensive hi-fi stereo unit. We are asked to accept that when someone says they cannot afford a particular item, they have not chosen instead to spend their money on something else that they regard as more essential (or desirable), but which does not appear on LWT's list.

A more subtle criticism made of the consensual model is that statements of 'necessities' so gathered are bound to be contaminated by 'consumer fetishism', especially int eh acquisitive society which Britain has become. However, the Breadline Britain investigations suggested strongly that the British population had not become tarnished with the 'there is no end of

72

wanting' brush and proved itself diligent in differentiating between aspiring want and authentic need (proper diet, warm hone, self respect, etc.) However, the most glaring of indictments levelled against the consensus approach in our type of social constitution is that there really can be no actual consensus at all. When it is considered that the opinions of the poor, of the rich, of the middle income bands, of the tax payers will almost certainly clash and differ, then the only confident conclusion that can be drawn is that the set of opinions that will dominate policy is wholly dependent upon the distribution of power in capitalist society - and there is no ambiguity or fanciful consensus over that. A more conceptual criticism lies in the view that an integral element of social life involves passing judgements on those around us on the basis of material possessions and command over resources and, inevitably, we identify, isolate and set apart some who are poor. Could it be that this sort of judgement is motivated by a desire (conscious or otherwise) on behalf of those making the judgement to bolster their own social position through presenting fellow beings as somewhat below him/her in terms of materialist criteria? These judgements can thus be seen as socially motivated and based upon a community consensus on common standards. Consequently, a plethora of individual judgements are generated and when these inevitably gel into common denominators, they are perceived as a consensual analysis.

Relativist and consensual approaches to defining poverty cannot be seen int he same polarised way as 'relative versus absolute' debates; rather, they are more accurately regarded as complimenting each other, due to the high degree of common features, particularly their rejection of the prescriptive nature of the absolute or budget standard approach and its perceived accompanying failure to accommodate social and psychological needs. Orwell pointed to the historical hypocrisy in absolute, subsistence poverty models by scathing 'the damned impertinence of these politicians, priests, literary men and what-not who lecture the working class socialist for his "materialism"'. (*Looking Back on the Spanish War*)

Neglected Problems

Thusfar, we have looked at a number of different approaches to measuring and defining poverty. No attention has been directed towards certain aspects of such exercises, some of which have been catalogued by Piachaud (1987, p. 12). For example, poverty is invariably equated with a lack of adequate cash and subsequent absence of proper command over resources. In constructing a poverty line, should we for example include a measure of home production, such as cooking, cleaning, making clothes, child care, vegetable growing etc., dependent as these are upon opportunity and time? Piachaud points to the example of chips. To make one's own, potatoes must be washed, peeled, decay gouged out, sliced, fried, tossed, drained and only then are they edible.

On the other hand, oven ready chips, which are about five times more expensive per pound than traditional chips, are simply laid out on a tray and heated in order to become ready to eat. The 'raw' chips cost only a fraction of the convenience chips because the consumer does not pay for the factory food processors' time; but they absorb far more time and effort in preparation. Which potatoes should be included in a standard of living for the poor? 'hat assumptions should be made about the level of home production and the input of time?' Similarly, in co9nstructing a poverty line, should new or second hand clothes be budgeted for? Should the poor be expected to wash clothes by hand or might they have a washing machine? Should an unemployed person walk to an interview or be allowed the cost of public transport fares? Clearly there are issues of stigma and social status involved in these questions, but equally, they are characterised by problems of time - e.g. second hand clothing must be washed and usually repaired and adjusted; washing be hand takes infinitely more time (not to mention wear and tear on the hands) than using a washing machine; walking takes more time then vehicular transport.

A factor which must surely influence decisions on these questions is the widespread assumption that the poor have, if little else, plenty of time on their hands. However there is an abundance of research on the time costs of caring for children and other dependents, on the time costs involved in making necessary journeys without private transport, and thus such assumptions have no factual basis whatsoever and may almost certainly be impertinent. An even more complex factor is introduced by Piachaud (1987, p. 13) who recognises that, unlike money, time has no common currency and there are many ways in which time can be 'spent' with very diffuse outcomes:

> Academics ... enjoy inestimable life advantages in terms of the degree of control over the use of time and the distribution of tasks and the opportunities to earn additional income. By contrast, for a lone mother, the degree of control over time is likely to be minute - the impact of an hour spent entertaining a child at 4 a.m. is rather different from that at 4 p.m; furthermore, the opportunities to supplement income with part time earnings are likely to be very limited.

Conclusion

Attempts to measure and define poverty have invariably occurred within the context of existing conventions. The Edwardian exercises to construct minimum subsistence standards were founded on designs to estimate costs of food, fuel, clothing, etc. against the back ground of commodities which were conventional within their era and location. the 1960s onwards efforts to measure poverty as an element of relative deprivation concerned themselves with the normal customs and expectations of that period. The crucial departure between these two paradigms does not lie, as is widely held, in their absolutism or relativity; rather the main differential characteristic features the question of from what quarter comes the decision as to what these minima are to represent. The absolute subsistence model centres on the assumption that, in constructing estimates of minimum requirements, the opinions of experts on how families should lead their lives and purchase their lifestyles is superior and more appropriate than those of the subjects themselves - poor people. Questions such as: which commodities and services must households purchase; what quantity of these items should they acquire; which foodstuffs, clothes, household durable, recreation, social activities etc. are not necessary for a poverty line standard of living, are all to be decided by experts, who, presumably, are not themselves poor.

Absolute subsistence standards concentrate on the weekly income required to provide nutrients, body coverings and household shelter; they do not concern themselves with mental food (as in social pursuits) which make up the physical/psychological wholeness of human beings. The main reason for this is that such experts are not yet expert enough to devise acceptable methods for measuring and costing these social and psychological requirements.

Switching to relativists notions of poverty measurement, the judgements as to what constitutes necessities, without which deprivation exists, lie with ordinary citizens. The intercession of experts occurs only when they are required to employ their talents in implementing social studies of the population to determine the income levels at which: (a) most individuals and households, successfully meet their socially defined needs and; (n) individuals and households are substantially deprived, the definition of this latter condition being determined by reference to social investigations, rather than by experts. In this sense, Veit Wilson (1985, pp. 17) explains: 'The work "poverty" means not having enough money to buy oneself out of deprivation/' Piachaud (1986, p. 19), in his usual empathetic manner, concludes:

> If the term "poverty" carries with it the implication and moral imperative that something should be done about it, then the study of poverty is only ultimately justifiable if it influences individual and social attitudes and actions. This must be constantly borne in mind if discussion on the definition of poverty is to avoid becoming an academic debate worthy of Nero - a semantic and statistical squabble that is parasitic, voyeuristic and utterly unconstructive and which treats the "poor" as passive objects for attention, whether benign or malevolent - a discussion that is part of the problem rather than part of the solution.

This argument has been advanced by Bob Holman (the *Guardian*, 12 January 1994) who suggests that 'experts' know little of the despair of countless job rejections, of children made sick through damp homes and the inability to afford power cards for electricity meters. He states: 'The silencing of the poor is a social mechanism by which inequality is upheld. The poor have to be kept out because their regular and powerful contribution would undermine the cosy consensus whereby politicians and media professionals - and their peers - enjoy both the fat of the land and the right to comment upon it.' Even the Labour Party sponsored Commission on Social Justice includes a chief executive from industry, a director of a large voluntary agency, a knight, an Oxbridge professor and a host of well heeled academics. But the poor, benefit dependents, the victims of social injustice, do not seem to be worthy of a single place on the Commission.

But if this moral imperative notion is valid, then measurements and definitions of poverty must take account of the readiness of the public at large to take some action of an anti poverty nature. If this readiness is not evident in a sufficiently large scale, then it could be that what has been monitored by consensual research is a concern with inferior, perhaps inadequate lifestyles - not poverty. 'Under a consensual model, elucidated in this way, poverty exists only to the extent that people are prepared to take action about it.' (Walker 1987, p. 215). However, poverty as defined only by a lack of adequate income apparently does not provoke the same emotive, passionate reaction among the population as starvation, homelessness and unnecessarily high infant mortality and therefore generates little impetus for governments to act. The message for poverty statisticians appears to argue that income/money poverty is only a singular facet of a Janus faced system of multiple deprivation, inequality and injustice and should not be presented as an isolated, solvable phenomenon and a problem which, when overcome by offering adequate weekly income, cures the plethora of social, economic and human ills inherent in capitalism.

Is it thus the least path of resistance to define poverty in a pluralist approach - i.e. subsistence to relative to consensual? If so, can it be confidently asserted that subsistence poverty has declined: can it be argued that, in relative terms, deprivation has not declined, and may indeed have increased? But this appears a blatantly apolitical, narrow sighted approach. Poverty is only one form of inequality and only one facet of the structure of privilege and disadvantage that is Britain in the 1990s. Those who profess similar sentiments should acknowledge that inequality is a different concept and indeed a different problem from poverty. The emotive symbolism of the term poverty exudes suggestions that it is an irregular abnormality for capitalist society, a source of discomfort and stigma for its victims and thus, an issue which society should be morally compelled to tackle and rectify. There is nothing radical in a concern for poverty and a commitment to tackling it at whatever level. The same degree of moral imperative is not attached to inequality, which, many believe, is a healthy motivation for a competitive society. Poverty carried an ethical obligation for society: inequality does not.

That would be much too 'dangerous' for many academics and politicians. Seabrook (1985, pp. 15-16) touches upon this dilemma be arguing eloquently that endeavours to establish a definition of poverty, particularly those of a relative nature, are clumped together by a common assumption that human needs are created by diverse cultures. The discomfort lies in the fact that, 'What poverty means in a society in which the creation and manipulation of need itself is a primary purpose, is the greatest conundrum, before which definitions falter an d remedies appear impossible. This is what happened with us; and thus it is that needs become measureless and unanswerable and the task of fulfilling them hopeless.'

Such issues have consequently negated any attempts to judge the constitution of poverty in capitalist societies. It is not possible to paraphrase or explain Seabrook's (1985) arguments in one's own words without diluting the impact of his forceful sentiments and thus he is quoted at length:

> What we are dealing with is the expropriation of need and its refraction, vast, moving, irretrievably lost in the panoply of capitalist selling, the spectacle that is capital to such a degree of accumulation that it becomes image. When we talk, as Townsend does, of poverty as the exclusion of people from the norms, standards and customary activities of their society that is beyond dispute; but then these norms and standards are themselves all centred on fugitive notions of increase - more, better, higher, bigger, all of them comparative terms detached from their positive degree - then any definition of poverty becomes a mobile and untenable as any gesture towards sufficiency. This preoccupation has been described as "a culture of wanting" in which commodities and marketed services cease to be straightforward objects, but are progressively more unstable, temporary collections of a mixture of objective and imputed characteristics - that is, highly complex material - symbolic entities, and easily escape practical attempts to define need.'

The definition of poverty in Britain has thus been metamorphosed in a manner which renders the calculation of a poverty line, below which people are poor, above which people are not poor, inconclusive and unattainable. Poverty is not measured in relation to human needs, but against a background of a limitless potential to produce and sell. As such, defining and measuring poverty is a problem without a solution. And the solution to the problem of the existence of poverty, however defined, is located, not in palliatives to compensate the poor, but in the realm of the affluent, 'in whose image the poor have been remade'. (Seabrook 1985, p. 87). Seabrook clarifies what he means by this by explaining that the reason for the failure of all serious endeavours to define poverty in non absolutist or beyond basic subsistence terms, is that poverty in the sphere of capitalism is an 'elaborate artefact', the product of the concrete relationship between money and social and psychological structures.

> Money is thus evolving; so that even as the income of the poor increases, it can always be recuperated by the rich through an even more complex process of adding value to the necessities of the poor (VAT on fuel) or of finding new and more expensive ways of answering basic need that will maintain and increase profit. It is the rich who control both the experience and measure of poverty.'

Capitalism's huge regenerative potential stems largely from the vast plasticity of human needs, the energy of which is exploited by capitalism for its own ends. Once it is generally accepted that the core problem is poverty and the core solution is increased production, then there becomes no limit to the expansion and growth of capitalism's stranglehold. 'Human beings are always being made, broken and remade in ways that perpetuate subjective feelings of expropriation and loss, the healing answer to which is offered only by a closer and closer identification of human needs with capitalist necessity. In other words, the malleability of human needs means that they can be tormented into any shape that may be required for the perpetuation of an economic system which was supposed to have satisfied them.' (Seabrook 1985, p. 174). Who better to turn to for reinforcement of Seabrook's arguments on the political economy of needs in capitalist society than Karl Marx, writing in his earlier works on the social definition of needs (1946, pp. 268-9):1.

> A noticeable increase in wages presupposes a rapid growth of productive capital ... (this) beings about an equally rapid growth of wealth, luxury, social needs and social enjoyments. Thus, in comparison with the state of development of society in general, although the enjoyments of the worker have risen, the social satisfaction that they give has fallen in caparison with the increased enjoyments of the capitalists, which are inaccessible to the worker (the law of increasing misery). Our needs and enjoyments spring from society; we measure them therefore by society and not by the objects of their satisfaction. Because they are of a social nature, they are of a relative nature ...

In other words, poverty can be regarded more as a basic lack of power, than a mere manifestation of a lack of money and consequently, exercises to measure it apolitically, particularly absolute standards, are misleading, incomplete and mystificatory. In their classic study of poverty in Nottingham in the 1960s, Coates and Silburn (1970, pp. 37-8) explain:

> Whilst it is true that socially expanded needs can displace the "natural" priorities of consumption, so that social pressures may persuade a person to go hungry rather than naked, or undernourished rather than lag too visibly far behind the Joneses, so that it becomes possible to find children

exhibiting many of the signs of malnutrition and yet families with every televised exploit of Batman or Tarzan, it is also true that the normal consequences of poverty in an advanced society are far more dire than physical results.

Poverty's strongest impact involves the loss of power because it is 'the most permanent' and 'self enforcing' aspect. Basic human needs are vulnerable to manipulation in the 'most cynical and conscienceless way', where citizens forfeit control over their joint activities. (Coates & Silburn 1970, p. 38). The core message is that measurements of basic needs (and indeed, the whole plethora of human needs) are controlled and exploited by the system of capitalism, both materially and ideologically and thus, any orthodox attempts to define poverty lines become tools for the expansion of exploitative production and inequality. But for all practical intents and purposes involved in the measurement (as opposed to the definition) of poverty, in terms of 'getting the message across ' to the general public, although the Church of England (1985) agrees that poverty involves much more than a shortage of money: it involves rights and relationships, treatment of people and self perception, powerlessness, exclusion and loss of dignity, it asserts, 'Yet the lack of adequate income is at its heart.' However, this loss of power, in a more practical sense involves, for poor people, a gross restriction of their access to the structures of decision making which influence and determine their lives and which attacks their citizenship rights. For example poor families often cannot afford the costs of getting to local authority council meetings, they cannot afford to attend school meetings, pressure group meetings, etc. and in this way, they are forced to forfeit the chances to challenge decisions and policies which determine their quality of life.

Academic debates and administrative complexities on the definitions of poverty and deprivation are arenas which are far from the concerns and interests of the poor themselves. What difficulties, sleeplessness, anguish and degradation that the next twenty four hours is going to bring would naturally constitute the limits of their concentration. In arguing for a more qualitative approach to understanding and raising awareness about poverty, Silburn (1988, pp. 11-12) states: 'The careful documenting of this actual experience (in all its variety and complexity), the monitoring of the consequences for health happiness and well being, and the chronicling of the multifarious reactions, responses and coping strategies that the poor must evolve; this task of description and analysis is the necessary qualitative counterpart to the more technical work we have considered.' Silburn points to a century and a half of social research of this kind, starting with *London Labour and the London Poor* by Henry Mayhew in early Victorian England; Booth and Rowntree in a later 19th century; Jack London's *People of the Abyss*; *The Road to Wigan Pier* by George Orwell in the inter-war era; 1960s and 1970s works by the CPAG; and in the 1980s, *'Landscapes of Poverty'* by Jeremy Seabrook and Paul Harrison's ' *Inside the Inner City'*. Silburn concludes (p. 13): 'We need sober, dispassionate, even ... bureaucratic analysis, but equally we need the more vivid, descriptive first hand account. The first without the second can be formal and sterile, the second without the first can be sentimental and lack theory. Together, the quantitative and the qualitative appeal to both our intellectual and our fraternal selves.' The concluding Chaper of this book will thus engage upon a review of the literature on qualitative accounts of poverty and will offer research evidence which exposes the grim reality of the yawning chasm between the basic, subsistence needs of the poor and the levels of poor relief handed down to themin Britain in the 1990s.

3 History of poor relief in Britain

Introduction

> *Doolittle:* I am one of the undeserving poor, that's what I am. Think of what that means to a man. It means that he's up agen middle class morality all the time. What is middle class morality? Just an excuse for never giving me anything. (Bernard Shaw, Pygmalion, 1912)

> We want people to help themselves to work - not help themselves to taxpayers' money to which they aren't entitled. (David Hunt MP, Employment Secretary, Conservative Party Conference, 1993)

The institution of poor relief in Britain predates the existing system of capitalism and certainly bears a much longer history then the welfare state as it became known. An historical journey is now taken through the emergence and development of state systems for 'relieving' poverty and a detailed discussion is embarked upon on the major studies of poverty and poverty lines which informed and significantly influenced such policies. The term 'poor relief' is selected consciously, as opposed to conceptual measures aimed at eradicating poverty. From the discussion on the theories of poverty causation, it can be seen that all schools of thought, either through analysis or through prescription, see poverty as playing a major important role in capitalist society. As such, there have never been any social policy attempts to eliminate poverty, as this would necessarily involve substantial upheavals in the social, economic and political order. All the major milestones in tackling poverty have thus concentrated solely on 'relieving' the worst excesses of the material deprivations associated with the phenomenon. It will also be a central task of this chapter to emphasise the nature of the measurement and definition of income levels for the poor. Chapter 2 looked at the different ways in which the 'poverty line' is or can be constructed - absolute, relative, consensual etc. This section will explain that the main rationales behind the calculations of poor relief income levels have been political and economic in nature and have had little to do with even an absolutist model of basic needs, far less a relative or consensual approach to defining a deprived lifestyle.

Responses to pleas for help from the needy have historically ranged from forcing applicants to enter the workhouse in much the same way that criminals were treated, to providing them with Income Support rates which have been insufficient in content to afford basic, necessary commodities of life and adequate only for a life of exclusion and stigma. The literature explains that many poor relief claimants were, in the past, beaten, branded, and forced, according to an 18th century piece of welfare law, 'to suffer pains and execution of death as a felon' and treated as 'enemies of the Commonwealth' (Novak 1984, p. 2). The poor of the 1980s and 1990s have similarly been charged with fecklessness, laziness, bad management of household finances and resources, inability to budget, waste, etc. It was argued (in the discussions on structuralist and Marxist explanations of poverty), that social policies to deal with the poor were functional to consolidating the privileged position of the ruling class. It was also proposed by the orthodox economic, minority group and culture/sub culture theories of poverty that financial provision for claimants should act as a deterrent for complacency and disincentive to work and as instrumental in encouraging the means to escape from poverty by availing of the opportunities of the labour market. All schools of theoretical thought on poverty hold that therefore, income provision for the poor in societies such as Britain either (analytically) WOULD BE or (prescriptively) SHOULD BE as low as possible and certainly below any acceptable standard. The following section will travel chronologically throughout the history of provision of relief for the poor by the state and will show that this has always been the case throughout the main stages of 'development' of poor relief, including the current scheme of Income Support.

The Poor Law 1834

The notion of the 'deserving' and the 'undeserving' poor is as old as the very notion of poverty itself. The dominant elites and powerful institutions have differentiated between acceptable and unacceptable forms of poverty since as early as the Black Death era. To prevent the spread of the lethal disease, the poor were dissuaded from travelling around the countryside in search of relief/work and forcibly returned to their home villages. The adoption of poverty as a national issue can be traced back to the Middle Ages when Britain began to develop as a nation state with its own national economy. Before this, the poor were the problem of the locality in which they were unfortunate enough to be found. In practice, the regulations on poor relief, beggars and vagrants were much more directed towards overt punishment than relief. The Poor Law of 1601 was the first endeavour to identify the 'deserving' poor, based on the perception that the poor were responsible for their own poverty because they would not work, could not keep a job or refused to save money, drank too much or indulged in 'excessive procreation'. The 'deserving' poor were those individuals and their families who had worked and saved, but had encountered unfortunate circumstances beyond their control.

As a result of the Industrial Revolution and accompanying decline in agriculture, the standard of living of the agricultural labourer dropped significantly, with a subsequent increase in applications for poor relief. Between 1760 and 1784, taxes gathered for relief purposes had risen by about sixty per cent. (Mencher 1967, p. 99). In the latter decades of the 18th century, the government had introduced legislation, known as the Speenhamland system, which compensated labourers for the differences between the wages they received from their employers and their cost of living, as determined by local boards, from public poor relief funds. This ancestor of current system of Family Credit is the earliest example of an official estimation of the required finances for the poor to acquire a certain standard of living, but unfortunately, there is no indication of how these local boards estimated such a cost of living. In view of the absence of such calculations, it can reasonably be assumed that these estimates of the cost of living were products of government financial budgeting, rather than measurements of the costs of basic needs.

The prevailing mood of the English taxpayer at the time however, was one of growing hostility towards the system and the recipients of poor relief because of the massive increase in taxes levied to finance such programmes. Corresponding with this trend in attitudes was the emergence of a new school of political economists which developed its own theories on poor relief. The doctrine of 'laissez-faire' achieved widespread acclaim with the publication in 1776 of 'The Wealth of Nations' by Adam Smith. Laissez-faire, as a set of beliefs, emerged in a particularly appropriate period for industrializing Britain, whose manufacturing sector was highly enthusiastic to achieve conditions in which it could maximise profit generated by the Industrial Revolution. The laissez-faire doctrine also proposed the withdrawal of state support for the poor because of its liability to create a disincentive to work, to interfere with the natural equilibrium of the free market economy to achieve a proper wage level and to syphon off resources required by capital. The government responded in 1832: (1) to the requirements of the manufacturers to be unfettered by taxes and regulations on wages levels; (2) to the dissatisfaction of the taxpayers and; (3) to the need to discipline the restless workers - by anointing a Royal Commission to examine the Poor Laws. The most effective method of dealing with these concerns was to encourage a strong work incentive in what were seen as lazy and deviant able bodied men. Theevil was held to emanate from the relief rather than from the situations which generated the request for relief.

The Commissioners recommended that the government should,

> '... devise means for rendering relief so irksome and disagreeable that none would consent to receive it who could possibly do without it (the "deterrent" factor), while at the same time, it should come in the shape of comfort and consolation to those whom every benevolent man would wish to succour - the old, infirm, idiots and cripples (the "deserving" poor). (cited in de Schweinitz 1943, p. 119)

The distinction between the 'deserving' and the 'undeserving' poor had been openly and officially established in legislation; the principle of 'deterrence' - making all system of poor relief so unpleasant and harsh that it would deter all but the most desperate had been operationalized; and the dye of what was to become the underlying philosophy of social security and poor relief for the next century and a half had been cast. The needs of capital, the power of the taxpayer and the disciplining of the workforce were the foremost considerations of the architects of the new Poor Law. The moral question of the quality of life of the poor was simply not on the agenda. Indeed, such a concern would have been in direct conflict with the aims of poor relief. The nature of the relief to be provided for the 'deserving' poor - 'the old, infirm idiots and cripples' - was 'to come in the shape of comfort and consolation' - i.e. the workhouse.

Armed with such virtues and confident that not only were 'wasters' being deterred, but that 'the necessitous are abundantly relieved', the Commissioners embarked upon establishing a principle which has subjugated the relief of poverty ever since:

> 'The first and most essential of all conditions, a principle which we find universally admitted, even by those whose practice is at variance with it, is that his situation as a whole shall not be made really or apparently so eligible as the situation of the independent labourer of the lowest class.' (cited in de Schweinitz 1943, pp. 120-4)

This statement, referred to as the principle of 'less eligibility', laid the foundations of British social security policies in the 19th and 20th centuries. It was established to ensure that the standard of living of even the lowest paid worker in employment was superior to that of recipients of poor relief, and that poor relief policies would certainly not act as a disincentive to work.

These philosophies discouraged policy makers from actually addressing the issue of a quantified standard of deprivation- prevention, subsistence or poor relief. According to E.P. Thompson (1968, p. 195), the Poor Law, ' ... was perhaps
the most sustained attempt to impose an ideological dogma in defiance of the evidence of human need in English history'.

The late 1980s

The latter half of the 19th century brought with it a conflicting force moving in other directions. Britain had experienced over a century of revolutionary change in industry and in society as a whole and this had begun to affect the way in which it perceived problems like poverty and poor relief. After three hundred years of virtually unaltered operation, the Poor Law began to address a social philosophy that, increasingly, would attack rationales and attitudes that before, had enjoyed almost total hegemony in the administration of relief. During the later stages of the 19 century, as now, a beleaguered Tory administration was drowning in the quagmire of the deepest recession for a long time, causing record levels of unemployment and crime. Crucially, in the 1860s, Victorian society was compelled to acknowledge that some poverty was beyond the control of the individual. The American Civil War had spawned a cotton famine and, as a result, entire workforces in the cotton towns of Lancashire were made redundant. Not even the most vehemently dogmatic conservative could argue that these unfortunates had brought poverty upon themselves.

By the 1880s, Britain was confronted with survey data which indicated the extent of poverty and deprivation in its midst and its underlying causes began to be recognized as lying outside individual pathology and personal responsibility. These factors started to manifest in growing demands for statutory intervention to create solutions, or, at least, remedies, to such an extent that they became irresistible, even to the dogmatic Victorians and Edwardians. An extremely important consideration in the discussions on poverty and poor relief which added momentum to this wave of public demand for centralized state assistance to give security to the standards of living of the poor was the social surveys of poverty. The famous investigations by Booth in London and Rowntree in York in the 1880s and 1890s exposed two major issues: firstly, the numerical extent of poverty; secondly, its fundamental causes which were seen to fall outside the scope of the individual (laziness, wasteful expenditure etc.) and could be located within the socio economic system. Thus, the responsibility for its alleviation was society's and not the individual's - i.e. it was a social problem requiring social action.

In 1883, the Reverend S.A. Barnett, vicar and a member of the Charity

Organisation Society (COS) described, in a paper called, '*Practical Socialism*', the living standards and expectations of the labourer on casual low wages in the 1880s, just a few years prior to Charles Booth's innovatory study of poverty:

> In the labourer's future, there is only the grave and the workhouse. He hardly dares to think at all, for the thought suggests that tomorrow, a change in trade or a master's whim might throw him out of work and leave him unable to pay for rent and for food. The labourers have few thoughts of joy and little hope of rest; it is well for them, if, in a day, they can obtain ten hours of the dreariest labour, if they can return to a weatherproof room, if they can eat a meal in silence, while the children sleep around and then turn into bed to save light and coal. (Mowart 1961, p. 118)

But, in tandem with this recognition that most poor people were deserving of relief, there was another more sinister attitudinal trend: that there continued to exist, the 'undeserving' poor, unwilling to work, feckless, idle, alcoholic, criminal and therefore, poor. This **'underclass'** were a 'teeming, barely controllable mass of humanity (who were) outside normal society. It certainly frightened the servants and the children. This was the undeserving poor.' (the *Observer*, 14 November 1993, p. 14). (The reader is asked to bear these descriptions in mind when reading Chapter 5 on 'The Underclass'.)

The survey of Charles Booth: 1886-1902

The object of Booth's enquiry was to, 'show the numerical relation which poverty, misery and deprivation bear to regular earnings and to describe the general conditions under which each class lives'. (Booth 1902, p. 6). He presented the first paper on his work in 1886, the same year as the hunger riots in London. His categories of 'poor' and 'very poor' were arbitrary. 'Poor' was taken to refer to those 'who have a sufficiently regular, though bare, income, such as, 18 shillings to 21 shillings per week for a moderate family'. (A 'moderate' family was assumed to be two adults and three children of unspecified ages). The 'very poor', according to Booth, were, 'those who, from any cause, fall much below this standard'. Booth stated,

> 'the "poor" are those whose means may be sufficient for decent, independent life; the "very poor" are those whose means are insufficient for this, according to the usual standard of life in this country. My "poor" may be described as living under a struggle to maintain the necessities of life and make both ends meet; while the "very poor" live in a state of chronic want'. (Booth 1902, p. 33).

His finding shocked Britain, especially as he had drawn his poverty 'cut off' point at a meagre 18-21 shillings a week, an amount thought to be 'inhuman' at the time.

Rowntree's survey - 1989

Benjamin Seebohm Rowntree motivated himself to establish whether similar levels of deprivation existed in provincial cities, using York as an example. In particular, Rowntree was also interested in natural science and was eager to determine whether this discipline could be exploited to illuminate the prevailing discussions on the causal factors of the phenomenon of poverty and the measurement of a poor lifestyle. It was this essential element which was to lead him to claim that he was, ' ... the first person to define poverty in scientific terms'. (Rowntree 1901, p. XIX.). Rowntree was also a vigorous advocate of state sponsored social security and emphasized his philosophy that the power of the state should be used to lay down minimum standards of living and to protect citizens from falling beneath them, free of the chance evils of the market.

To arrive at a numerical level of people living in poverty, Rowntree went beyond Booth's arbitrary selection of a specific income level as a cut off point. Rather, he established, for various families sizes, the indispensable requirements for 'a minimum of food, clothing and shelter, necessary for the maintenance of merely physical efficiency'. Once these were costed and a weekly monetary amount calculated, it was compared with each family's income and when the latter fell below the former, the family was deemed to be living in a state of 'primary poverty'. (Rowntree 1901, pp. 76-7). Throughout the entire survey, Rowntree was at pains to point out that in establishing his cut off level, no allowance was made for any expenditure other than that absolutely required for the maintenance of merely physical efficiency. Adding up his figures for allowances for food, rent and sundries, (including clothing), he obtained the final minimum standards for each family.

Thus, for a 'moderate family' of two parents and three children, 21s 8d was the minimum expenditure needed per week in York to maintain physical efficiency. This was made up of: food, 12s 9d; rent 4s. 0d; clothing, light, fuel, 4s 11d. The poverty line exclusive of rent was 17s. 8d. Rowntree's rates for a female adult were set at 67 per cent of the male adult rate and for the first child, at 34 per cent of the male adult rate. Although Rowntree introduced other important concepts and models in his studies - causes of poverty, the poverty cycle, etc. - it was the construction of his minimum subsistence standard which attracted most attention and criticism. This will be discussed in much the same way as Rowntree presented his estimates.

Nutrition

Through the use of advice and guidelines from 'neutral expert authorities', Rowntree was able to calculate the average subsistence dietary needs of adults and children of both sexes and translate these into quantities of various foodstuffs, which were, in turn, translated into the cash equivalent. In establishing a specific diet, Rowntree looked towards, 'the diets provided for able bodied paupers in workhouses, as the object of these institutions is to provide a diet containing the necessary nutrients at the lowest cost, compatible with a certain amount of variety'. Rowntree chose only the cheapest rations, and so, no butcher's meat was included in his dietary. He concluded, '... the standard adopted here is therefore less generous than that which would be required by the Local Government Board for the Workhouse.' (Rowntree, 1901, p. 130-131). According to his calculations, the cost of a weekly subsistence dietary for an adult was 3s.0d., for a child aged between eight and sixteen, 2s.7d and for a child aged under three, 2s.1d. For the sake of simplicity, in his final presentations, Rowntree averaged the weekly cost of feeding a child at 2s.3d.

Household sundries

The main items in this category were fuel, clothing and footwear. Rowntree gathered his information on these items from a 'a large number of working people'. He based his estimates of the minimum necessary expenditure on clothing by asking respondents,

> What, in your opinion, is the very lowest sum upon which a man can keep himself in clothing for a year? The clothing must be adequate to keep the man in health and should not be so shabby as to injure his chances of obtaining respectable employment. Apart from these two conditions, the clothing must be the most economically obtainable.

For the other items in this category - e.g. fuel, light, soap, replacements etc. - similar methodology was used. This use of lay opinion among poor people themselves meant that Rowntree's approach to measuring the minimum standards for these household items was neither 'scientific' nor 'objective'.

But, for other sundries, he admitted, '... information as to the average sum required for other household necessities proved to be very difficult to obtain.' So Rowntree chose the characteristic line of least resistance by stating, 'It will not be overstating facts if we allow 2d. per head per week to cover all household sundries other than clothes and fuel.' It seems that he was forced into this further arbitrary measurement because his questions on these items were met with replies which indicated the impossibility of budgeting for these articles on a low and fixed budget: 'If we have to buy anything extra, such as pots or pans, we have to spend less on food, that's all.' (Rowntree, 1901, pp 139-141).

Housing

Rowntree was highly critical of his own method of estimating the minimum necessary expenditure for rent. He claimed that he would have preferred to have been able to establish a reliable standard of accommodation, conducive to health and welfare and then to employ the average cost of such accommodation in York as the minimum expenditure allowed for in his poverty standard. However, such an approach would have involved the assumption that this adequate accommodation was available to every family who sought it which, in reality, was not the case. For these reasons, Rowntree used the actual sums paid for rent as the necessary minimum expenditure for rent. By employing such methodology, Rowntree had introduced a serious degree of negative circularity, by allowing the amount paid by the poor for rent, as the minimum necessary. By his own admissions, he did not establish a standard of accommodation conducive to physical efficiency, let alone health and welfare. Nor did he consider the argument that actual spending on accommodation probably reflects limitations generated by income restraints rather than choice. Rowntree gave a graphic description of the totally inadequate nature of the vast bulk of working class housing in York at the time - the overcrowding, the insanitary conditions, the dampness and lack of ventilation and light - the 'slums'. (Rowntree 1901. pp. 181-192)

John Veit Wilson (1986) has rounded on the main critics of Rowntree's subsistence measurement because of what he perceives as gross misunderstanding and misinterpretation of what Rowntree was attempting to do. Veit Wilson explains that Rowntree's central aim was to address the question of whether the appearances of poverty were the results of individuals wasting their incomes which were, in nature and in quantity, sufficient for preventing the effects of poverty, or whether they were the inevitable manifestations of, simply, insufficient income levels. Consequently, Rowntree was forced to confront the inescapable problem of what was 'insufficient income'. Recognizing that no answer was possible which was free of value judgements, Rowntree endeavoured to measure a level of 'sufficiency' which, under no reasonable circumstances, could be attacked for generosity. Rowntree was therefore not in the business of prescribing what minimum, subsistence measures of poverty should be; he undertook this exercise to counter the prevailing beliefs which held individual fecklessness as the main causal factor of poverty and to provide irrefutable evidence that widespread deprivation was caused by incomes insufficient for physical efficiency. Veit Wilson concludes:

It was state officials, and not Rowntree himself, who turned his eye-opening minimum levels into blind maximum incomes. After 80 years, Rowntree's concerns are still lively in any consideration of the boundaries of the tolerable.' (Veit Wilson 1986, p. 82)

Yet, this poverty standard, void of any traces of generosity and scope for providence, constructed to expose the utter deprivation and destitution in which the poor in Britain lived at the end of the 19th century, came to constitute the basis for measurement of the extent of poverty and the nature of the lifestyles of the poor and was transformed by 'state officials' into a prescriptive yardstick upon which to build social security provision for the unemployed.

Liberal reforms 1906 - 1911

The publication of Rowntree's survey in 1901, it was claimed, not only forcibly removed the ideological blinkers of many in the population and decision makers in Edwardian Britain, but it became, what Bruce (1961, p. 146) called, at least one of ' ... the driving force(s) of the Liberal reforms'. A Royal Commission on the Poor Laws and Relief of Distress was appointed in 1905. There were two fundamental issues which the Commission agreed upon: (1) the acceptance of the new terminology, 'public assistance', in relation to poor relief, which basically rejected the principle of 'deterrence' - i.e. the provision was so unpleasant (the workhouse, the means test) as to deter those in need from claiming it) and; (2) the introduction of a previously unheard of principle, with a duality of purpose - prevention and social provision - i.e. preventing demands on the state for assistance, not through deterrence, but through positive policies such as labour exchanges, greater clamp down on child labour, cutting down on the number of working hours in a day, etc., all of which were seen as spreading jobs and reducing unemployment. Social provision was to materialize in the form of a system of insurance against unemployment and invalidity. (de Schweinitz 1943, pp. 197-8) The concept of blind individualism which blamed the poor for poverty, it appeared, was being seriously challenged for the first time, at this level, for centuries.

In Parliament, Lloyd George was to signal the changes in attitudes towards poor relief and to set the scene for radical policy measures in social provision. His statement in 1906 epitomized his own commitment and the movement of forces within the country:

> ... the law which protects those men in their enjoyment of their great possessions should, first of all, see that those whose labour alone produces wealth, are amply protected with their families from actual

need, where they are unable to purchase necessaries owing to circumstances over which they have no control. By that I mean, not that they should be referred to the scanty and humiliating fare of the pauper, but that the spare wealth of the country should, as a condition of its enjoyment by its possessors, be forced to contribute first to the honourable maintenance of those who have ceased to be able to maintain themselves. (cited in de Schweinitz 1943, p. 201)

Thus, for the first time in the history of social security and poverty alleviation, the concept of state provision of income necessary to meet basic human needs was referred to. But did it underpin the construction of the levels of provision? The two main pieces of social security legislation enacted were: 1908 - The Old Age Pension Act and; 1911 - The National Insurance Act and the National Health Insurance Act, providing for protection against ill health and unemployment. The primary architect of the pensions plan was Charles Booth who suggested a basic state provided income of 5s. per week, subject to the consideration that no one would receive a pension whose income rose above a specified level - 14s.6d. a week. It was thus automatically assumed by Booth and his cohorts that 14s.6d. plus 5s. was a weekly sum sufficient to meet most basic needs - there was no attempt to calculate a measurement of needs, nor to monitor the standard of living which 19s.6d. would purchase. The Old Age Pensions Act 1908 was the first means tested income maintenance provision on a national scale.

The National Insurance plans of 1911 consisted of two major parts: (1) health insurance; (2) unemployment insurance. Both schemes contained the contribution principle, with the employee, the employer and the state all contributing to the central pool. Those few workers covered by the scheme would receive weekly unemployment benefit of 7s., for a maximum of fifteen weeks in any twelve month period. This, in 1911, constituted approximately one third of average weekly earnings of the lowest regularly paid industrial worker. (Gilbert 1970). There is no suggestion that this sum was the product of any estimates of the costs of basic needs or that the lifestyle afforded by this amount was a consideration for policy makers. Rather, the objective inherent in the level of provision was encapsulated by Churchill in 1909: 'Nothing in our plans will relieve people from the need of making every exertion to help themselves, but, on the contrary, we consider that we shall greatly stimulate their effort by giving them for the first time, a practical assurance that those efforts will be crowned with success.' (cited in de Schweinitz 1943, p. 208). Thus, the ideology of self help and individual reliance was paramount and preserved, and far from being abandoned, as was claimed, was enshrined in legislation. The 1911 system of unemployment insurance had deliberately avoided all pretence of meeting basic needs. Veit Wilson (1989) summed up the nature and level of the scheme as follows:

... benefits were explicitly not intended to do more than prevent income for a relatively short time from falling far below unskilled workers' wage rates in the limited employment they covered. They could not equal or exceed such rates for the simple reason that this would have introduced the disincentives of "moral hazard" ... contribution and cost were set in terms of political considerations of economic factors. Adequacy was thus judged in terms of the appropriate political and labour market context of income maintenance instead of extraneous criteria of poverty or need.' (Veit Wilson 1989, p. 27).

There was no attempt to justify the levels of insurance benefits in terms of meeting standard requirements.

The first world war to the 1920s

Prior to the war, poor relief to the unemployed was a secondary matter but the entire system almost crumbled as a result of the pressure exerted on it by increasing unemployment after the war. As a response, unemployment insurance was extended to cover most of the working population in 1920 but there was stern opposition at the time in the Ministry of Health to consider setting scale rates for poor relief, mainly on the grounds, they argued, that they limited, ' ... undesirably, the discretion of a Relief Committee; and further, if a scale is once published, there is a grave danger lest the recipients may begin to regard the gift as a right.' (cited in de Schweinitz 1943, p. 211). It also believed that the establishment of definitive weekly assistance levels would be misconstrued as the state's estimates of the costs of subsistence living for the unemployed. From the 'privileges' granted by the 1911 provisions, the system of social security in Britain had, by 1920, been transformed, in theory and principle, into 'a prerequisite of citizenship, a right to a national minimum that had been arrived at in an unspoken compromise between
british politicians and the citizens who elected them'. (Gilbert, pp. 31-2).

This unspoken agreement also involved an understanding that the 'dole' was not, any longer, merely a supplement to whatever savings the unemployed had managed to accumulate - rather, it came to be regarded as a subsidy to assist the attainment of a respectable standard of living and as such, the level of provision took centre stage in the debates. Addison, the Minister of Reconstruction, argued that provision for the unemployed should move beyond simply a gratuity to supplement savings, to actual maintenance. This principle came to be accepted by the Government, although it was careful not to openly state that it had conceded to provide cover at this level, for fear that it would come to be perceived as a national Government approved minimum. Gilbert

(1970) presented the pertinent questions at the time: ' ... was the amount of money that the guardians of the public purse felt the state could afford, adequate in terms of human needs? Would it satisfy the moral obligation that society had to those in distress? ... was 15s. enough to maintain the average unemployed worker and his family, now that many had been without work for nearly a year and had exhausted many savings and trade union benefits they might have possessed?' In responding to these questions and to growing working class pressure and violent street disorders, the Cabinet conceded that 15s. was not adequate for a basic living standard for a man and his family. There was no indication of how the Cabinet arrived at this conclusion. It is not apparent that they possessed some measuring stick: rather, it appears that such a decision was taken in response to political pressure, which itself was a diluted representation of the serious unrest and disorder among the working class.

Unemployment assistance, 1934

The Unemployment Assistance Act received Royal Assent in June 1934. The regulations permitted the Unemployment Assistance Board (UAB) significant discretion in proposing the benefit scale rates and modifications to them for individual special needs. The law simply referred the Board to the needs of the applicant and his/her dependents. And, in this sense, the rates that were eventually established by the UAB constituted the first official national minimum income levels which were presented as affording a subsistence lifestyle. On of the major factors which influenced the Board in its deliberations at the time of setting the rates was the Unemployment Insurance benefit rates. It was generally believed that these levels were determined by calculations of the costs of the basic needs of claimants and, therefore, any attempt to set the assistance scale rates at: (a) a lower level would attract the criticism that basic needs were not being met and; (b) the same, or a higher level would undermine the insurance principle, if the non insured were seen to be reaping the same fruits as the thrifty insured population. It was generally believed that the Board set more political importance by the latter. Concern over this issue raged in the House of Commons, with Robert Hudson MP arguing that the insurance scales should not constitute an upper limit for relief payments. 'If anything, they (should) form the ground floor', while another Labour member argued that if relief payments were to be made on the basis of need, then they would inevitably rise above the level of insurance benefits. (cited in SBC 1977, p. 37)

The Report of the UAB in 1935 emphasized a crucial dilemma for any scale of assistance for the unemployed - i.e. the issue of the relationship between: (1) welfare payments provided during unemployment and; (2) the general wage levels and the normal earnings when employed. Such concern was tantamount to a fear of generating a financial incentive to idleness and voluntary unemployment and the policy to emerge from it was an updated version of the Poor Law's less eligibility principle - i.e. a wage stop - which was to survive until 1975. This reflected a rule which disallowed unemployed claimants from receiving more than their wage levels in the six months prior to unemployment. However, wage levels, and particularly those at the lower range, were not calculated on any basis of needs, and so to permit them to dictate assistance provision in many cases, exposed the political and economic agenda behind the Unemployment Assistance scale rates. And, of course, the UAB had no control over the relatively low levels of wages: these were left to the forces of the market economy, in line with the philosophy of orthodox economic theory.

Although the Board stated that it was concerned with such primary needs as those of food, fuel, shelter, clothing etc., and that it considered expert opinion on the cost of living from the British Medical Association's Report on Nutrition, it remained, in practice, highly dubious about the scientific establishment of a minimum income scale. However, in a clear expression of apparent adherence to a relative definition of poverty, they stated in July 1934: 'There is no absolute criteria or scientific basis of need. The comforts of one age become the necessities of the next and any minimum standard must be determined largely by time and place.' Strohmenger also argued at the time that the problem of under nourishment was not a phenomenon for the lower classes only and that its causal factors lay more within the scope of income mismanagement than in the low levels of welfare allowances. He said that 'general malnutrition' was not within the terms of reference of the Board's responsibilities. (cited in SBC 1977, pp. 43-4). In this rather dismissive way, the Board attempted to veto any meaningful discussion on the level of an acceptable minimum income and on why it had rejected such an approach.

The human needs of labour, B.S. Rowntree, 1937

This attempt by Rowntree aimed to estimate incomes necessary to enable families of different compositions to secure the necessities of a healthy life. Rowntree commenced his report by referring to 'the low standard of health obtained by a large section of the population', which was 'simply and solely because the fathers of families are not in receipt of incomes large enough to provide the necessities of physical fitness for themselves and those dependent upon them.' And thus, Rowntree's task was to construct 'a measuring rod to enable us to assess the wage necessary for physical efficiency'. Concentrating upon the 'moderate family' of two adults and three children, he estimated the level at which such a minimum income was required. By employing the latest nutritional data and surveys into consumer behavioural patterns in York, Rowntree estimated the costs of the minimum requirements for diet, fuel, clothing and household and personal sundries at 1936 prices. Again, it must be stressed that Rowntree was not prescribing minimum income levels; he was, similar to 1899, endeavouring to establish the weekly costs of living, below which, no one could remain physically fit: this was not Rowntree's definition of poverty per se, only a measurement of a type of utter deprivation. Nor was Rowntree prescribing the level of physical efficiency as the standard of living that should be provided through social security for the poor - again, one of the primary determinants of his approach was a desire to pre-empt any criticism which may have been levelled against his allowances on the grounds of generosity and subsequent disincentive to work.

His minimum nutritional needs were based on expert opinion as expressed in a report of the Nutrition Committee of the British Medical Association (BMA) in 1933. Although this standard was constructed rather differently from that of 1899, the more recent one was, by no means, set at a more generous level than the previous one. Controlling for price constancy, Rowntree's food standards on both occasions were roughly the same. Holding prices constant again, the clothing standards between 1899 and 1936 were drawn at a very similar level. The minimum subsistence standard set by Rowntree at 1936 prices was approximately 40 per cent higher in real terms than the 1899 allowances, given price constancy. At 1936 prices, the poverty line of 1899 would have been drawn at 30s.7d., exclusive of rent. This apparent increase can be attributed, in the main, to a liberalization in the calculations of the sundries group of basic needs. Even so, Rowntree still did not make any allowances in 1936 for, e.g. conventional insurance payments, shaving soap, toilet paper etc. On the positive side, he did make provision for savings towards household furniture and fittings, although he did not allow for expenditure on replacing these items. The more generous 1936 level was a reflection of the belief by Rowntree that the 1899 subsistence allowance required modification in the light of economic and social progress in the intervening thirty seven years. As Rowntree put it himself, the 1899 researchers would not have classified as, 'obvious want and squalor', circumstances classified so in 1936 and they would not have regarded many families living below the 1936 subsistence standard as, 'showing signs of poverty'. (Rowntree 1937, p. 461). Rowntree, by 1936, had come to perceive his f ormer poverty line as indefensibly low, 'a standard of bare subsistence rather than living'. (Rowntree 1937, p. 102). However, such an improvement, when measured against a reliable indicator of economic progress, emerges at a much more modest level. Compared to the average earnings of male manual workers,in 1899, Rowntree's subsistence standard for a family of five stood at 79 per cent, while in 1936, it had risen quite modestly to 84 per cent. And if both these standards were to be compared with measurements of economic progress across the entire population, and not just the working class, then its possible that there was no improvement at all. (George 1968, p. 47)

In 1936, Rowntree again used expert opinion to estimate minimum nutritional requirements, this time, a special report from the BMA which listed daily food needs in terms of 3,400 calories and 100 grams of protein per man per day, with the needs of women and children relatively decreasing. In fact, the terms of reference of the BMA's project was, ' ... to determine the minimum weekly expenditure on foodstuffs which must be incurred by families of varying size if health and working capacity are to be maintained'. (cited in Briggs 1961, p. 296). These recommendations were minimum, not optimum standards, and indeed, cost little more than the 1899 levels would have cost at 1936 prices. Rowntree then converted the BMA's recommendations into a set of highly detailed menus, assisted by some domestic scientists. They did contain 'protective foods', such as vitamins and minerals and Rowntree also considered palatability and choice as influential factors in his dietaries. He professed, 'In this country, almost everyone takes a mixed diet - even the poorest try to get a certain amount of meat; and though undoubtedly health can be maintained without it, we cannot, in selecting our dietary, ignore the fact that meat eating is an almost universal custom. So is the drinking of tea and coffee ... ' But he clearly stated that his nutritional levels represented, 'a standard, below which no class of worker should be forced to live' But he went on to qualify this meagre quality of his subsistence diet by saying, 'Indeed, I do not put it forward as the kind of dietary that I consider entirely satisfactory for unskilled workers.' (Rowntree 1937)

In calculating his estimates for allowances for clothing and footwear, Rowntree attempted, ' ... to arrive at the minimum sum which a working class family must spend on such clothing as is necessary to keep the body warm and dry, and to maintain a modest respectability'. Rowntree's allowance for fuel and lighting was based on his conclusion that there was little or no difference in the average weekly fuel bills, no matter what type of heating was used by the household. To cover requirements such as washing and cleaning materials and the costs of replacing linen, pots and pans, he estimated a sum of 1s.8d. for a moderate family, land for personal sundries, the lowest sum he could establish was 5s.11d. for an unemployed man, his wife and three children. Rowntree again qualified this by saying, 'I feel almost ashamed to put forward so low an estimate for personal sundries', but such was necessary so as to establish a level, 'which is unassailable'. (Rowntree 1937). This Rowntree's poverty line of 1936 was referred to as a Spartan' and based on a 'fodder' standard.

Beveridge report, 1942

The release of the findings of Rowntree's 1936 study, (as with his previous surveys), generated significant shifts in public opinion and in policy approaches towards social security. Another impetus for the Beveridge examination of social security policies appears to have been the experience of economic decline in the 1920s and especially the early 1930s and the social consequences which this created. By the end of the 1930s, a whole range of conditions were being covered by contributory insurance schemes - old age, unemployment, sickness, widowhood etc. But these schemes tended to be organized separately from each other and governed by a broad range of rules and qualifying criteria. The Beveridge exercise was, ostensibly, instigated to amalgamate these provisions into a single comprehensive structure. The importance of the subsequent plans and proposals was, however, not the wide scope of exigencies for which insurance cover was to be offered, but the stated, if only theoretical, commitment to adequate financial provision, obtainable as of right and without exposure to a means test. Beveridge also planned a non contributory means tested scheme for those who fell outside the protection of national insurance, in the form of National Assistance, but this was foreseen as a marginal scheme, continually decreasing in size as the economy and the insurance schemes progressively improved.

Beveridge insisted that social security should make no provision above and beyond a minimum subsistence level, not only because this was appropriate to economic circumstances, but also as a positive characteristic and one of the core merits of the entire scheme. He said,

> Provision by compulsory insurance of a flat-rate benefit, up to subsistence level, leaves untouched the freedom and responsibility of the individual citizen in making supplementary provision for himself above that level. (Beveridge, 1942, Appendix F, para. 16)

As such, he stressed the importance of co-operation between the state and the individual. He believed that, although independent insurance schemes should take a back seat to state provision, they had an important function to fulfil. Beveridge's plans aimed to encapsulate national cohesion with individual initiative, a duality which has survived to the present era of discussions on social security. Thus a central practical principle for Beveridge's proposals was the benefit levels for physical subsistence only, with any improvement on this bare standard being achieved through private arrangements with insurance societies. His rationale was that the standard of provision should be so low, that those who had the means would turn to the private sector for real protection and security. Those who had not the means would simply have to exist on a meagre subsistence lifestyle, supplied through an assistance scheme.

In his approach to defining and establishing a subsistence income,

Beveridge relied significantly on the methodology applied by Rowntree, who, still regarded as the leading authority on poverty, was a member of the small sub committee which advised Beveridge on the levels of benefits to recommend. Beveridge agreed that Rowntree's methodology in measuring poverty was the appropriate basis for paying benefits in a social security system designed to abolish want. It is useful to examine in a little detail, the considerations Beveridge took account of when he chose to apply a plan for a subsistence based system and the methodology he employed to define 'subsistence'. During the period of the Labour Party's administration from 1945 to 1950, it consistently extolled the virtues of the social security system and particularly, the 'adequate' nature of the level of benefits. It attempted to justify this claim by invoking Beveridge's 'scientific', authoritative definition of subsistence. Since then, successive governments have sprang to the defence of their records and have attempted to validate their lack of re-evaluation by arguing, rather superficially, that National Assistance/Supplementary Benefits/Income Support, at whatever state, provided a superior lifestyle than the subsistence income of Beveridge. Therefore, it is highly appropriate to emphasize the rather parsimonious lifestyle which Beveridge referred to as a subsistence minimum.

Beveridge stated that

> ...the plan leaves room and encouragement to all individuals to win for themselves something above the national minimum, to find, and to satisfy and to produce the means of satisfying new and higher needs than bare physical needs... But it must be realized that nothing materially below the scales of benefit here suggested can be justified on scientific terms as adequate for human subsistence. (Beveridge, 1942, p. 170)

Thus, science was exploited to defend this definition of subsistence. Liberal principle argued what was desirable and science was used to justify this as adequate. Beveridge was expected to do more than establish the central themes of a reconstituted social security system. The Treasury, in its eternal fashion, demanded minutely detailed estimates of the bills of the different benefits and this forced Beveridge to put down in precise terms, the actual amounts in £.s.d. which he had calculated were necessary for the weekly subsistence of various households. Veit Wilson (1989) argued:

> This discussion formed an unconscious and unremarked milestone in the development of the British confusion between poverty lines and social security scales. These officials and experts had muddled up their task of finding standard minimum necessary income for households (which was necessarily average) with the design of social security benefits (which had to be done at the lowest possible aggregate cost)... This confusion between an individual's minimum income needs, and the

Exchequer's view of the maximum to pay them, has unfortunately persisted from then on in the British discourse on these topics. (Veit Wilson, 1989, p. 32)

After careful consideration, Beveridge established the minimum weekly incomes which his scheme needed to satisfy. He exploited a number of sources in his quest to set these standards and his proposed benefit level for a non-pensioner couple with no children, at 1938 prices, was 22 shillings a week. (Beveridge 1942, pp. 84/90) Rowntree's 'human needs' minimum for a family of five cost £2.90 at 1938 prices, yet the Beveridge plans proposed a subsistence level of £2.65 in 1942 for the same family and this was to include the family allowance which Beveridge advocated as an adjunct to his scheme. The central explanation for the difference in his and Rowntree's scales was that Beveridge allowed absolutely nothing for the items which Rowntree listed as 'personal sundries'. He attempted to justify this by arguing that state insurance contributions would be waived when a man was unemployed; he would also have no need for the 1s which Rowntree allowed each week for travel to and from work, but as far as the remaining items were concerned - newspapers, postage stamps, radio, presents for the children, occasional entertainment, haircut etc. - Beveridge simply ignored these needs; they would, it appear, have to be done without.

As Beveridge was concerned with policy making, he found it necessary to allow a margin to cater for the lack of expert nutritional knowledge among working class housewives. As Kincaid (1973, p. 56) put it, they '...do not prepare the family meals with reference to a BMA table of calorific values and with a committee of domestic science teachers available to advise'. Thus a margin was required over and above the maximum efficiency diet. Kincaid also explains, 'The scientific values of the nutritionists are presented as a realistic norm and deviations are patronizingly referred to as inefficiency.' (p.57). Beveridge stated,

> The foregoing calculations, particularly that for food, assume complete efficiency in expenditure, i.e. that the unemployed or disabled person buys exactly the right food, and cooks and uses it without waste. This assumption is clearly not likely to be realized. Some margin must be allowed for inefficiency in purchasing, and also for the certainty that people in receipt of the minimum income will, in fact, spend some of it on things not absolutely necessary. (cited in Kincaid, 1973, p. 87)

To compensate for this weakness, the allowance for food was established at a mere one sixth above that which absolute necessity demanded. When Beveridge said subsistence, he meant it in the strictest sense of the word. In establishing his proposed minimum incomes, Beveridge relied relentlessly on the 1937/8 Ministry of Labour survey of working class household spending patterns which gave him detailed data on actual expenditure. But throughout his calculations, he estimated sums for each component of expenditure that were less than the corresponding figure in the government's data tables, arguing that, 'subsistence expenditure can clearly be put below these figures, which relate to household living well above the minimum.' (cited in Kincaid, 1973, p. 87). The benefit levels which Beveridge arrived at were the product of a series of stringent calculations on a very narrow range of apparent necessities which bore no identifiable relationship to actual spending patterns. When Beveridge said, 'Determination of what is required for reasonable human subsistence is, to some extent, a matter of judgement', he meant it.

Beveridge was of the opinion that the most appropriate method for alleviating poverty was to provide individuals and families with an adequate income and allow them to spend it as they wanted. He wrote, 'Management of one's income is an essential element of a citizen's freedom.' (Beveridge, 1942, para. 23). Beveridge's adequate income however, was a standard of subsistence minimum which was even lower than the level below which Rowntree, in 1936, said, it was not possible to maintain mere physical efficiency. There was little freedom afforded by his meagre sums, and purely to exist, Beveridge would have required any recipients of his estimates to spend their income in exactly the manner in which his calculations implied - so much for food, so much for fuel, etc. Such lack of freedom became a dominant characteristic of the social security schemes which have stemmed from the Beveridge Report in 1942. Indeed Veit Wilson (1992) went on to examine the working papers from the Beveridge Committee of 1942 to account for the exchange of ideas among the members about measurements of needs and poverty. Because the Committee referred to 'human needs', the 'principle of adequacy of benefit' and social participation, it is assumed that these considerations determined the poverty line social security scale rates. Veit Wilson's investigations proved that the Beveridge Committee were fully aware that social participation was beyond the affordability of its proposed benefit levels.

> Because it is consciously implemented the principles of minimum subsistence and less-eligibility in the face of inadequate wages, the proposed scales were arguably more austere even than Rowntree's "primary poverty" standard which both he and Beveridge acknowledged were not sufficient to meet human social needs. (p.269)

But this muddle over the nature and quality of Beveridge's proposed scale rates has mystified the policy making process, social policy analysis and critical comment and research into the adequacy of poor relief scale rates ever since.

National Assistance 1948

In 1946, the Assistance Board (AB) wrote a memo that

> The adequacy of any scales of allowances must, to a large extent, depend upon considerations of habit and, social policy not capable of being measured by a scientific yardstick, the current scales did provide a reasonable margin over the cost of the bare necessities of life. (AB, 1946, para. 1)

But they considered that a re-evaluation of the existing scale rates was required in order to 'discover whether for "scientific" reasons or on wider grounds of social policy, they ought to be revised'. As the mechanism for establishing 'whether the current scales satisfy scientific tests based on the analysis of minimum human requirements in the bare necessities of life', they selected the proposed minima in the Beveridge Report. By doing so, they had adopted the subsistence basket of goods approach of Beveridge and Rowntree as the most 'scientific' test of the nature of their scale rates. As a basis for these estimates, the relevant authorities had divided the scale rates into detailed breakdowns of expenditure on various bare necessities. The assistance rate for a single pensioner in late 1945 was 20s. per week. This estimate makes no provision for a variety of 'non-essential' items such as: bus fares; renewals of bed linen, furniture, crockery or any other household equipment; church collections; cinema; subscriptions; holidays; tobacco; beer; firewood and firelighters; pills and ointment; magazines; fruit; and extras such as cake, meatpie, sausages etc. (AB, 1946, Appendix)

When the National Assistance scale rates were established in 1948, they were set at slightly lower levels than the insurance rates; but they were also set, in many cases, below the standard proposed by Beveridge as an irreducible minimum. And it should be remembered that Beveridge, in turn, set his standards below what Rowntree, in 1936, set as his basic human needs floor. Adults were estimated at a higher level than Beveridge's minimum, but children were given less under the National Assistance scheme. It is clear that Beveridge's proposals were not really implemented in the way he had foreseen, neither in benefit levels nor in their format. With over fifty years of hindsight, it is difficult to resolve the question of adequacy objectively, but there is reason to believe that the standards set for insurance scales were below any reasonable measure of subsistence at the time. The Labour administration accepted this and established National Assistance at levels just below insurance rates, but provided an allowance for rent which had the effect of lifting assistance allowances to a substantially higher payment. The 1948 calculations were founded, in part, on estimates of the cost of food, fuel, clothing, sundries etc., reached by officials of the NAB, but these calculations were never officially published. Similarly, it was never publicized just what amounts of money, or what proportions of the total income were allocated to meet the various needs of each member of the claimant family. A central stated theme of the regulations was that individuals should, as far as possible, have the scope and freedom to decide how to spend their income and what proportion to allocate to meeting the various needs. Lynes (1985) explains:

> No doubt, it was felt that publication of a "shopping list" of necessities would lead to continual pressure for increases in the amounts allowed for particular items and the addition of new items to the list. The absence of public information of this kind served to emphasize the political nature of decisions on the timing and amounts of increases. If there was no objective measure of adequacy, there could be no objective criteria for deciding at what point, price increases had rendered the existing assistance scale inadequate. (Lynes, 1985, p. 2)

Thus, it can be seen that the scale rates of 1948 were a hotch-potch of various approaches, methods, measurements, assumptions etc., but were firmly stepped in the subsistence basket of goods construction, as employed by Beveridge and Rowntree, but dominated by political and economic criteria. As such, the structure, upon which the current poor relief system is based, was, in theory, the product of the 'scientific' measurement of bare subsistence needs, but, in practice, contaminated to accommodate existing wider factors and environments. For the system that was founded in his name, Beveridge was to disclaim responsibility. He had always stressed throughout that his subsistence level was irreducible, the most frugal imaginable. Unlike those who implemented the insurance and assistance schemes, Beveridge emphasized that a crucial element to the entire planning of a National Insurance system, was that it should provide a level of subsistence as a right and without being subject to a means test. But insurance benefit standards were significantly inferior to Beveridge's subsistence measurements in 1948, and this disparity was to grow in the coming years. The most appropriate elegy for the downfall of the subsistence principle was provided by Beveridge himself, addressing the Commons in 1953, shortly before his death:

> ... either the Government will have to raise the benefit rates to adequacy for subsistence or to say ... that they have formally abandoned security against want without a means test, and to declare that they drop the Beveridge Report and the policy of 1946.' (cited in Kincaid, 1973, pp. 60-61)

Supplementary Benefits, 1966

In 1964 the NAB stated:

> Although the Beveridge Report had been hailed as opening up new vistas

in the development of social services, the subsistence levels proposed
therein, viewed from the vantage point of 1964, seem very tight
indeed... However valid the reasons therefore, the point remains that the
Board's scale rates in 1948 were meagre... As regards the actual level
of the rates, our enquiries led us to the conclusion that we could not
regard as satisfactory, the standard of living provided by the scales in
operation in 1964. (NAB, 1965)

Despite generating concern over the existing inadequate system by arguing
these points and despite making it clear that the provision for poverty relief
was in need of major changes, the practical actions of the government
amounted to little more than a renaming of the system, with a few minor
alterations. The poor were to remain just as poor. In 1964, the government
announced that a substantive review of social security provision was to be
carried out under the Chair of Houghton and was to establish ways of co-
ordinating the business of the social services to facilitate the abolition of 'the
scandal of poverty in the midst of great potential abundance'. The review
operation went on for three years, but did not produce any substantive
outcome or material guidelines for forthcoming social security policy. For
Britain's poor, it was to be more of exactly the same medicine. As a result
of the recommendations of this report, a number of purely administrative
changes were administered. An under the new Act, for the first time,
legislation was enacted to confer legal entitlement to poor relief, i.e.
Supplementary Benefits (SB). The concern which had been expressed for
some time about the benefit levels and the underlying subsistence framework
was largely ignored and demands for a whole new system to be implemented
in 1966 when the Labour government had the opportunity to do so, fell on
unreceptive ears.

The Department of Health and Social Security (DHSS) in 1975 rejected any
responsibility for the adequacy or inadequacy of the SB scale rates and argued
that such issues were the subject of historic basis and processes. They
suggested that,

> The use of minimum income levels in existing legislation is not
> appropriate for assessing the adequacy of these same minimum income
> levels ... Questions about the adequacy of the SB scale rates ultimately
> involve questions about the adequacy of the original Beveridge
> recommendations and the up-rating procedure. (DHSS, 1975)

It seems an unreasonable assertion to argue that a minimum income level,
measured almost thirty years previous and recognized ever since as highly
insufficient (even by the DHSS), should form the basis of an adequacy test of
existing levels, rather than current scientific criteria and opinion. It may well

have been that these 'don't blame us, blame Beveridge' statements were aimed at avoiding any movement towards an acceptable assessment of the level of poor relief in the 1960s and were designed to lay the responsibility for inadequate provision on the door step of individuals and governments who were unable to explain their approaches and challenge the DHSS's assumptions. It may well have been that such statements were another attempt to hide the issue of the lifestyles of the poor from view, to prevent discussion on it, or to render any discussion invalid because of inaccessible information.

In 1976, the Secretary of State for Social Services, David Ennals obliged a small group of DHSS officials to embark upon a review of the SB system, but they were restricted in their terms of reference, in that they were instructed to formulate ways by which the scheme could be improved without additional resources, either in money or staff; in other words, to facilitate the adoption of SB to its new 'mass role' - providing for millions of unemployed households who were without any other means of subsistence. When the review team presented their plans, the Supplementary Benefits Commission (SBC), (SBC, 1979), and the Child Poverty Action Group (CPAG), (Lister, 1979), both rejected the assumption that positive and effective reforms could be formulated on a nil cost basis and both lamented the absence of any discussion on what they perceived as the most important issue - i.e., the standard of living of the poor. The review team did not share their prioritizing and failed to address this question at even modest length. And the SBC, making its own response to the review proposals, emphasized its dissatisfaction at the nil cost approach, and publicly disassociated itself from it. It was undoubtedly the major weakness of the review, that it carried no detailed analysis of the poverty existence afforded by the scale rates of the SB system for the different categories of claimants. As NACAB (1979) put it, 'we must reject the Review outright because ... of its failure to put sufficient money where it is needed most, in the claimants pocket.' (NACAB 1979, p. 38)

Social Security Acts 1980

In November 1980, two pieces of social security legislation were passed which significantly changed the operation of the SB system. They were to manifest at the time, in the latest reforms in a process of metamorphosis which, over the preceding half century, had evolved into a complex system of means tested assistance in Britain. According to the DHSS, the 1980 reforms were the most searching analysis of the role of social assistance in this country since the NA Act 1948. But most concern was expressed over the nature of the reforms and particularly, their failure/refusal to address the deprived lifestyles generated by the SB scale rates, which even after the November 1979 up ratings, stood at: for a child aged under five a daily level of 74p and; for a child aged five to ten, 89p. One of the major changes generated by the reforms was the substantial reduction in eligibility for single payments for one-off expenses not covered by the weekly scale rates. As claims for single payments for the likes of clothing would automatically fall as a result of the restrictions and the Government would (and did) argue that this was an indication of the scheme working more efficiently, this did not mean that claimants were **managing** any better or that this could be taken as a firm indication that benefit levels were more in keeping with the basic needs of the poor. As Walker (C. 1983, p. 198) put it,

> The danger is that when problems fail to manifest themselves in the form of requests for help from the SB scheme, policy makers and politicians will believe the problem has been solved. In fact they will merely have been legislated out of out of "official" existence.

This very terse approach to welfare threw up three central themes: the first was whether the cuts represented a temporary setback or a permanent diminution of the role of social security; the second question was whether the distinction between means tested and contributory benefits would become less clear cut; and an equally serious issue was that making means testing apparently more acceptable would strengthen the hand of those who argued that the proper role of the state lies in the provision of no more than a basic minimum income for those unable to support themselves. Thus, 'targeting' limited amounts of cash on 'those in greatest need' would manifest in providing the barest skeleton of an income to a minority of encumbrants. Throughout the reforming process, emphasis was centred upon: the performance of the economy and the dependence of the standards of living of claimants on economic expansion; the need to maintain the work incentive; decreasing the welfare burden to allow revenue to be used for industrial progress; ensuring that strikers were not subsidized in their actions by the state; administrative simplification; and on financial savings. The standards of living of S.B. recipients were not discussed in any significant or positive/negative way - the lifestyle which S.B. afforded to claimants appeared to be of interest to the government only insofar as it functioned to achieve the above objectives. In what was claimed to be 'the most searching analysis' of the benefit system since 1948, the issue of meeting basic needs was totally ignored and marginalized by preoccupation with freedom for wealth accumulation, economic prosperity, disciplining the workforce and imposing moral standards.

Income support 1988

In 1988 alone, cuts in benefits as a consequence of the April reforms, in which S.B. was replaced by Income Support (I.S.) - which, as far as the basic benefit levels were concerned, amounted to no more than a change in name and a further reduction in the standard of living for many poor households - saved the Treasury at least £5 billion which was in start contrast to the tax cuts to the top one per cent of income earners in the 1988 Budget which amounted to a total of £4.5 billion. Field (1988) concluded that,

> 'This finding helps to explain why the government depends so much on rhetoric about what is happening to the living standards of the poor, while initiating a series of moves reducing the amount of publicly available information on the "condition of the people" ... Now that it is clear that the poor have not benefitted from a period of extraordinary economic growth, it becomes more, and not less important, to have an informed debate about what is happening to those at the bottom of British society.'

As such the remnants of the basic, underlying principles of the Beveridge proposals, especially the centrality of social insurance and the residual role of social assistance, were firmly laid to rest. And, via the hierarchical premium system which emerged from this new system, whereby those of retirement age and those with disabilities received a higher level of benefit than the unemployed and single parent families, the historical and traditional distinction between the 'deserving' and the 'undeserving' poor had, once again, been enshrined in poor relief legislation.

Summary

In the midst of the changing environment generated by the Industrial Revolution, social investigations into poverty and other phenomena abounded throughout Britain. They sought to 'scientifically' measure subsistence in terms of the income required to attain physical efficiency and to show to the nation, the numbers of citizens of one of the most wealthiest countries in the world who could not even achieve this standard due to poverty income. Rowntree certainly was the first to approach the question of subsistence by breaking down the various major items of needs - food, fuel, clothing etc. - instead of simply reaching an arbitrary weekly sum, as Booth had done some years before. In doing so, he set a precedent which became the springboard for the major re-evaluations of social security in the 20th century and which became the accepted methodology for reaching a measurement of subsistence. Whatever the weaknesses of Rowntree's exercise in 1899, he formed the basis of the major deliberations of the British poor relief systems of the 20th century and his approach is central to any analysis of poverty and poor relief systems. (See Stitt & Grant 1993). It is generally agreed that the findings of Rowntree's survey provided at least part of the impetus for the first major pieces of social policy legislation this century, the Liberal reforms of 1906/11. Although the concept of public assistance, rather than deterrence, emerged during this period, the emphasis was on means of helping people to avoid requesting financial assistance. The major reform was undoubtedly the introduction of state covered insurance. However, these were not designed as a humanitarian response to an obvious need, nor were they constructed on a basis of meeting living needs. There was no attempt to carry out a similar exercise to that of Rowntree in order to establish a subsistence income - rather, the introduction of the provision and the level of benefits were products of moral dogmas and economic restraints. The insurance scheme strove to ensure that it did not interfere with the esteemed attribute of self-help and this, again, was reflected in the level of benefits and contributions. The insurance scheme overtly rejected a subsistence approach to providing benefits and publicly assumed no obligation whatsoever for meeting the needs of claimants.

During the First World War and the 1920s, there was little practical movement towards change or examination of benefit levels, with any alterations which did take place being of an administrative nature. However, conceptual discussions and theoretical evaluations caused some shifts in perceptions of policies for poor relief. Financial provision for the needy was no longer seen as supplementary to savings but rather as a means within itself for attaining an independent standard of living and as such, the quality and level of provision dominated discussion. Such sentiments, however, were implied by central government rather than officially stated. There was distinct apprehension concerning the introduction of identifiable scale rates in case these were regarded as the subject of rightful entitlement and not a gift from a benevolent state and for fear that such scales might be perceived as constituting a stepping stone to an official national minimum. Still, there was no attempt at defining the nature and quality of lifestyles, the constituents of a subsistence standard of living, or the money required to attain this. Continually throughout this period, the Treasury strove to influence the level of benefits by introducing evidence of national economic difficulties.

The benefit scheme was to experience in-depth crisis in the early 1930s as the result of spiralling unemployment and increasing demands placed on the central funds during the Great Depression. Consequently, the newly elected Conservative administration responded by reducing the level of benefits payable by ten per cent, increasing the contributions by employees and employers, introducing a means test and limiting the period of entitlement. All these measures were implemented without any concern being expressed on their impact on the living standards of the already poor and without any attempt to establish a minimum income below which no one should be allowed to fall, regardless of other variables. These measures served to provoke a growing realization that the existing system of provision was inadequate and inappropriate to deal with the demands being placed upon it by a changing society.

As a consequence of this dissatisfaction, the first concrete, organized and structured system of poor relief, with its own brand of calculated basic scale rates, was introduced in 1934 - i.e. Unemployment Assistance. The levels of benefits paid were the product of a number of different considerations: (1), the level of insurance was generally perceived as sufficient to meet basic requirements and thus, setting assistance provision below this standard would render them clearly inadequate, while setting them above would naturally undermine the insurance principle; (2), the level of wages paid to those in work would have to be superior to any assistance least the latter might generate a financial incentive to idleness and so, the introduction of the 'wage stop' cut the level of benefits paid to many claimants down to their subsistence, although it was stated that this did not represent a scientifically determined minimum income and, indeed the Board never made public its approach to establishing these rates, although comparisons with basic needs scales at the time exposed the meagre nature of the UA rates.

Rowntree's survey in 1936 was his second attempt to measure and establish an income level, below which individuals could not maintain even the standard of physical efficiency. Rowntree again divided up basic subsistence needs, rather than follow the example of the UAB who simply set an aggregate weekly amount to cater for all the basic requirements of claimants. Rowntree's latest piece of investigation provoked significant swings in public attitudes towards poverty and poor relief, no least Beveridge in his proposals for a benefit system. There was a stated commitment by central government to improve the standard of living for the poor, the needy and the working class in general, who constituted the vast bulk of those who were depended upon to defeat Nazism and win the war. Being a committed disciple of individualism and self reliance, Beveridge planned insurance payments at a level concordant with subsistence living only, in order to encourage individual private provision, with NA provided for those outside the coverage of insurance or in receipt of inadequate insurance payments. NA was to be the ceiling above which no beneficiary could rise, not he floor below which no one should fall, implying that assistance rates would afford claimants to meet all basic needs. Beveridge asserted publicly that nothing below his minimum could be scientifically justified. Although Beveridge was highly influenced and continuously advised by Rowntree, his breakdown of weekly benefits was also a response to a demand from the Treasury, concerned about the financial costs, for detailed explanations of the components of each benefit. The format, presentation and outcome of the entire review was determined by

108

liberal conscience and financial soundness, not the needs of poor families and once these factors had decided what to pay, science was used to justify the levels.

The major outcome of Beveridge's plans was the National Assistance Act 1948 which drew up weekly scale rates, broadly based on Beveridge's calculations, but in parts, up-rated in line with inflation since 1938. The NAB admitted that insurance benefit levels were below subsistence standards and assistance payments were to be located even lower than these. Their ad hoc response to this dilemma was to allow the payment of rent in full to NA recipients, above and beyond their basic scale rates, thereby lifting them above the insurance level in many cases. Throughout the early 1950s, in an era of national thriving affluence, there was no public statement laying out the justification for linking benefit rises merely with the general Retail Price Index, nor was there any open analysis of the appropriateness of the existing scale rates. Poverty was regarded as a disappearing phenomenon, lost in the impetus of national wealth accumulation and as such, its relief was a rather marginal issue. When a Labour government was eventually put into office in 1964, expectations were optimistic for a real improvement in the standard of provision for the poor and this optimism was fuelled by Labour's (unfulfilled) pronouncements on the need for a national Income Guarantee for all. Upon election, their attention switched from meeting basic needs to a preoccupation with economic growth and industrial planning and ministers made it clear that the provision of social security had to be measured against financial resources. During this period, the numbers in receipt of N.A. were gradually, but significantly, swelling, but this did not prompt the government to examine the standards of living of the lower income groups nor the provision of existing benefit levels in meeting the needs of the poor.

When the N.A. scheme was replaced by SB in 1966, the only changes involved were administrative, attempting to simplify some of the minor parts of the system. There was no suggestion of any substantive re-evaluation of the structure of the level of provision, nor any examination of the living standards which poor relief afforded to claimants. NA had changed in name only and the basis for measuring needs in the 1930s and 1940s continued to underpin the system of poverty line benefits in the 1960s. As Britain moved into the 1970s and its economy began to feel the effects of the smouldering world wide recession, unemployment crept steadily upwards, levels of poverty increased and the numbers in receipt of SB rose in tandem. It was during this turbulent period that the DHSS denied any responsibility for tackling the question of the lifestyle provided by the SB scale rates by arguing that such issues must refer back to the approach of Beveridge when he set the guidelines for the existing system. This reaction was feeble on two related counts: firstly, measurement apparatuses established in war time Britain in the 1940s to calculate the basic needs of the poor might not be the appropriate mechanism for dealing with benefit levels in the 1970s and; secondly, the DHSS failed to justify their apparent unwillingness to carry out a similar analysis of the basic needs of claimants.

A review team was set up to examine ways in which the SB scheme could be adopted to its new mass role; but because no resources could be found to finance alternative to SB reliance, then similarly, no money was available to improve the standard of benefits and thus the review team was given a nil-cost remit. This allowed them to examine issues such as simplification, efficiency and discretion - it did not permit any analysis of the scale rates or the basis for their construction. As it was generally agreed at the time that the standard of living afforded by the scales of SB was parsimonious, then there was grave disquiet at the refusal of the government to facilitate a detailed, critical examination of the question of standards of living by the review team. It appeared that the needs of the administration and the desire to exercise some form of economic common sense in the face of the recession, were placed before the needs of the poorest section of the population. Benefit levels were cut to facilitate growth in output and economic expansion with the sugar to sweeten the medicine being the promise of improved benefits when these had been achieved (the 'trickle down effect'). They never were and benefits were further reduced in real terms. Social security policy and the basic needs of the poor were, once again, subordinated to economic growth and industrial promotion.

With the election of the Tories in 1979, social policies were adorned even more with free market philosophies and the requirement to reduce public expenditure, regardless of the impact on the dependents of social services. Social security was the first area to be tackled with a re-evaluation which did not include discussion on what was recognized to be the most pressing issue in the entire ares of income maintenance - i.e. the deprivation suffered by welfare benefits claimants. The perennial statements about preserving the income gap between the employed and the unemployed, the need to generate economic prosperity before the requirements of the poor could be considered, the extent of fraud and abuse of the system, etc., dominated discussions on social security. These were the pivotal points around which the debates centred, not the declining standards of living of the poor. As David Donnison (1980) explained: 'It is the working poor whose living standards impose a political ceiling on what you can do for the people out of work.' And as Walker et al (A. 1983, p. 17) were to conclude, the standards of living of the rapidly expanding legions of the unemployed were, in a nutshell, ' ... the conscripts in the battle against inflation ... and the casualties of economic restructuring.'

All of the major pieces of social security legislation and the more important research exercises since 1834 can be understood in terms of responses to various crises which were brought about by economic change and the pressure to expand, by political necessity and by ideological shifts. Once these factors had been absorbed into the deliberations on benefit levels and had determined the standard of financial support which the state should and would provide for the poor, then the concept of subsistence income was introduced to justify and legitimate the meagre provision. Poverty line benefit levels were: not calculated, as they were claimed, from the bottom up - i.e. basic needs measured by some mechanism and the finances required to meet these established, but; from the top down - i.e. the state, subject to a range of forces and pressures, decided how much it was going to allocate on an aggregate level and then reformulated the scale rates to adopt to this.

In the very latest reforms to the poor relief systems in Britain, the S.B. system was replaced in April 1988 by Income Support, as a result of what was described as a major reevaluation. In the Green Paper to the Commons in 1985 on his proposals for the restructuring of the social security system, Normal Fowler wrote, 'There have been many attempts to establish what would be a fair rate of benefit for claimants. But it is doubtful whether an attempt to establish an objective standard of adequacy would be fruitful.' (DHSS, 1985). This was to be the sole reference to the issue of standard of living in the entire proceedings surrounding the reforms of social security and it came in the form of a rejection of any necessity for discussion on the question of whether the scale rates were sufficient to meet the needs for which they were ostensibly designed to cater. The review team behind the reforms failed to attempt to offer a single justification for their argument that and objective standard of adequacy was not measurable and Fowler would not be drawn on the relationship between a 'fair' rate of benefit and an 'adequate' one. In their evidence to the review team in 1984, the Citizens' Advice Bureaux (CAB) explained: ' ... the standard and style of life which is accepted in the 1980s as being the minimum that will provide for a dignified existence within the community, is not made possible by the existing scale rates.' They continued:

> We make no apology for repeating our view that the most important issue for the Review Team to tackle is the general inadequacy of the rates. Many clients simply cannot survive financially ... the rate of S.B. is based on assumptions about the amount of money required to subsist. Since Beveridge, there have been major changes in society. The expectations of individuals and families have risen, and eating and living habits have improved. We recommend that a major piece of research is commissioned, or a new review appointed to establish the true costs of participating in today's society. (NACAB 1984, p. 25)

These sentiments and volumes of similar messages presented as recommendations to the review team, were rejected out of hand by Norman Fowler in the two brief sentences quoted above. This reflects the current consideration and concern attributed to the issue of the poverty line benefits scale rates in meeting basic human needs and the deprivation experienced by the poor in Britain as the 21st century beckons. This historical journey has generated an account of a 'nothing has changed' process in the 'development' of attitudes towards poverty and the poor and the systems of poor relief in Britain spanning a period of over 150 years. The only things that have 'changed' are explained succinctly, yet tellingly, by Seabrook (1985):

> The images of hardship inherited from the past obscure the emerging outlines of the new landscapes of poverty: no longer the sweatshops, the infants selling matches, the men besieging the hiring foremen at the docks., In the new landscapes of poverty, the wind whistles through the metal hoardings, the streets are empty under the sulphur lamps, and up the dark stairs of the two b locks, the grey-purple pallor of the T set flickers through the lace curtains.

It may be as pertinent and illustrative way to conclude this chapter on the history of poor relief by, as the *Observer* did (14 November 1993, p. 15), cataloguing what Victorian/Edwardian commentators had to say on the dominant values towards poverty and by comparing these to the sentiments of the Conservative government in the 1990s, in order to identify and record similar, underlying beliefs and to lay open the 'morality' of the 'back to basics' crusade:

THEN

> A certain percentage ... are almost beyond hope of being reached at all. Crushed down into the gutter, physically and mentally by their social surroundings, they can but die out, leaving, it is hoped, no progeny. (H.M. Hyndman, leader of the Marxist Social Democratic Federation, 1887)

> The average guardian divides his paupers into two classes: the undeserving wastrels who have only themselves to blame for their misfortunes, on whom kindness is wasted; the industrious poor. (Robert Blatchford, *The Clarion*, 1892)

> With regard to the treatment of the ... deserving poor, it is felt that persons who have habitually led decent and deserving lives should, if they require relief, receive treatment different from those whose previous habits and character have been unsatisfactory, and who have

112

failed to exercise thrift in the bringing up of their families.(Local Government Board, 30th Annual Report, 1988)

The unemployable are the "can't works" and "won't works" ... of incurably parasitic or criminal disposition ... flotsam and jetsam of our industrial life. (Royal Commission on the Poor Law, minority report, 1909)

NOW

I've got a little list ... (of) of young ladies who get pregnant just to jump the housing list. (Peter Lilley, Social Security Secretary, Conservative conference, October 1992)

It must be right, before granting state aid, to pursue the father and see whether it is possible for him to make a financial contribution. (John Redwood, Welsh Secretary, July 1993)

Everyone who is a dole cheat is taking money away from the unemployed and training councils. WE cannot afford to allow that to happen ... Everyone wants to see law and order restored and the weeding out of people who do not respect it. (David Hunt, Employment Secretary, Conservative conference, October 1993)

Social security benefits all too often appear as an entitlement rather than something which should be earned. (Michael Howard, Home Secretary, Conservative conference, 1993)

Putting girls into council flats and providing taxpayer-funded childcare is a policy from hell. (Stephen Green, chairman, Conservative Family Campaign, 1993)

Being interviewed on BBC Radio's Today programme on 9 November 1993, a Conservative member of the Social Security Select Committee stated: 'The social security system is losing widespread popular support because it does not appear to meet the deserving, er, poor.' The hesitancy in his regrettable statement is understandable, given that the MP had used a concept synonymous with Victorian values, soup kitchens, the workhouse, ragged schools etc., but a concept which underpins the poor relief policies in the 1990s' back to basics drive. As journalist Michael Durham (*Observer*, 14 November 1993) claimed:

It is not a phrase many politicians choose to use openly. But whether spoken aloud or not, the notion of the "deserving poor" is back in fashion. A century after it was invented by Victorian social engineers, worried at the ugly turn society was taking. It has returned to the political agenda. Forward to the past.

4 Gender, race and poverty

Introduction

This chapter does not attempt to account for the substantial diversity of the poverty experiences of women from ethnic minorities (other than very briefly), or white women and black women from different social classes, with and without physical and mental disabilities. It does not attempt to prioritize the various factors which cause and influence poverty - class, race, gender etc. Obviously, a white, middle class women is less likely to confront poverty than a black, working class man. Women and poverty, and race and poverty are thus dealt with separately on the basis that it is not pertinent to gather all of these variables into a unitary snap shot of poverty or affluence. Class, gender, race, as with disability, age, sexuality, appearance etc., are all highly influential features which determine the life experiences of the working class, women and blacks - but in heavily diverse and varying manners, although writers like Delphy (1984) suggest that the exploitative relationship between male and female partners is similar in nature to that between the different social classes. The societal forces which generate and consolidate racism and racial discrimination are somewhat at variance with the ideologies and practices which manufacture the nature and extent of poverty among women, among the disabled, older people etc. In order words, not all women and not all ethnic minorities are equally poor. Class, race, gender etc. all make their own contribution to the nature and extent of the exploitation. In both of the following sections, it is argued that poverty among women and among ethnic minorities has, historically, been largely invisible and that poverty has become feminised and racialized only in the sphere of public awareness, official acknowledgement and academic research. But if women's and ethnic minorities' poverty has been invisible, then poverty for the Black or Irish or

115

Jewish woman, for the working class Pole, for the woman with a sever disability (and all the bivariate and multivariate combinations which can be generated) has been far more invisible.

Gender and poverty

An oft quoted reference from a United Nations report calculates that one third of the world's paid workers are women, four fifths of the world's unpaid work is done by women, but women receive a mere ten per cent of the world's income and own less than one per cent of the world's property. Yet, throughout the heyday of the most recent phrasemongering, esoteric battle over the definitions and measurements of poverty, little reference was made to the gender variations in the extent and distribution of poverty. Even given the overwhelming and conclusive research data recently uncovered by feminist writers, which demonstrates the financial disadvantage of women compared to men, academic discussions of poverty have remained, until relatively recently, 'gender-blind' and guilty of generating 'presentational invisibility'. For example, the *Journal of Social Policy*, Britain's most widely read publication on social welfare issues, published a special edition in 1987 devoted entirely to a debate among leading commentators on the definitions and measurements of poverty. There was no single direct reference to the feminisation (or indeed, racialization) of poverty thesis in the entire journal. And in official circles, the area is virtually ignored in many government publications, such as the DHSS/DSS's 'Low Income Families' and 'Households Below Average Income', neither of which gives any analysis by sex. The Low Income Families 1985 Report (DHSS 1988) presents figures which show that 3,150,000 single pensioners and 570,000 lone parents were living on or below the poverty line of 140 per cent of SB scale rates: but they did not indicate how many of these were women and how many were men. In reality, in excess of 80 per cent of single pensioners and 88 per cent of single parents are women. The 'hidden' nature of women's poverty in relation to academic discussion and research has led writers in that field, such as Glendinning & Miller (1991, Chapter 2) to talk about 'Poverty: the Forgotten Englishwoman', an analogy to the classic 'Poverty: the Forgotten Englishman' by Coates and Silburn (1970). Indeed, what relatively little research which has been carried out by the general academic and official world into women and poverty had concluded that:

> Women's poverty is simplistically attributed to sex - to women being women - rather than to gender - to the economic and social processes which are constructed upon this basic biological distinction. (Glendinning & Millar, 1991, p. 25)

116

Where the literature (e.g., Glendinning & Millar, 1987, p. 15) refers to a feminisation of poverty, it appears in a rather ambiguous fashion. In empirical terms, there has been no such trend if we take the data at its face value. Poverty has always been much more of a problem for women than for men: according to the date that exists, at the beginning of the century, 61 per cent of all adults who were recipients of poor relief were females (Lewis & Piachaud, 1987). In 1990, 62 per cent of all adults in receipt of poor relief - i.e. Income Support - were females (Oppenheim, 1990, p. 93). On the surface, it would seem that the gender balance in the distribution of poverty has remained unchanged throughout the 20th century and thus, no empirical evidence has emerged to substantiate the 'feminization of poverty' thesis. (This is the conclusion of Jane Lewis and David Piachaud, 1987, p. 50). Only its composition has changed, from clustering among married women, widows and the elderly at the beginning of the century, to being concentrated among single mothers, lone women and the elderly today. Indeed, most feminist research has argued, and this chapter agrees, that women's poverty has historically been invisible and has only begun to become more visible since the 1980s. Bettina Cass (1987, cited in Glendinning & Miller, p. 15) agrees that women and poverty is not a new problem; rather a recently recognised problem. This may be the result of: (a) the myth that women are financially dependent upon men being exploded and; (b) the feminisation of research into poverty and other social issues. Rather, it seems that the feminisation of poverty has been a trend that has witnessed such extensive poverty becoming identifiable, coming under public, official and academic scrutiny and becoming more unacceptable than previously. It is perhaps less ambiguously labelled the feminisation of the study of poverty, rather than of poverty itself.

Estimates of the numbers of women experiencing poverty have tended to be rough guesses via manipulating other primary data. For example, in 1987, if we equate poverty with receipt of the safety net benefits - Supplementary Benefit/Income Support - then 4.5 million women, 3.2 million men and 2.5 million children were living in poverty. In addition, in 1988, women's incomes amounted to only 86 percent of mens and retired women were much more dependent than men upon welfare benefits, being less likely to have pensions, annuities and investments (Oppenheim, 1900 p. 94). This excessive dependency on welfare payments among retired women is the product of lower wages, intermittent employment patterns and inferior rights to occupational pensions.

The economic disadvantage and poverty suffered by women has traditionally been invisible but can be identified in the trinity of channels to material provision: (1) paid work; (2) income maintenance and; (3) family and household distribution. All of these forms of inequality, leading to greater poverty among women, are the product of the patriarchal set of values which sees women as being economically dependent upon men. Firstly, women in employment, whose numbers have dramatically increased in the post-war era, leading to a 'feminisation of work', is examined. The drift towards part time work is understood as an integral element in the quest by employers to 'attract' an inexpensive, exploitable source of labour. As such, married women have become an instrument, a 'pawn in the game' (Bryson, 1992, p. 203). It is frequently assumed that, because of their 'natural' domestic roles, women do not need their own independent incomes as they are, and should be, economically dependent upon the male 'breadwinner'. It is therefore not necessary to pay them an adequate, fair renumeration for their labour. The role that the image of female financial dependency upon men plays in encouraging and consolidating work incentives among male labour at the lower end of the income scale, is not difficult to identify. All research into this area points to women receiving an average wage which falls in the region of 67 per cent of men's wages. More specifically, in 1990, British women in full time employment earned on average, 77 per cent of their male counterparts (Department of Employment, 1990). Because of restructuring in the labour market to accommodate economic and ideological shifts, the feminisation of work process has operated and has led to female employees being clustered more and more in low paid, low status posts. In the mid 1980s, 52 per cent of all married women were employed on a part time basis, compared to less than one in twenty men and compared to a mere ten per cent of married women in work in 1931 (Close, 1989, p.8). The Labour Force Survey showed that: 77 per cent of male employees worked full time and 4 per cent part time; 51 per cent of females worked full time and 40 per cent part time; 43 per cent of married women employees worked full time and 48 per cent part time (Department of Employment, April 1990). By 1989, women employees represented almost nine out of ten part time workers, in employment conditions which did not qualify them for the National Insurance scheme and where employment protection did not apply. This trend is, of course, exacerbated by the effects on women's earnings of interruptions to their employment by periods of childbirth, child care and indeed, care of other dependants. Heather Joshi (1987) reckoned that, on the basis of a female employee's career being divided into a eight year break having children and then twelve years of part time paid employment, the lost wages would amount to £135,000. A woman with two children would lose £122,000. But, of course, women care for and tend more people than their children and this adds to the domino effect on their lost earnings. Elderly, sick, disabled relatives are usually looked after by a female adult. In 1985, among the six million carers in Britain, 3.5 million (15 per cent of all women) were carers, compared to 2.5 million men (12 per cent of all men). The likely loss of income each year for a woman sacrificing her job in the later stages of life to look after an elderly or disabled person was estimated at £8,500 for a woman with no children and £7,000 for a woman with children. What caring for another adult actually entails is indicated by the finding that 45 per cent of all carers devoted 50 hours or more a week to their caring chores (Oppenheim, 1990, p. 98). The paradox lies in women being protected as the dependants of men, but the reality is that it is women whom others depend upon, whilst they are rewarded by questionable forms of gratification. Leifbried and Ostner (1991, pp. 165-166) add: 'Furthermore, those who care daily will be those who, in their future, can seldom rely on being cared for themselves ... caring thus marginalises the carer and cared for in a mutual relationship of dependency.' In 1989, 6.34 million women were low paid (defined by the Low Pay Unit as less than two thirds of median male earnings) which was 71 per cent of the total number of people on low wages. More than 4.25 million women were employed in part time jobs, of which 79 per cent of them were low paid. Almost one million men had part time jobs only, of which 72 per cent were low paid. Average hourly wages for women were 68 per cent of mens (including overtime) and 76 per cent of mens (excluding overtime) (Oppenheim, 1990, p. 95). Women not only make up the bulk of part time employees, but they also constitute the substantial majority of low paid workers, exposing a distinctive gender division of labour in 1989:

- in education, health and welfare - 14 per cent of women compared to 5 per cent of men - 20 per cent of the full time female workforce earned less than £160 per week;
- in clerical work - 30 per cent of women compared to 6 per cent of men - 56 per cent of full time female workforce earned less than £160 per week;
- in catering, cleaning, hairdressing and other personal services - 21 per cent of women compared to 4 per cent of men - 82 per cent of the full time female workforce earned less than £160 per week;
- in retailing - 10 per cent of women compared to 5 per cent of men - 73 per cent of the full time female workforce earned less than £160 per week (Oppenheim, 1990, pp. 100-101).

An unseen feature of the above data is that women employees are clustered in occupations which reflect the roles that they generally carry out within the home - caring, servicing for others, nurses, cleaners, clothing workers, attendants and home helps. What many women do in the home for no pay is replicated in the labour market for low pay. The skills that they require to carry out these low status jobs are as under valued as those which they possess in carrying out their domestic chores. The sexual division of labour is exposed in all its tentacle like, permeating omnipotence. Paid employment, and the absence of it, is largely dependent upon the availability and affordability of childcare facilities. Many mothers would opt for employment or longer working hours if suitable and affordable childcare was provided. In terms of state funded childcare provision, Britain has an unenviable position within the European Union, being third from the bottom in childcare for the 0-2 year olds and second from the bottom for 3-4 year olds. In 1986, only 2 per cent of British children aged 0-2 years old and only 44 per cent of over 3 year olds obtained state provided pre-school care. The corresponding figures for Denmark were 44 and 87 per cent, for Greece 62 per cent for 3 year olds upwards and 66 per cent in Spain (Oppenheim, 1990, p. 100).

The feminisation of work thesis surfaced in material events on May 13th 1993 when the Swan Hunter Shipyard on Tyneside (the last of its kind) shut its gates for the last time to 2,200 male employees, swelling the official male unemployment ranks to 2.3 million. But on May 10th 1993, three days before this inglorious event, the Secretary of State for Employment, Gillian Shephard, told a group of women entrepreneurs in Bristol that there were 'new horizons for women's opportunities' and she gave examples of 'what can be achieved if women take full advantage of the opportunities that are available'. According to Cohen and Borrill in an aptly named article in the *Independent on Sunday* (p.19), 'The New Proletariat':

> This contrast - between the bleak future of male manufacturing workers on Tyneside and the supposedly bright prospects for women in the South West - echoed the most dramatic and far reaching change in the late 20th century Britain.

In other words, with the decimation of the male dominated heavy manual labour, women are becoming THE most important source of labour power. Since 1970, almost nine out of ten new jobs created in Britain have been filled by women. In 1979, there were 13.1 million male workers and 9.4 million female workers. By April 1993, the imbalance had been almost eliminated - 10.7 million men and 10.1 million women in paid employment. As we approach the 21st century, for the first time ever, Britain can increasingly assert that the typical British worker is a woman. But, as this chapter has already shown, this trend is no source of celebration for women workers. Almost half the women working in 1993 (4.6 million) were in part time employment and a substantial proportion of their full time colleagues are in low paid, low status posts. Cohen and Borrill (Ibid) provide figures which show that British Home Stores paid its female till operators £3.08 an hour and its cleaners £2.50 an hour. Women check out assistants at Sainsbury's earned £3.57 an hour - a company that in May 1993, announced record annual profits of £733 million.

Secondly, because of their greater dependence on low paid, part time employment, and because of their careers being punctuated by childbirth, child care and other caring obligations, and because the social security system assumes male centred, full time, uninterrupted employment, then women face the greater risk, in periods of unemployment, of either, dependence on safety net, means tested benefits, or on lower rates of contributory benefits. The

Beveridge Report of 1942 planned the social security system on an assumption that women would be financially dependent upon their husbands, would not require welfare benefits in their own right and would be available to carry out unpaid domestic duties. Although the past 50 years have brought about significant changes and improvements, couples living together continue to be assessed along the female dependency line and women are still assumed to be available for unpaid caring. In 1988, over two million women were employed in jobs in which the wages levels were too low to permit them to pay contributions towards national insurance, thus distancing them from the range of contributory benefits. At the same time 1.19 million women over pension age, compared to 350,000 men were in receipt of Income Support, a multiple of over three. (Woman's longer life expectancy also means that a higher proportion of them live out their lives in a state of subsistence poverty). Over 727,000 single parents (88 per cent of whom are female) were dependent upon Income Support, equivalent to approximately two-thirds of all single parents. A full 96 per cent of single parents on Income Support were women (Oppenheim, 1990, p. 96).

Thirdly, it is assumed that food and other resources are equally distributed among the family members. But research has shown that there continues, a system of unequal distribution of domestic resources within the family, with women receiving less than their 'fair share'. Such is the case regardless of the employment status of both the male and female partners. It is assumed that, because the role of the male is one of the 'breadwinner', then he should take decisions on the distribution of household resources. Thus the male deploys what he decides should be given to the female for household maintenance (a sort of housekeeping allowance), and then she is responsible for managing and budgeting the financial affairs of the household. Such a situation appears to be more common among low income families than other better off households. But being in change of the family coffers does not necessarily involve power to spend it fairly. Pahl (1989) puts is simply: 'If a pound entered the household economy through the mother's hands more of it would be spent on food for the family than would be the case if the pound had been brought into the household by the father.' Failure to maintain an acceptable standard of living on an inadequate income is thus perceived as 'a matter not of public policy but of private failure' (Parker, 1987, p. 258). Women have been left with the central obligation of managing the financial (and emotional) consequences of the unemployment of their male partners.

> She would take as many critical financial decisions in the course of a week as the wealthiest entrepreneur, and manipulate as elaborate a pattern of income and debt ... the strategic dispersal of inadequate resources still required unceasing mental effort. (Vincent, 1991, p. 187)

Thus by understanding poverty on a household aggregate, rather than an individual level, the measurement of poverty and the cloaking of women's poverty is subject to two factors:

1   women are included in the measurement of poverty only if the household income level falls below whichever poverty line is applicable. Family income may be above that cut off point, but because of the unequal distribution of power and command over resources, women may fall below and individually defined poverty line. Because of the patriarchal structuring of conjugal relationships, men may have larger and more expensive consumption practices - e.g. income is withheld for personal benefit such as smoking, drinking, hobbies. (Graham 1987);

2   women in lower income households are more likely than in better off families to be delegated the core responsibility of weekly budgeting. The sexist nature of the distribution of the burden of poverty within households generally means that women suffer far more sacrifices than men (or their children, whether there is a male head of household or not) in trying to make ends meet. (Graham 1987).

The problems inherent in the budgeting responsibilities for women have been exacerbated by the late 1980s reforms of the social security system. Examples of these are:
- the loss of entitlement to free school meals and the inadequacy of the compensatory amount of 60p (payable through Family Credit) means that women in poor households will be further stretched in trying to feed their children on a reduced weekly budget and being forced to spend time and effort making packed lunches;
- the abolition of single payments and their replacement by repayable Social Fund loans has added weight to the burden women bear in budgeting on an already parsimonious income;
- non-recipients of Income Support and Family Credit and mothers under 16 years of age are no longer entitled to the non means tested maternity grant of £25. Under the Social Fund, mothers can claim a maternity needs grant which is less than half what they would have received under the old SB scheme;
- carers of elderly and disabled people, who are in the vast majority of cases, women, are the sole category who will forfeit the higher long term rate of Income Support.

The current social security system permits a care allowance to be paid to women who look after a dependant who is in receipt of an attendance allowance - but no such benefit is payable to the legions of women who care for children, presumably because this is perceived as their 'natural' duty for

122

which no financial regard is expected. For the women looking after an adult dependant, the care allowance does not alleviate her poverty as it is paid at a level below that of contributory unemployment and sick pay. There is therefore no entitlement to 'compensation' for the earnings sacrificed through the loss of the opportunity to seek a paid job. There are a number of reasons why women are more likely than men to fail the criteria for entitlement to unemployment benefit:
- they have not been in paid employment long enough;
- they have not been working sufficient hours to pay contributions;
- they have opted for paying the 'married woman's contribution' (before 1976);
- they cannot register as 'available for work' because they have children or because they cannot travel anywhere in the country in search of work. (Abbott & Wallace 1990, p. 200)

Another feature of the social security system which reinforces the idea of women's economic independence upon men is the 'cohabitation rule'. Under present arrangements, if a woman claimant is known to have a male friend visiting and staying in her home on more than three nights a week, she is regarded as being financially supported by him and her benefit entitlement is reduced accordingly. Such decisions are confirmed if she isfound to be washing and cooking for him. The thus assume that the woman in such cases is, or should be, 'paid' by the male in return for sexual and domestic favours, leading to allegations that such assumptions introduce criteria akin to prostitution. In order to prove their case, the AD employ officials who have become known as 'sex snoopers' (for obvious reasons), often found parked outside women claimants' homes in the early morning, watching for male visitors leaving 'the morning after'. They are also entitled to, and do, interrogate women claimants suspected of cohabiting on their sexual activities - with whom, how often, when, where etc. The sexist nature of this piece of social security legislation lies in the fact that the process is rarely reversed - i.e. women visiting male claimants, where the latter is subjected to the cohabitation rule in principle, but very seldom in practice. Caroline Glendinning (1987, p. 60) concludes: 'While the history books will record Mrs. Thatcher's major achievement in becoming Britain's first women prime minister, testimonies such as these demonstrate that, ironically, it is women who have had to bear the brunt of the increased poverty over which she has presided.'

If decision making and control over resources within the family are unequal, so too is the pattern of intra-family consumption. As stated above, it is a common practice for males, whether employed or not, to withhold part of the household income for their own exclusive consumption - e.g. for alcohol, tobacco, hobbies etc. No so common is the withholding by the mother of income for her own use; any such boxing off is normally restricted to munal benefit - e.g. holidays, savings, clothing for the children, furniture And, Millar and Glendinning (1987) found, even were communal benefit ls are purchased, it is usually 'his' car, and BAR 'her' washing machine, exposing the inequality of freedom which such purchases offer. And even within essential expenditure on commodities such as nutrition, domestic heating etc., women also tend to lose out during the distribution. Again the image of the male breadwinner (whether it is borne out by employment status or not) legitimises the privileged niche accorded to him and allows him to enjoy steak while the mother and children eat sausages, milk while the others receive tap water, the domestic heating system turned on or up while he is at home, while it is off or lowered while he is out. Indeed, the study by Charles & Kerr (1988) into the distribution of food within the family exposes the finding that the best quality meat, the largest portion, the biggest steak usually found its way on to the man's plate. When income is scarce, a relatively easy way out is for the manager of household resources - the woman - to withhold food, heating, clothing, niceties from herself so that firstly the male can be satisfied, then the children, and what is left is consumed by the mother.

An element of this phenomenon is that participating in many social activities outside the home among low income families appears to be, relatively, a male domain. Bradshaw & Holmes (1989, Chapter 6) carried out a comparative analysis of social activities engaged in by women and men. Against he background of low income severely restricting such participation, the findings showed that women were far less likely than men: to go out for a drink - 3 per cent compared to 18 per cent; participate in sport - 8 per cent compared to 18 per cent. Pahl (1989) found that 44 per cent of men in her survey compared to 28 per cent of women had personal spending money, while 86 per cent of men compared to 67 per cent of women spent money on leisure activities. These crucial indicators inherent in the control over household resources, have yet to be extensively incorporated into the main body of research into relative definitions and measurements of poverty.

Such reality presents serious challenger to the dominant ways in which poverty has been conceptualized and measured. It causes problems in identifying the unit (individual, family, extended family) for measuring poverty in the sense that for a woman to be included in the measurement of poverty, she must belong to a household whose income falls below whatever the poverty line may be. If this income is at a level above the poverty cut-off point, she is not quantified as being poor, regardless of whether she has equal access to that income. For example, a woman may live in a family whose income is above the poverty line, but where the male 'breadwinner' or claimant withholds a portion for his own personal use. Household poverty is created for other members of the family, particularly the woman, but is disguised and hidden from public and seemingly, much academic scrutiny. What has been suggested so far, and what the relevant research has upheld, is that a woman can live in a household whose income is, perhaps, substantial, above the poverty line, yet because of inequality in the distribution of resources **within** the household, she may, herself, live in a state of deprivation. As David Vincent (1991, p. 6) succinctly put it: 'This is why many women, previously married to or living with a man, even in relatively well paid employment, find that they are financially better off living on their own and claiming benefit in their own right.' Hilary Graham's research (1987, p. 59) indicated that 20 per cent of the females in her study who left a marriage in the 1960s, even where it resulted in a lifestyle on the poverty line, felt that they were economically and socially better off. Of those who separated or divorced in the 1980s, this had risen to 67 per cent. And Mary Daly (1989) also found an average awareness of feeling better off after breaking up with their male partners, even though their household income decreased. This it becomes clear how poverty within couple relationships can remain invisible and it is only when women become lone parents that their poverty is brought into public and official recognition. Lone parenthood can be characterised as a shift from poverty that women cannot control to one which they can.

Rowntree, although credited with the foundation of the absolute measurement of poverty, implicitly (and probably unintentionally) absorbed into his research the gendered, unequal distribution of resources within the household via his differentiation of 'primary' and 'secondary' poverty. His perception of secondary poverty illustrated a household income which was adequate but which was financially mismanaged through unwise expenditure on non-necessities. Such a model facilitates an acknowledgement of poverty caused partly by inequality in the control (as opposed to the management) of access to family resources. Rowntree exemplified this concept of secondary poverty by referring to spending on alcohol, tobacco, gambling etc. Seen in this way, secondary poverty could be perceived as reflecting the position of the woman within the family, where the adult male's superior share of household income leads to an unequal distribution of resources, and therefore poverty, within the household. But more specifically the 'consensual' method of poverty definition (mentioned in Chapter Two) assumes that a consensus exists on the notion of a poverty cut-off point. There must clearly be a broad range of diversity on perceptions of 'necessities' within the capitalist, patriarchal and racist society. Males and females will frequently differ in attributing priority to items of household needs, and thus in the constituents of poverty, particularly when cash is scarce. For example, men are more likely to suggest that some item of personal consumption, such as a night out, a football game, is a more significant indicator of deprivation than, say, an item required for family welfare, such as a cooked dinner or fresh fruit and vegetables. In this way, Millar and Glendinning (July 1989, pp. 368-381) argue: '... a consensus definition of poverty may well mask gender based differences of opinion and conflict of interest, unless these differences are made explicit and incorporated into the research design.'

A particularly sexist analysis of poverty causation within the intra family model argues that the sacrifices made by women resulting in them being at greater risk of poverty, are normal and valid in that they are a constituent of females' natural concern for the welfare of others, especially their own dependants (Land & Rose, 1985). Thus these sacrifices mean that poverty itself is unequally distributed within the family, with the adult female in the low income household making more sacrifices than other family members and subsequently at greater risk of poverty. Furthermore, as women are, in the vast majority of cases, financial managers of the household budget, when 'things go wrong' and deprivation emerges, women are blamed for 'causing' the poverty through their irrational spending. Poor families have been on the receiving end of advise for centuries on sensible dietaries which take account of their nutritional needs and their income constraints. Lentils, bread, cabbage, porridge, have all had their virtues extolled to poor households, without considering the restrictions that following them would impose upon the adult female. Firstly, the extra burden of preparing such foodstuffs would land on the shoulders of the mother. Piachaud (1987, pp. 147-164) argues that: 'Any definition of poverty implies some assumption about the time inputs into home production.' Discussing the 'cost' of cooking chips, he explains that a pound of potatoes costs a lot less money than a similar quantity of frozen chips, but in terms of temporal costs, they require a lot more investment of time and effort. This investment is expected, in the vast majority of cases, of the woman, as are other time and effort consuming domestic activities, such as seeking the most cost effective shopping, repairing clothing rather than purchasing new articles etc. It is women who '...maximise the benefits to be derived from available income through efficient consumption' (Miller & Glendinning, July 1989, p. 377). These burdens are all the more cumbersome and unjust when looked at against the background of, in 1989:

- 50 per cent of women were mainly responsible for shopping compared to 7 per cent of men (the rest shared);
- 77per cent of women were mainly responsible for cleaning, compared to 4 per cent of men;
- 88 per cent of women were mainly responsible for washing and ironing compared to 2 per cent of men;
- 67 per cent of women looked after children when sick, compared to 2 per cent of men. (Oppenheim 1990, p. 97)

These forms of 'home production' - time spent in attaining a certain lifestyle - are generally disregarded in poverty studies. Glendinning and Millar (1987) find that: 'The value of time - both in the generation of resources and their use - has hitherto been ignored in poverty studies. If time were included, it

126

would almost certainly point out substantial differences between men and women.' Thus poverty is about more than just WHAT level of income; it is as much about HOW income and other resources are obtained. It may require a woman to work 50 hours a week to earn an adequate amount of income to attain a certain standard of living, whereas it may require a man to work 40 hours a week for the same standard of living. Thus, the hours spent attempting to acquire an adequate living is a crucial factor in that woman's poverty. The man working 40 hours may earn a wage that many people would regard as non poor. The woman, earning the same wage, can be regarded as poor because she has to work 50 hours a week. Other examples include going on frequent visits to small shops because there is not sufficient cash to justify a weekly visit to a supermarket, preparing packed lunches as there is not enough money for hot dinners at school - these involve substantial investment of time and effort. Oppenheim (1990, p. 99) suggests that not having sufficient money, or a washing machine, or a car, all mean that it takes much more time and work for someone in poverty to achieve the same standard of living as someone who is comfortably off.

It is likely in many cases that the male 'breadwinner' would not succumb to sacrificing his 'just rewards' as easily as this approach assumes. If men are held responsible for 'causing' poverty through not providing for their dependants (bad providers), women are to blame for 'causing' poverty by unnecessary expenditure on 'luxury' foods - e.g. convenience foods (bad managers). The assumptions which underpin this rationale are reflected in the late 1980s reforms of the poor relief system and are referred to by Millar & Glendinning (1989, p. 372): 'The recent changes to social security both reflect and reinforce this difference - in families it is likely to be men who must satisfy the very restrictive "availability for work" test as a condition for receiving benefit and women who must explain their budgeting practices to Social Fund Officers.' Reinforcing this perception that much poverty is 'caused' by bad budgeting by women has been the 'caring profession' of social work, which has, historically, also contributed to the assumption that women are responsible for family management and welfare. Since the Poor Law era, social work has intervened in the lives of working class families who have been labelled as 'inadequate' rather than victims and the nature of this intervention has invariably been designed to bolster the domestic talents and caring skills of women. Indeed, the birth of modern day social work stems from the post-war objective, planned by Beveridge, of remoulding working class family life - i.e. white, middle class, nuclear, full time male breadwinner, full time female housekeeper. With the virtual extinction of publicly funded childcare facilities, those mothers who sought paid employment risked falling foul of statutory services like social work and being regarded as neglectful. Bechy Morley (1988, p. 227) explains: '"Maternal deprivation", "latchkey children" and the rise of juvenile delinquency became

127

linked to mothers' abandonment of the family and through paid work and divorce.' And the recent official drift towards 'community care' requires social workers to deploy informal caring networks - in other words, women's unpaid caring.

Historically, and more so in recent decades, Trade Unions, in expressing their underlying male domination, have campaigned for the 'family wage', a level of income paid to male workers which is sufficient to cover the need of himself, his wife and children. Many Trade Union activists perceive the 'family wage' as a means of securing a decent wages standard for workers. But, as this discussion has indicated, the 'family wage' would not necessarily ensure that the woman received a fair and sufficient slice of that income. 'The price for increasing working class income in this way was increasing control for men and increasing dependency for women.' (Alcock 1987, p. 34). The assumption that women are economically dependent upon men has underpinned the practice of retaining the income gap between the earnings of men and those of women. The argument that women's financial dependency on the male breadwinner insulates them from poverty through men sharing 'heir' income with women, may have some superficial, if sexist, validity to it, but not for definitions of poverty which emphasise non-monetary indicators of deprivation such as powerlessness and social exclusion. For Glendinning & Millar (1991a, p. 31): 'It is strange reasoning which argues that women are not in some way impoverished by dependency itself and by the relative powerlessness which accompanies this dependency.'

If the impression portrayed so far has suggested that women are more vulnerable to poverty than men in three separate spheres: the labour market; the state sponsored welfare systems; the family - this is erroneous and misleading. In order to comprehensively understand the feminisation of poverty thesis, requires analysis of interaction between all three worlds and their propensity to generate poverty. As more female labour has entered the labour market, there has been a greater increase in the numbers of married women with children seeking employment than any other category. The work they find is generally in the low paid, low status sectors of the service industries. For most married or co-habitating couples, both males and females work in paid job s. But the patriarchal nature of the sexual division of labour dictates that the jobs occupied by women are inferior to men's because: (a) the male is THE breadwinner of the family and provider of the main household income, while the money brought home by the mother only bolsters this; (b) the female's 'natural'duties lie in her home caring role and any position outside of this is merely subsidiary. Women take on mainly part time work as this is the type least inconvenient for fulfilling their domestic responsibilities and that most sought after by employers. And this is correspondent with the changes in the labour market which now offer more part time, low wage, low status jobs than at any other period this century. The relationship between the

128

labour market, the state and the family in generating the conditions most conducive to the feminisation of poverty are explained by Buswell (1987, p. 90):

Labour markets which recruit cheap full time youth labour and part time female labour are actually structured around the assumed dependency of these groups within a family context. It is assumed that both of these groups belong to households where the main expenses are borne by a high earner (the male, whether actual or otherwise). Changes in the labour market therefore, are not simply about employment but about the connection between employment, home, class and gender.'

Even though the income of many employed women is still perceived in abstract form as being subsidiary and not as important as that of the male 'breadwinner', because of the effects of the current economic recession, women's 'secondary' earnings have become crucial to many families who, without such income, would be unable to pay mortgage rates which increased massively in the 1980s, would not be able to afford the consumer durables which have become necessities in today's acquisitive society etc. Hilary Land calculated in 1983 that without the earnings of married women, four times as many families would be in poverty. Millar & Glendinning (July 1989, p 373) conclude: 'Thus we have the further paradox that women's earnings from paid work help to prevent family poverty (and homelessness), but no personal poverty.' Women impoverish themselves in order to prevent or lessen poverty for their family in three main ways:
- women 's domestic work, for which they are not paid, contributes to creating conditions which free the male partner to seek and obtain renumerative work, by helping him to avoid the time consuming responsibilities of the whole range of home chores. The male also benefits from not having to pay for an 'outsider' to perform the domestic and caring tasks;
- the, albeit generally low, wages that women workers contribute to the home's purse are, in many cases, the means by which families escape poverty or even worse poverty. As far back as 1980, official data suggested that poverty would quadruple without the earnings that women contribute to the household budget (CSO, 1980, cited in Glendinning & Millar 1987, p. 6)
- by sacrificing the satisfaction of their own nutritional clothing, personal needs (as discussed above), women act to protect their partners and children from poverty or worse deprivation.

The cumulative effects of poverty on women's health have been well documented. Rates of premature births, disabilities, low birth weights, congenital malformation, miscarriage, perinatal mortality etc. are all higher in births involving low income mothers. Problems with conception are also greater among low income women. Research suggests strongly that the effects of women's poverty on their dietaries during pregnancy and during childhood are significant, influential factors in future obstetric outcome. (Payne 1991, pp. 151/2). The experience of poverty imposes demands upon women's time and energy at a physical level, but also at a mental level. The sapping effect of guilt and worry over the management of scarce household income and prevention of substantial deprivation f or children and male partners generates high risks to the health of women: stress and anxiety; a poor diet; lack of recreational exercise; health damaging behaviour, such as smoking as a means of stress release and relaxation; housing and environmental hazards; the roll on health of both paid and unpaid labour; fewer opportunities for position experiences and pleasure. 'Poverty and its effects, particularly on their children, dominates the conversations of women struggling to survive on a low income.' (Payne 1991, p. 153). The story told by research of the impact of poverty on women's mental health involves increased levels of anxiety and depression generated by the constant struggle to make ends meet.

Thus, the study of women and poverty involves much more than simply adding the gender variable to data analysis and presentation. It necessarily involves investigating and discussing the access that women have to incomes and other resources, the time that they spend in acquiring income and resources and the distribution of resources within the household, which usually leaves the woman with the short straw. In other words, it involves studying the framework of gender inequalities which permeate the various life stages of women. As Townsend (1979) concluded: 'Many people, and overwhelmingly married women and children, are not in poverty by virtue of any **personal** characteristics so much as indirectly by virtue of the labour market, wage and social security characteristics of the principal income recipient of the family unit.' Some ideological assumptions about women's 'natural' roles and responsibilities are operationalized to mould their employment opportunities - what jobs, what wages - which, in turn, militate against their potential for fulfilment. These ideological structures assuming the budgeting and household financial management roles of women also function to hide the level and nature of women's poverty by generating ideas about their financial dependence upon men. Sacrifices made to facilitate the maintenance of family standards of living usually fall on the shoulders of the mother. Where this is not possible - e.g. children wanting toys, pocket money, clothes which cannot be afforded - it is normally the mother's stressful and unpleasant role to be the bear of the bad news. All of these stresses, on top of, perhaps, a dietary lacking in sufficient nutrients, constitute a greater risk of illness.

Presently, there are over one million lone parent families in Britain, and rising, ninety per cent of whom are headed by a mother. Lone mothers are defined simply as those who have no adult (usually male) partner and who have been separated, divorced, deserted or widowed, whilst single mothers,

130

included in the category of lone mothers, are usually those who have never been married.   Contrary to the popular image that lone mothers are contravening social conventions, data shows the incidence and composition of one parent families and demonstrates that the vast majority of lone mothers are divorced, separated or widowed, with single mothers representing a small proportion. In 1971, 15.8% of all one-parent families were 'single mothers', and this had risen to 22.8% by 1986. The figures for separated mothers were, respectively, 29.8% to 18.8%; divorced mothers, 21.1% to 40.6%; widowed mothers, 21.1% to 7.9%; all mothers, 87.8% to 90.1%; all fathers, 12.2% to 9.9%. (George V. & Howard I. 1990, p. 40)

Thus over fifteen years, the numbers of single parent families have doubled in Britain, (from 570,000 to 1,010,000 or 8% of all families to 14%) in tandem with most Western countries, generating a radical increase in the social security bill.   Between 1981/2 and 1988/9, inflation proofed spending on income related benefits for lone parents increased from £1.4 billion to £3.2 billion. (Millar 1992, p. 156).   Most research puts the proportion of lone-mother families who live in poverty at about one third.

This section so far as argues that poverty among women living in a male headed household is hidden because of the assumption that the male 'breadwinner'/claimant will provide for the female.   Single mothers in poverty are thus much more visible. These categories of families are, in the views of the Right, the 'less deserving' poor. This and other questions are discussed in much more detail in Chapter 5 on 'The "underclass"' and explain that the perceived disincentive effects of welfare dependency are understood to contribute towards the generation of an 'underclass'; one parent families figure high in this thesis. Central to this argument is the concern that welfare payments and housing provision are in some ways encouraging women to leave the 'normal' family home, to break up the family.   There is also a parallel fear that absent fathers are easily avoiding their family obligations and leaving the state to pay for their dependants. Thus recent legislation has been passed to compel many lone mothers to disclose information about the father(s) of their children, under pain of withdrawal or reduction of benefit. However, the Child Support Act 1991 is largely regarded as leading to: (1) a very small increase in the abysmally low level of maintenance paid to lone mothers and; (2) increased moral pressure, stigma, degradation, fear of retribution and trauma for mothers who wish to banish their relationships with the fathers of their children into the realms of unpleasant memories. And, of course, many absent fathers may have incomes below the levels which compel them to pay maintenance. But the most important factor which shows that lone mothers will not generally benefit from the legislation is the fact that any income received from maintenance payments is automatically deducted from Income Support entitlement. For those lone parents on this benefit (75 per cent), there is no financial gain whatsoever. The rationale for this policy is obviously to avoid generating a work disincentive - i.e. Income Support plus maintenance payments would bring many lone mothers above the level of wages that they might expect to earn in the labour market.

The increase in the spread of one parent families can be largely attributed to long term alterations in economic arrangements which have led to greater economic independence for women, and to liberalised legislation from the 'permissive moment' of the late 1960s which allowed for easier divorce. The incomes of these families are sourced as follows (1990):

assistance benefits ....45 per cent

employment earnings .... 22 per cent

maintenance payments .... 10 per cent

pensions, investments, etc. .... 23 per cent

(George & Howards 1990, p. 41)

Also, Bradshaw & Miller (1991) found that the major source of welfare benefits for unemployed lone mothers was Income Support, with 85 per cent being in receipt of this benefit at some stage and 72 per cent dependent upon it in 1991. Half of these had been dependent upon t for over two and a half years. Throughout the 1980s, there was a greater concentration of lone mothers in the lowest quintile of the income distribution. In 1979, 29 per cent of single parents had net income levels which were less than half the average income By 1988, this had levels which were less than half the average income. By 1988, this had risen to 59 per cent, representing 1.6 million adults and children. In 1979, the average disposable income of lone parent households was £70.46 compared with £123.30 for couples with two children, representing an equivalent income of 57 per cent. By 1989, the comparable figures were £1344.61 and £339.71 - i.e. 40 per cent. (Millar 1992, p. 15)). There are two main reasons why this deterioration in the poverty of lone mothers has taken place throughout the 1980s and into the 1990s:

1   their reliance upon welfare benefits, particularly Income Support. In 1979, 45 per cent of all lone mothers were dependent upon SB. By 1989, 70 per cent were in receipt of Income Support;

2   their increasing inability to obtain paid jobs, particularly full time posts. In 1977/9, 22 per cent of lone mothers had full time jobs and 24 per cent part time. by 1986/8, the full time figure had fallen to 17 per cent and the part time figure to 22 per cent. (There has been an increase in the numbers of married women in paid employment in the same period, but both categories continue to be over represented in the low paid sectors.) (Millar 1992, p. 151)

Of course, greater access to adequately paid employment would contribute

132

significantly towards improving the standards of living of many lone parents, as well as offering increased opportunities for extra family contact and social interaction. In Bradshaw & Millar's (1991) study, they found that two out of every three lone mothers on Income Support expressed a rejection of paid work immediately, preferring to concentrate for the time being on their children. The issues which emerged included: caring for very young children; ensuring that the break up of the family did not traumatize the children too much; trying to be both father and mother to the children; and most importantly being hampered by the absence of proper and affordable child care facilities. The general standards of living of one parent families compare unfavourably with the two parent family: they run a higher risk of poverty; they are less likely to own their own house; they are more likely to live in inferior accommodation; they are more likely to be homeless; the children are more likely to suffer ill health, to be taken into statutory care, to experience educational problems etc. Lone mothers may feel that they are capable of holding down a paid job while they continue to care for and nurture their children and maintain their homes. But the benefit system is such that, frequently, they discover that there is little financial advantage in earnings from employment. Because of the aforementioned sexual division of labour, many lone mothers will be offered low paid work only, and from this, they will almost certainly have to pay for the expenses of child minding and of getting to and from work. After this, it is likely that many will find that they are caught in the poverty trap and are better off, or no worse off, drawing benefit. From the academics who have contributed most to the feminization of the study of poverty in the 1980s and 1990s:

In a decade in which women, more than most, are experiencing increasing poverty in all areas of their lives, it is vitally important that the traditional invisibility of that poverty is urgently challenged. The key starting point is no longer to ignore the sexual division of labour. Instead, we must make it explicit, analyze its consequences for women's and men's differential access to resources, and hence their differential inequality and poverty.' (Glendinning & Millar 1989, p. 10)

Race and poverty

(The term black is used to identify people of Afro-Caribbean and Asian origins, whilst the term ethnic minorities is employed to describe those who are not black, but who are a numerical minority and relatively powerless vis-a-vis the majority ethnic group - such as the Irish, Chinese and Arab communities.)

Whilst the feminization of poverty thesis has attracted much recent academic and official attention, much less acknowledged, researched and documented has been the correlationship between 'race' and racism, and poverty and inequality. If the debate has acknowledged that poverty has become more feminized, this has not been met with anywhere near the same level of acknowledgement that poverty has become more racialised. For example, the main government publications of data on low income households - Households Below Average Income and its predecessor, Low Income Families: the Family Expenditure Survey - hold no informative and much needed breakdown of statistics by ethnic origin. And in writing their chapter on 'Race and Poverty' (in Becher & MacPherson 1988), Vaux and Divine opened with the statement: 'The most notable point when researching this chapter is the paucity of information that is available.' Whether this 'colour blind' approach has been due to the views and activities of official bodies, the poverty lobby or academics in unclear.

Racism at both the personal and institutional levels appears to have the effect of decreasing life chances - e.g., discrimination and harassment in employment, inequalities in the labour market - for Black people and other ethnic minorities, consequently increasing their propensity towards poverty. What research does exist (and the amount is, thankfully increasing in the 1990s) shows unequivocally that black and ethnic minority groups demonstrate a greater than average likelihood of experiencing poverty. On all fronts, they are much more vulnerable to poor social security rights, high unemployment, low pay and unacceptable working conditions. These features themselves have been the product of immigration policies which deny immigrants access to welfare provision, employment practices which stream ethnic minorities into low paid, low status jobs, institutionalised racist discrimination within the social security system and societal racism. Amin and Leech (1988) forcefully argue that:

> Blackness and poverty are more correlated than they were some years ago. In spite of government concern with racial disadvantage, and the undoubted limited success of positive action and equal opportunities in helping to create a black middle class, the condition of the black poor is deteriorating.

Between 1987 and 1989, Black and other ethnic minorities had a male unemployment rate of 14 per cent, compared to 9 per cent among whites. The corresponding figures for females was 13 per cent compared to 8 per cent. For young people (aged 16 to 24), the differences are even more marked: 25 per cent of Caribbean, 16 per cent of Indian, 27 per cent of Pakistani or Bangladeshi, compared to 12 per cent of whites. Among those with 'higher qualifications', the rate was 7 per cent of black and ethnic minorities and 4 per cent of whites. For those with 'other qualifications', the rates were 17 per cent compared to 9 per cent.

At the beginning of the 1990s, the proportion of black people unemployed is, approximately, twice that of white people. Consequently, there are higher proportions of black groups claiming unemployment benefit: 17 per cent of Caribbean, 16 per cent of Asians and 7 per cent of whites in the same period (Oppenheim, 1990). But the social security claiming scene is one which can be alarmingly hostile to many black and ethnic minority groups and therefore, even though greater proportions of these communities are forced to rely upon benefits than are whites, these figures **underestimate** the accurate scenario of poverty. Many non-English speaking people report major difficulties in claiming their social security entitlement, leading to greater under claiming of benefits among ethnic minorities than whites. Gordon and Newnham (1985) argue that access to social security benefits can be dependent upon the racist values and assumptions of staff in DSS offices and that ethnic minorities particularly suffer from the complexity of the benefit regulations, again leading to under claiming and greater poverty. Clare Blackburn (1991, p. 19) suggests that many Asian claimants' benefit levels are reduced because of erroneous assumptions about the organisation of family and community support networks, about dietary practices and clothing requirements, about health standards. For example, prior to May 1987, the DHSS refused to acknowledge that sickle cell anaemia (which almost exclusively affects black races) was a 'serious illness'. This significantly affected many black claimants who had applied for additional cash to help with the extra heating costs of treating an illness which is exacerbated largely by coldness. Such a decision was not the product of merely ignorance on behalf of the DHSS, as medical science has been aware of the sources and causes of this illness for a long time. And Vaux and Divine (1988, p. 212) state:

> It is not an easy process to claim full entitlement and negotiate the complicated DHSS system... limited literacy and limited use of English language serves to aggravate the process even more and results in a considerably lower take-up compared to other groups of claimants. For example, in contact with the Bengali community, it was apparent that people were not claiming child benefit in contrast to English speaking claimants were take-up of this benefit is high.

The high level of under claiming of benefits among black and other ethnic minority groups can be partly explained in ideological terms also. Like any other community in the Western world, there exists among black groups, a belief that welfare provision weakens the resolve, the spirit of self help and the imagination of black people. Dependency on 'hand outs' from the 'white state' can be thereby regarded as inert internalisation of inferior status and of reliance upon a racist establishment. This perception is particularly widespread among young blacks, marginalised by society, rejected by the labour market, but who still refuse to approach state agencies with their hands outstretched. Vaux and Divine (1988, p. 212) explain that this process means that: 'such people cease to exist ... (and) the whole debate on race and poverty is therefore skewed because the views of key people are effectively discounted.'

But the problems of ideology lie beyond the realms of belief among the ethnic minorities; indeed the problem is largely one created by and for the white community. Generally, in our racist society, there exists a widespread fantasy of the black or the Irish dole hopper, the welfare scrounger who, along with a large family of children and in-laws, sponges off the British economy. This colonial imagery is, of course, fed and encouraged by many sources of public media and by societal institutions. But one of the most worrying features is the extent to which such racial prejudice prevails among social security staff, which, if at all visible to or perceived by ethnic minority claimants, will undoubtedly act as a deterrent to applying for benefits and further deepen existing poverty levels. Explained by David Vincent (1991, p. 181) in his comments on a 1985 report on the behaviour of DHSS staff:

> Working in a bureaucratic culture which distrusted the motives and morality of able-bodied claimants, they (the DHSS) were more concerned to ensure that public money was not wasted than that the private citizens were not denied their full entitlement. Claimants were categorised as deserving or undeserving on the basis of appearance or demeanour and the offices were no more immune to racial prejudice than the population from which they were drawn.

Documented evidence of the historic discrimination and intimidation within the social security system against black people can be found in the guidelines provided to DHSS officials investigating claims for benefits, such as asking '...a claimant who **appears to have come from abroad** for the circumstances of his entry and any immigration conditions imposed. Examine his passport...' The enforcement of the 1980 Nationality Act deepened the collaboration between the social welfare agencies and immigration control, scared ethnic minorities away from applying for support from these bodies and multiplied the risk of poverty. For many black people, social security and social work services are seen as an executive arm of the immigration control. According to a study of DHSS practices when dealing with claimants, the findings of which are kept from the public for over a year because of opposition from the social security agency, and released after stringent vetoing of any reference to racial prejudice (Cooper, 1985): 'Racist remarks were common from manager to doorman.'

Oppenheim (1990, pp. 89-90) has pointed to a number of ways in which the social security system disadvantages black families and adds to their propensity to find themselves living in poverty:

1   contributory benefits are payable to people who earn enough to pay national insurance contributions. But because of the concentration of black people in low paid jobs and unemployment, a greater proportion than white workers find themselves earning below the national insurance threshold or not earning at all; thus they pay no contributions and receive no benefits. And as large numbers only began to make contributions relatively late in their lives, they have not paid the required level of contributions to entitle them to the full retirement pension, and so face reliance on the poverty line Income Support benefits;

2   means tested benefits have become more and more discretionary, with fewer, if any, rights of appeal, thereby opening up greater opportunities for racist discrimination. Concern over being seen as a trouble maker, worry that any problems might affect residence, little information in native language etc., have added to an atmosphere of deterrence for many ethnic minorities seeking assistance from the social security system. The extension of the means test fuels the difficulties for black people who are confronted by the twin obstacles of protecting their immigration status and obtaining their benefit entitlement. As Oppenheim (p. 90) concludes: 'The further social security intrudes into the minutiae of individual circumstances, the more room there is for racism. Some black people, excluded from help under the new system, find themselves placed firmly in the category of the "undeserving poor"'

3   The following information indicates the disadvantage placed upon black and other ethnic minority claimants through legislation which governs the conditions of residence for entitlement to non-contributory social security benefits:

Child benefit	- present in UK for 6 months
Severe disablement allowance	- residence in the UK for 10 out of the previous 20 years
Invalid care & attendance allowance	- residence in the UK for 26 weeks in the previous 52 weeks
Mobility allowance	- residence in the UK for 52 weeks in the previous 18 months
Non-contributory widows benefit and category C retirement pension	- resident for 10 years in the period July 5th 1948 to November 1st 1970 or date of claim
Category D retirement pension	- resident in the UK for 10 years in previous 20 years.

(Skellington & Gordon, 1992, p. 75)

137

The residence question was briefly referred to in the Fowler reforms of the social security system in 1985 and served merely to deepen the hostile suspicions towards black people:

> We are concerned that the present conditions can allow too ready access to help by those who have no recent links with this country. Claimants will therefore need to satisfy a presence test; that is, the claimant will need to have been in the country for a set period to qualify for Income Support. (HMSO, June 1985, para. 2.87).

But the research which does exist certainly points to a lack of basic knowledge about benefits and a widespread perception that they are not entitled to such benefits among black and other ethnic minorities as the most crucial explanations for non-claiming of benefits. Vaux and Divine (1988, p. 214) cited the following experience:

> They (the Bengali community) were confused by the available information and wary of approaching local authority DHSS services for advice. Fears were expressed of the consequences of claiming anything that might bring attention to them and cause trouble... there was fear that their right to stay might be affected by claiming.

In addition, government policies which have resulted in cuts in the levels of Child Benefit (in real terms) and entitlement to Income Support for young people have particularly increased the levels of poverty among ethnic minorities, as the age profile of every major black community in Britain is younger than the white race. This factor is compounded by data which show that, in the mid-1980s, young black people had an inferior chance of obtaining a post after a YTS placement and were less likely to obtain a place on employer led YTS programmes, which apparently create a better opportunity for gaining employment. Another demographic feature pertaining to the extent of poverty among ethnic minorities is the higher level of single parent families among, particularly, Caribbeans. In 1988, 43.4 per cent of Caribbean families were single parent, compared to 11.8 per cent of white families (Oppenheim, 1990, p. 86). As the section on women and poverty demonstrated, generally, the risks of poverty are much greater for single parent families, given the low level of earnings for women and the paucity of affordable childcare amenities. Poverty studies have also shown that extended families are more at risk of deprivation. Brown (1984, p. 45) found that 22 per cent of Asians and 17 per cent of West Indians, compared with 6 per cent of whites, lived in households with more than three adults. Among other forms of disadvantage, this meant, for example, that with the imposition of the Poll Tax, 75 per cent of households with three or more adults were estimated by the Department of Employment to lose out, compared to only 25 per cent who gained

138

(Skellington & Morris, 1992, p. 75). Thus, the relatively large proportion of: (1) West Indian households headed by women and (2) Asian households with three or more adults, renders black families much more at risk from poverty.

Even for those black and ethnic minority people who are in employment, racist inequality manifests in greater levels of poverty. Evidence shows clearly that black employees find themselves concentrated in low paid jobs, this being a legacy of the availability of jobs during the labour shortages of the 1950s and 1960s, when black labour, particularly from the West Indies, Pakistan and India, was 'attracted' into the labour market to take up those low paid, low status, part time jobs which white labour was becoming less inclined to do, mostly in the public transport, textile and iron industries and hospital services. This clustering of black and other ethnic minority labour into the lower end of the industrial sector, in terms of conditions, pay and job security, was compromised and facilitated by widespread racial prejudice and has left ethnic minorities especially vulnerable to the recession, the decimation of manufacturing industry, ensuing unemployment and poverty. As Novak (1988, p. 147) points out: 'The employment of black workers ... provided capital with a level to offset the potentially disruptive effect of full employment on wage levels and factory discipline.' Confronted by racism in the labour and housing markets, black communities have become clustered and ghettoised around the industrial kernel of the large cities of England but, as a result of the flight of capital and employment from such areas, a trail of unemployment and deprivation has been the consequence for many black workers. Little wonder that Brown (1984, p. 232) concludes: 'Britain's well-established black population is still occupying the precarious and unattractive position of the earlier immigrants.' Isolated in where they live and in where they work or once worked, neglected by the labour movement, subjected to state and street abuse and violence, ethnic minority communities have become more introverted, hostile, isolated - and, naturally, rebellious.

In traditionally low wage sectors such as distribution, hotels and catering (over half of whose employees earned less than £130 a week), the New Earnings Survey for 1988 showed that 53 per cent of ethnic minority males were employed here, compared to 36 per cent of white males. In general, in industries where 30 per cent or more of the employees earned less than £130 a week, 55 per cent of ethnic minority males were employed here, compared to 33 per cent of white males (Oppenheim, 1990, p. 81). At the beginning of the 1990s, generally speaking, black employees earned up to 20 per cent less than white employees (Becker, 1992, p. 80). For women, Asians earn less than whites, who earn less than Caribbeans. Explaining this in positive rather than negative terms, Oppenheim (1990) states that Caribbean female employees are more likely than white women to be in full time jobs, involved in more shirt work, and members of large public sector unions whose relative strength has ensured higher wages. Additionally, female employees in general

139

are clustered in the low wage strata of the labour market, where there is less scope for disparities based on ethnicity. This abundance of low wages among black and other ethnic minorities has been reflected against the receipt of welfare benefits. In the 1980s, only one per cent of white households claimed Family Income Supplement (the predecessor of Family Credit), while, two per cent of Asians and five per cent of Caribbean households claimed the same benefit (Oppenheim 1990, p. 83). Future employment conditions and opportunities for escaping poverty for ethnic minorities seem no less pessimistic, given the imminent abolition of wage councils and the privatisation of public services. Both of these developments will generate the scope of employers to cut their wage bills, particularly in sectors of employment in which ethnic minority workers have been clustered - e.g., hospitals, public and private transport, catering etc.

Racist immigration policy has also contributed to the higher degree of vulnerability to poverty among black and other ethnic groups. Immigration policies and practices have historically focused on 'problem' groups - blacks, Jews, Irish - whose numbers have had to be controlled. For example, the 1988 Immigration Act stated that the immediate families of Commonwealth immigrants were entitled to come to Britain only if they could prove that they would be materially and financially supported and housed without having to claim from 'public funds' - i.e., social security and council housing. With the state thus freed from providing cash and accommodation for immigrant families, the ensuing poverty has been inevitable for many families and has, in a large number of cases, compelled families to live apart, as the Afro-Caribbean or Asian male, working in low paid employment in Britain, cannot afford to bring his family to him without assistance and support from the state, leaving his wife and children living in their homeland. After having worked and paid taxes for, perhaps, many years, a great number of people from different races are not permitted to be joined by their families. And, of course, the ideological environment generated by such policies creates a public perception of the black person as an uninvited, unwelcome foreigner in UK society, a body of opinion that leads to racial tension, conflict, prejudice and violence. Gordon and Newnham (1985, p. 43) conclude:

> Black people are not only subjected to the injustices and indignities of the entry clearance system, but also, when these have been overcome, face discriminatory treatment by the welfare system. They are not just treated as second-class citizens - as are most claimants - but they are second-class citizens even among claimants ... the sponsorship provisions ... create a class of people who may be in the UK quite lawfully - but who are entitled to welfare on the same basis as other citizens only if they are prepared to risk legal action against relatives who have sponsored them.

140

This point leads us to a crucial debate in social welfare policy since the late 1980s which has centred on the citizenship issue, invigorated by the resurrection of the works of the founders of social administration - in this case, T.H. Marshall. Yet this debate has largely been characterised by the relative absence of discussion of the effects on citizenship rights of ethnic minorities as a result of their over exposure to poverty and subsequent exclusion from political and civic structures. If poverty equates with exclusion from meaningful participation as citizens, then, as more and more people from ethnic minorities become 'poor', then fewer and fewer can enjoy their citizenship rights. A practical manifestation of this lies in the fact that people on Income Support or other low incomes cannot obtain any assistance from the DSS to pay for the substantial citizenship registration and naturalisation fees (currently over £200). It is thus beyond the reach of the vast majority of poor black families and individuals to afford even their basic citizenship rights. As Salman Rushdie (1982) concluded: 'Britain is now two entirely different worlds, and the one you inherit is determined by the colour of your skin.'

The very status of ethnic 'minorities' carries an implication of discrimination and disadvantage which acts to separate and distance the groups from the mass of indigenous citizens. The consequence of this can be that the poverty suffered by blacks and others is assumed to be a normal feature of 'our' social organisation, in a similar way to the famine and devastation of 'Third World' African nations being taken for granted as their 'normal' fate. The present social arrangements which generate poverty among ethnic minorities are thus not up for challenge. This set of perceptions bears substantial consequences for both communities. The majority, wishing to maintain the current social order, consciously or otherwise, cuts off the escape routes from poverty for the minorities (social closure), who, in turn, react with either: (1) acquiescence, by rejecting the incentives to climb up the social ladder out of poverty or; (2) more frequently, rebellion and rejection, this time of the very fabric and values of the society which has condemned them to a life of poverty, inequality and oppression. Defeatism perpetuates the existing order, whereas rebellion creates further distance from the rest of society; both avenues lead to the continuation of poverty.

It was ridiculous to expect in excess of one million immigrants from the crumbling British Empire to arrive in this country and to assimilate themselves into 'our' culture and social and economic arrangements without major micro and macro difficulties. A government White Paper (Department of Environment 1977) 'Policy for the Inner Cities' acknowledged this very point when, on the one hand, it accepted that the decline in the urban ghettos was due to poverty and consequently, the policy response would need to involve capital investment and job creation, whilst on the other hand, it concluded that a substantial number of inner city dwellers were not suitable for the industries to be introduced and consequently, such people should move out of these areas

141

into the peripheral estates (the dispersal and unacceptable minority communities). John Rex (1988, p. 35) summarises the issue by saying: 'It would seem that ... it is the presence of (ethnic) minority people which constitutes the problem rather than the notion that they themselves have problems.' Even policies based on the concept of 'positive discrimination' for racial minority groups living in poverty can function to perpetuate the problem in three ways: (1) black and other racial poor are absorbed into and treated the same as a single group of poor people; (2) the perception is created that ethnic groups are being allocated more than their fair share, generating the risk of a racist backlash; (3) 'beneficiaries' of anti-poverty grants would become agents of the state and forfeit their potential for political effectiveness in confronting the socio-economic forces operating within government agencies which cause poverty, including institutionalised racism.

As with the 'underclass' (see Chapter Five) the lessons to be learned from the black and other ethnic minorities' experiences of poverty expose an intensity of feelings of anger and foreboding and are long overdue. In his evidence to the Liverpool 8 Inquiry into Race Relations, chaired by Lord Gifford in 1988/89, Eric Lynch, a council employee issued the following warning:

> The time is coming when we, Liverpool-born blacks, can no longer tolerate the situation which we are forced to live in. The time is coming, in fact the time is very close, when more and more of us realise, and through the realisation act collectively to take that which is rightfully ours into our own hands... We demand the right to work, we demand the right of promotion in jobs. We demand an equal opportunity and equality alongside the working class white people of Britain... No longer are we prepared to be the underling, the plaything. No longer are we prepared to be used, to be picked up and dropped. We have seen our own people throughout the world used and we have seen that they have reached the point in their lives when they said, enough was enough. They said it is better that we die, men, women and children, as human beings. It is better that we preserve our dignity and that we will take no more. (cited in Gifford, 1989, p. 49)

5 The 'underclass'

The notion that there has been a layer at the very base of the societal structure which has been characterised and commented upon in isolation from the mainstream social system and even from the working class and which has been systematically marginalised by social structural processes, is not a 1960s-onwards idea. It is an issue that certainly dates back at least 500 years. With almost boring repetitiveness, vehement efforts have been exercised to impose a cleavage among the poor: those who are poor due to socio-economic and demographic factors outside of their control and; those who are poor because of their own inadequate, deviant behaviour. It has been a common theme that this latter group of recalcitrant and wayward, pathological individuals and families constitutes a destabilising force. Such a model has been especially embraced by the Right-wing orthodoxy, as it comfortably accommodates their fundamental assumptions about the virtues of individual responsibility and minimalist state welfare intervention. And many on the Left also hold the concept of the 'underclass' as being synonymous with Right-wing social policy commentaries in the United States.

Chapter Three on The History of Poor Relief explained that in Britain, individual behaviour has historically been regarded as the primary causal factor of poverty and unemployment: the repression of vagrancy under the Elizabethan Poor Law; the Victorians distinguishing between poverty and 'pauperism' which described a condition of long term dependency on welfare relief; the residuum of the 1890s; the social defectives of the 1920s who would have been treated by the eugenics movement at the time by the sterilisation of 'defectives' displaying 'degenerate tendencies'; the genuinely-seeking-work test of the 1930s; the problem family of the 1950s; the cycle of deprivation of the 1970s; the voluntary unemployment rules, YTS and Restart programmes of the 1980s; and the proposed (by both Labour and Conservative parties) workfare schemes of the 1990s. All of these, in tandem with the search for the 'underclass', were characterised by a uniform objective: to identify an endogenous basis for explaining poverty, be it biological, pathological, mortal, social - anything but structural or institutional. Even Marx (1976, p. 797) spoke of '...lowest sediment of the relative surplus population (which) dwells in the sphere of pauperism. Apart from vagabonds, criminals, prostitutes, in short, the actual lumpen proletariat...' In the same way that 'homeless' people have been labelled 'roofless' or 'rough sleepers', the poorest sections of the population have become the 'underclass' in a yet further addition to the library of terms involved in the poverty debate. Yet Spicker (1993) has made the very pertinent observation that the problematic area lies not in the appropriateness of different terminologies: rather the discussion ought to concentrate upon those stigmatised people who constitute the 'underclass', the 'abyss', the 'submerged tenth', the 'hard to reach' etc. Commenting that semantic debate has inevitably led to the term becoming a term of abuse, Spicker argues that:

> There is nothing in the term 'underclass' which is inherently insulting, and the term is usefully descriptive: it refers to a group of people at the bottom of the class structure. The central problem is not what they are called; it is that they are at the bottom.

Back in 1978, Stuart Hall et al spoke of the colony culture in many inner city districts, with institutionalised racial prejudice interacting with class inequalities to create 'race-specific forms of subordination'. MacNicol (1988, pp. 293/318) proposed that, historically, the idea of an 'underclass' has been characterised by five features:

1 a false 'administrative definition relating to contracts with particular institutions of the state and welfare agencies, social workers, the police etc.' (Many studies, for example, Becker and MacPherson 1988, prove that there is nothing deducible from the obvious fact that the poor are more likely to come into contact with welfare workers, simply because they are poor);

2 transmission of values from one generation to the next, either hereditary or through the socialization process;

3 whilst acknowledging that some behaviour patterns are unacceptable, many others are overlooked. (The street corner drug and alcohol abusers of the ghettos are more visible and attract more attention than the same trends in higher class societies. Similarly, male adults deserting their families and female adults choosing to remain unmarried are not idiosyncratic to the poor.);

4   emphasis on the distribution and provision of resources and the implications on this of the relatively high demand for services by identifiable categories of clients;

5   'it tends to be supported by those who wish to constrain the redistributive potential of state welfare and thus it has always been part of a broader conservative view of the aetiology of social problems and their correct solutions.' (p.316).

It is somewhat unsurprising that the 'rediscovery of poverty' in Britain in the 1960s would be followed relatively shortly by a 'rediscovery of pauperism'. In the US in the mid 1960s, commentators on urban deprivation turned their attention to an old (not new) question: the existence of a substantial 'subpopulation', made up of unemployed or low paid households and whose behavioural traits were in direct conflict with those of the population as a whole. Although it was clear that significant levels of poverty abounded in many pockets of deprivation and decay throughout the first half of the 20th century, a number of trends attributed to this subpopulation - teenage pregnancies, unemployment, illegitimate births, violence and crime, reliance on state benefits - were not evidenced as crises until the mid 1970s. The sociological view of inner city communities, up until this period, had been one which identified features of social organisation - sense of community, positive identification with the neighbourhood, internal sanctioning against deviant behaviour - similar to those of the other societal systems. But from the 'discovery' of this subpopulation in the 1960s and 1970s, various symptoms of ghetto life were researched and 'proven' - illegitimate births (the rise in 'the casual creation of human life'), crime ('the rise in anti-social conduct'), drug abuse, heavy drinking, low educational achievements, high incidence of illness and premature death, low aspirations, family tension and conflict, divorce and separation ('the abandonment of children before they have been fully raised') etc. (quotes in brackets by David Green 1992, pp. 68-87).
   The typology of poverty which had existed from the early 19th century - i.e., the 'deserving' and the 'undeserving' poor - is, for many, inappropriate to contemporary analysis of current scenarios. Kosa and Zola (1975, pp. 29-31) are willing to replace this scission with a new one of the 'underclass' and the 'respectable' poor. The latter live in a state of 'acute' poverty and are exemplified by older people, who are encountering deprivation after living most of their lives above the poverty line. They have lost or have had reduced their 'acquisitive abilities' but retain some modest elements of privilege. 'The memory of former days is much alive and stimulates an active desire and effort to restore former state.' They are mainly unfettered by the nasty characteristics which the middle class find so repugnant and, similar to those higher up the social hierarchy, they resent being classified as

145

poor and lumped together with the 'underclass'.

The other layer live in long term 'acute' poverty, probably multi-generational. Their 'acquisitive abilities' have always been significantly narrow and deprivation in all its forms is perceived as the normal lifestyle, out of which there is little realistic chance of escaping. There is consequently no actual experience of the norms and values and behavioural expectations of living outside the world of poverty. The 'underclass' is 'self-perpetuating and preserves all the negative traits of pauperism. Its characteristic response to the existing state of affairs is either acquiescence or periodic and essentially futile rebellion.' (See the section in Chapter Four on Race and Poverty). The core essence of the 'underclass' problem is believed to lie in 'perverse incentives rooted in misguided paternalism' (MacGregor 1990, p. 85). These 'perverse incentives', in Britain, have been taken to mean unemployment benefit, income support and housing eligibility as it applies, mainly, to lone mothers. The then Social Security Secretary, John Moore, in January 1989, referring to a young woman in his constituency who received special benefits and a local authority flat by becoming pregnant, argued that the Government needed to be 'wary of providing incentives to obtain a particular benefit which can erode a sense of personal responsibility and adversely affect behaviour'. The debate centred on reducing the quality and nature of accommodation for lone mothers and their children to basic institutional care (shades of the poorhouse), 'to discourage others' (cited in MacGregor 1990). Spicker (1993) refers to this approach in terms of the response to incentives and challenges the validity of this explanation in a debate with the views of Charles Murray. (This general debate will be dealt with in greater detail later in this chapter).

In addressing the question, 'How Many Classes are there in Contemporary British Society' (August 1990, p. 388) W.G. Runciman defines the 'underclass' as those individuals and households who subsist, more or less permanently at a level where the state provides them with economic assistance because they are incapable of participating in the labour market. He proposes that there are identifiable features of the members of the 'underclass': their attitudes and behaviour exclude them from the labour market; these attitudes and behaviour are reinforced by receipt of welfare benefits; their example may influence others, especially their own children; their existence alienates 'respectable' workers and consequently puts in danger, state support for those deserving cases in genuine need. This individualistic explanation is confronted by Spicker (1993) by arguing that, of course, the poor act differently from the non-poor: 'that is part of what poverty is. People who are poor don't do the things that other people do, because they can't afford them.' The importance of this point emerges when poor people are held responsible for the conditions in which they live - e.g., the slum dwellers are compelled to accommodate inadequate living standards and observations of these conditions are often used

146

to object to any attempts to use public funds to improve the quality of housing provision for these areas. In refreshingly clear terminology characteristic of Spicker, he gives another example which challenges the pathological explanation:

> Likewise, people who are poor might be accused of lack of thrift. It's true; many poor people don't save anything. This is generally because they don't have any money to save. The odd thing about this statement is that people believe it somehow reflects on the morality of people who are poor.

In the US, the 'underclass' became synonymous with poor Blacks living in inner city ghettos, exposing the level of institutionalised racism in America through the proneness towards 'racially-based scapegoating' (Fainstein 1986, pp 403-451). An awesome combination of fear and ignorance among the white majority leads to the term 'underclass' being employed as 'a racial codeword that subtly hides anti-black and anti-Hispanic feelings - a convenient codeword that gives a veneer of liberal racial tolerance (by not explicitly referring to race) but which may serve to promulgate racism and conceal the issue of racial discrimination' (Gans 1990, pp. 271-277). Kenneth B. Clark (1965, p. 27) introduced the race element in his study of Black ghettos: 'But because Negroes begin with a primary affliction of inferior racial status, the burdens of despair and hatred are more pervasive.' The uniqueness and centrality of studies like Clarks was their endeavour to debate the process in which the social and economic conditions which many poor Black people live under generate ways in which they adapt to such circumstances, build up norms of behaviour and this leads to a 'self-perpetuating pathology' (Clark 1965, p. 81). It was only a few years after Clark's work that one of the then gurus of Right-wing philosophy in Britain, Keith Joseph, stirred the public and academic attention to what he called, the 'cycle of deprivation'. This mode of thought fits neatly into the culture/sub culture of poverty thesis, as explained in Chapter One, in that the norms and values of a deprived lifestyle are presented as being transmitted from parents to children, a no-hope mentality resounding around the ghetto which discourages young people from attempting to acquire the necessary attributes to escape from the cycle of deprivation. Such a perception, of course, gives credence to the individualist approach to poor relief.

These early reports on the conditions in the inner cities actually deterred further professional research between the mid 1970s and the early 1980s because progressive researchers were reticent about examining and publishing behaviour patterns which would be perceived by society as negative, critical and further stigmatising of cultural minorities. There was concern that such research might inadvertently generate grounds for racist arguments and provide fuel for those who wished to further a 'blame the victim' perspective. This lull in the process only served to cause a major shock when researchers returned to look at the inner cities, mainly as a result of the street riots in many areas of Britain. They were somewhat taken by surprise at the depth and extent of the deterioration that had occurred and few theorists proposed explanations for the phenomena. In the context of this void, Right wing policy makers and advisors uncovered and introduced the concept of the 'underclass'. Whilst liberals wallowed in confusion over the nature of the causes of the developments in the inner cities, Right wing analysts constructed a 'social dislocation' paradigm, based upon a set of assumptions which have attracted considerable public compulsion. It is worth quoting Jeremy Seabrook (1985, p. 86) in full to appreciate the societal function that the inner city poor play in maintaining the status quo of privilege, and thus the importance to conservatives of fostering a pathological perspective on inner city and 'underclass' lifestyles:

> When the poor attack each other, fire the ghettos, mutilate others and damage themselves with drugs or alcohol, it has this advantage to the rich, that the connection between them and the poor has been so effectively shrouded, that they cannot be accused of complicity in the damage that is done to the poor. The poor can be safely left to demonstrate to the world their instability and violence; and to show that they are poor because they deserve nothing more; while the wealthy proceed, serene and inviolable in the enjoyment of their just deserts, going about their business and only dimly aware of the red glow in the night sky, barely perturbed by the sirens of the ambulances that fetch out their freight of torn and wounded humanity from the impenetrable ghettos. The rich have been delivered from the consequences of their own actions.

Thus the functional nature of the 'underclass' lies in advanced capitalist Britain having its population which has a distinct material interest in marginalising and expelling the poor from the process of the distribution of income and power, leading to a scission in the social structure between the comfortable majority and an 'underclass' minority. Cooperation and participation in social arrangements is beyond the bounds of concern for such a group and consequently, it is regarded by 'normal' society as, at best, burdensome and at worst, threatening. As a result, according to Jordan (1989, p. 19): 'Welfare provision is gradually transformed into mechanisms for control and punishment, while the passivity of the underclass changes to conflict, crime and disorder.' Another interesting function of the usage of the term 'underclass' is that it has become synonymous with the most disadvantaged blacks in inner cities. British writers on the subject have concentrated more upon social, political and economic apartheid of black and white poor, rather than racial apartheid. The retreat of the liberal perspective has also involved a reluctance to employ the term the 'underclass'. Such a popular, emotive label is regarded as confusing and negative as it presents as an umbrella grouping for different problems confronted by different people. By concentrating on individuals' features and pathology and by stigmatising the deprived for their lifestyles, the 'underclass' stands alongside such previous terms as the 'lumpen-proletariat', the 'undeserving poor' and the 'culture of poverty'.

In the US, many black liberals began to detract attention away from the negative, pathological experiences of the inner city, and towards the positive elements of life in the ghettos and the strengths and resilience that the inhabitants required and indeed possessed to survive in such adverse, oppressive, social, economic and racial conditions. By revising the approach from one of racial isolation and discrimination and class exploitation, to one of the 'successes' of the black communities, attention was focused away from economic issues, such as the need for greater financial investment to create jobs, better the need for greater financial investment to create jobs, better housing, education, health provision etc. According the a US black academic, William Julius Wilson (1987), 'In short, such arguments effectively diverted attention from the appropriate solutions to the dreadful economic condition of poor blacks and made it difficult for them to see how their fate has been inextricably tied up with the structure of the American economy.' Poverty, caused by a move from commodity production to service provision, resulting in the loss of many millions of unskilled jobs, and social isolation has led to a severe form of evolving social disorganisation. Wilson became uncomfortable with the term 'underclass' because of its stereotypical nature but he generally defended the use of the concept on the pragmatic grounds that a concentration of poverty had existed and 'no amount of wishful thinking or semantic tinkering by well meaning liberals can change that reality.' (Robson & Gregson 1992, p. 40) Frank Field (1990, p. 38) suggests that there is no racial element in Britain's 'underclass' Although many black people swell the ranks of this group, they are there less because of race and racism and more because of their highly vulnerable class status in UK society. What Field does not address is the rather apparent theme that black people are proportionately much more clustered in the deprived groups than whites - because of their race. As such, there is little variance between the black ghetto dweller of South Chicago and the black inhabitant of Toxteth.

Three of the main explanatory theories discussed in Chapter 1 on Theories of Poverty Causation have their own views on the 'underclass' which largely correspond with their ideas on poverty in general - individualist orthodoxy, Marxist and cultural:

The **individualist orthodoxy** appears insensitive to the idea that the non poor can be persuaded to cooperate in policy responses to deal with the problems of the inner city, the 'underclass' and poverty, on the basis that such factors diminish the claim of Britain to be a civilised nation. The

Thatcherite revolution targeted the values of the successful in society and conditioned them to perceive the failure of others as evidence of a refusal to avail of the opportunities open to all members of the community. Field (1989, pp. 155-6) concludes: 'This "closed drawbridge" mentality from those who have safely gained access to the good life, or at least a better life, is itself, one of the factors that is having a "ghettoising" effect on the underclass. With the Thatcher government, and now to a larger extent, the Labour Party appealing to the better off, this trend, if anything, is likely to be reinforced.' The orthodox policy response to the problems of the 'underclass' can be classified under five strategies:

1   the role of the state should concentrate on creating an economic climate which encourages economic growth and assists people to escape from poverty;

2   the poor should be categorised according to the 'reasons' for their poverty - the elderly, able-bodied unemployed, disabled, single parents etc. People who are poor due to self damaging conduct - the underclass - should live in a condition worse than low income along. Money alone will not sure poverty for all groups;

3   understanding the personal life strategies which have proved successful in enabling people to escape from poverty - i.e. complete education, once an adult, get married and stay married, stay employed, even at a wage and under conditions below their ultimate aims;

4   tried and tested methods and institutions of self-improvement are not being followed by the underclass - e.g. the church, voluntary bodies, the family, all of which teach values life personal responsibility, hard work, duty, integrity, self control and impulse restraint;

5   recreation of a two sided ideal of self reliance and community. The ethics of personal responsibility combined with a personal sense of obligation to render service for the good of all is essential to a fulfilled life. David Green, director of the Tory think-tank, the Institute of Economic Affairs (1992) elaborates on this:

Instead of seeing people as bearers of rights or claims on the public purse, people are seen as contributors to the common welfare. Someone who fails to support himself also renders himself incapable of giving service to others ... welfare recipients (should) be viewed, not as victims of circumstance, but as potentially free, responsible, choosing, valuing citizens who need temporary help in order to restore them to fully functioning citizenship. To send them cheques through the post is to fail to respect them. To draw attention to the flaws in their own conduct, however, is to respect them as capable of more and thus to encourage an increase in self-esteem. Government almsgiving keeps people going, but for most breadwinners, no amount of insistence that the cheque is sent as a human right will given them the self esteem that comes from their own efforts or the self fulfilment that flows from surviving in the face of challenger in the workplace.

The central contradictions in the explanations offered by the orthodoxy is that:

a) their arguments are based on morality. Murray perceived himself as 'a visitor from a plague area come to see whether the disease is spreading'. Dahrendorf analysed the 'underclass' as a 'cancer which eats away at the texture of societies' and its future development as 'critical for the moral hygiene of British society'. (both cited in Lister 1990, p. 25);

b) this 'morality' fails to present a convincing justification of the reality of poverty for millions of families within a 'common welfare'.

Claiming that the state strives to assist those in most need, this set of arguments is unable to coherently explain the consequential reality which is a system of parsimonious benefits, minutely administered and complimented by powers to force the unemployed to labour for the state for safety net welfare incomes. The 'morality' of the orthodoxy's views is further diminished by the contrast between this scenario and that of the relative affluence and freedom of choice which dominates the world of the market. Robbed on the incentive to join the competitive social process, the alternative is for the state to threaten and coerce the unemployed into low paid employment. As Green (1992) states above, society requires a social responsibility for all to labour for the common good of the labour market; yet this obligation exists only for the 'underclass' and not for the market sphere where the choice to work or not is dictated by self interest. The existence of an underclass casts doubt on the social contract itself. 'It means that citizenship has become an exclusive rather than an inclusive status. Some are full citizens, some are not.' (Jordan 1989). These 'forces of expulsion' are: unemployment; widening class differences; the exclusion of the vary poorest from the rapidly rising living standards; and a hardening of public attitudes.

The poll tax is a social policy point in question here. MacGregor (1988) agues that inevitably, to avoid paying the tax for low income families, particularly those living in 'high spending' areas, many will be forced into official oblivion, by removing themselves from public records and perhaps keeping them on the move to avoid detection. In the US, city census exercises can add notional numbers to their actual collected data to make up the shortcomings of such non recording. MacGregor concludes that the same may have to happen in Britain. The passivity of the 'underclass' often converts into semi-organised resistance to the coercion and harassment employed by the state. The previous absence of coercion and harassment employed by the state. The previous absence of any motivation to participate in the socio-economic arrangements then converts into identifiable justification for opposing any enforced cooperation and the collective drift is to remain outside the state's control. For Jordan (1989, p.103), 'From being a neglected substratum of society, they turn into an oppressed underclass, whose domination by the majority, through the state agencies, is a source of resentment and conflict.'

For **Marxism/structuralism**, the concept of the 'underclass' is generated by the hegemony of capital and the requirement of the capitalist system to produce more marketable commodities at decreasing costs - i.e. numerically less, but qualitatively superior (better skilled), workers. This leads to a section of the working class becoming misfits, unnecessary, superfluous to the normal relations of the market society. The 'underclass' is thus NOT a precise class in Marxist concepts. As Nick Buck (1992, in Smith D., p. 89) put it, the members of this group are 'not so much stable members of an underclass, as unstable members of the working class'. It is a layer of the working class, either permanently or on a long term basis, excluded from the established structures of production, victims of the process of capitalist manipulation and exploitation of the labour force. This group is not needed at present, nor do they figure in the future plans for the economy. The 'underclass' is the fate awaiting the working poor when they become unemployed. (Marx 1970, pp. 600-3). Such a rationale is used to question the very validity of the term 'underclass on the grounds that:

a)   this section of the population are members of the working class and, at this stage of capitalist development, it incorporated the most oppressed members. This group is 'in no sense a detached and isolated group cut off from the rest of society. They are just the same people as the rest of our population, with the same culture and aspirations, but with simply too little money to be able to share in the activities and possessions of everyday life with the rest of the population'. (Bradshaw & Holmes 1989, p. 138);

b)   'the use of a concept so imprecise, emotive and value laden could serve simply o weaken further the poor's claim to citizenship in the eyes of the rest of society, even though this approach is effective as a means of putting poverty in the headlines.' (Lister 1990, p. 24).

Within the Marxist explanation, the equivalent of the 'underclass' on an international basis is the Third World. The parallels between the 'underclass' in britain being not needed by the national economy and the very poor countries being not needed by the global economy represent and analogy. The degree to which the poor in Britain do not figure in the political agenda and the low level of concern for underdeveloped countries among richer nations both reflect a common denominator central to the 'underclass' debate.

'Underclass' commentators, like Frank Field (1989 , p.4) complicate traditional Marxist analysis by suggesting that the bottom sections of the working class are distinguished from, not only other groups in receipt of low, fixed income, but, even more crucially, from the working class as a whole. With the other socio-economic classes, the working class now hold similar aims of improvements in their material standard of living. 'These aspirations now appear as a more powerful uniting agent than the personal and political differences arising from the massive disparities in income and wealth in this newly formed coalition.' A large section of the working class has thus, for Field, become embourgeoised. But Field does concede that the 'underclass' constitutes 'a subtle form of political, social and economic apartheid'.

Whereas Marxism would regard such an 'underclass' as a revolutionary threat to the capitalist order, bearing the brunt of only so much exploitation and degradation, Dahrendorf (1989(disagrees by explaining that groups who are so utterly poor are incapable of organising themselves to generate political upheaval. He points to the presence of conservative (often extreme) stances taken by many poor people and the extent of revolutionary objectives prevalent amongst the employable sections of the 'underclass' can and have presented as a threat to social integration: the inner city riots in Toxteth, Bristol, London and most recently, Los Angeles. By arguing that, if liberals had been asked in 1979 what were their views on an unemployment rate of three million and its effect on state functioning, they would have agreed that 'democratic government' would fall and society would become unstable. However, Ralf Dahrendorf points out that Britain is still a relatively peaceful nation. But, he warns, this is the case relating only to the extent of large scale, community, street riots. Widened to take account of crime in general, he concedes that there, ' … may not be official no-go areas for the police in our cities (?), but there certainly are such areas for the rest of us'. (Dahrendorf 1987, p. 13).

Many political activists of the Left have advocated the need to 'empower the poor'and to facilitate their political participation, in order that they may organise in such a way as to stake their claims on society and to obtain their full citizens rights. Welfare rights movements, anti -poverty groups, equal opportunities bodies etc., pursue this strategy. B ut the Thatcherite ideological revolution of the 1980s invaded and colonised this concept and remoulded it to suit its own values. In the place of the 'enabling state' and the model of collective empowerment, what has been witnessed has been moves to encourage greater individual consumer choice, limited, voluntary self-help welfare activity and 'community care' - individual empowerment.

A **culture of poverty** explanation would concentrate upon some of the observed features' of the 'underclass', which would include inferior standards of educational achievements, prematurely leaving school without the skills to advance in the labour market, broken or single parent families, slum housing. And, on top of this, Ralf Dahrendorf (1987, p. 13) argues that the 'underclass' has constructed a value laid-back sloppiness, association in changing groups or gangs, congregation around discos or the like, hostility to middle class society, particular habits of dress, hairstyle, often drugs or at least alcohol - a style, in other words, which has little in common with the work society around.'

The main pitfall in such an approach is, of course, that, in **describing** traits and patterns among some of the poor (the most visible), such features become perceived as the basic causal factors of poverty lifestyles and lead comfortably and inevitably to a 'lame the victim' response. Within this understanding, the poor self-perpetuate norms which provide the seeds of their own downfall. Of course, such characteristics do hold valid for the minority of the poor, but to view these as representing the normal behavioural patterns and values of all the poor and to base policy responses on these features, is to further isolate this section of the community from society in general and to perpetuate their status as an 'underclass' - which appears to be the hidden agenda of policy directed at poverty. It also fails to take account of the extent of 'deviation', 'irresponsible' and 'abnormal' behaviour - such as being 'aid-back', a contemporary fad; group association, like the Sloan Rangers; frequenting discos, like Stringfellows in London; hostility to other classes; habits of dress and hairstyle, like suits, red braces and ponytails; drugs and alcohol, like cocaine and bottles of wine or Peruvian beer - are as prevalent among the better off groups, if not more so, than among the poor, who, most of the time, cannot afford most of these pursuits anyway. Dahrendorf's comments epitomise the class prejudice which is the very cornerstone of the concept of an 'underclass'.

The culture of poverty thesis is not held valid by the findings of Anthony Heath's research (1992 in Smith, D. pp. 32/47). He found that there were no identifiable differences between the attitudes of the 'underclass' and those of mainstream society, particularly in relation to children and the family. Parts of his research show that families in the 'underclass' are more likely than employed family units to 'lace a higher value of children'. Also 'underclass' families are likely to hold more positive attitudes towards single parenthood than others. Members of the 'underclass'are much more likely than non-employed members of employed family units to want renumerative employment. Although political participation was lower among the 'underclass' in terms of voting, this difference was fairly small. These 'deviant cultures' are, in reality adaptive survival strategies.

There is thus a 'structure versus culture' debate, an intellectual struggle to provide an explanatory framework within which to understand the nature of the 'underclass'. David Smith (1992, p. 7), explains this as follows:

1   **Structural**: alterations in the make-up of the economy - e.g. eliminating large numbers of manual posts; institutional structures - e.g. inadequate education and training provision; poor facilities - e.g. nursery places for the children of single mothers - all of these combine to withhold from a population group, the chance and skills to enter the labour market and seek employment on a competitive basis. It may be that there is also a spatial element encouraged by the sale of council housing, as indicated by research which demonstrates that local authority tenancy bears a stronger correlation with the 'underclass' than other social classes or educational attainments. Those tenants who can afford to purchase their accommodation in the better quality areas leave the remaining stock concentrated in multiply deprived estates which are increasingly inhabited by the long term unemployed and single parent households. Thus the UK council housing stock takes on a similar stigmatising mantle as that of the USA's 'welfare housing', with a similarly deteriorating social structure and extraordinarily high crime rates. The practice of Westminster council in 1993 of selling off council housing to better off, and thus potentially Tory voters, will have a clear impact on the 'yuppification/gentrification' of some areas and the 'marginalisation/residualisation' of other areas, deepening and extending the inequalities and injustices experienced by the 'underclass';

2   **Cultural**: a group of people have given up the struggle to compete within their cultural context and environment, albeit as a result of: (a) the unequal nature of such competition and; (b) this culture being, at least partly the product of structures and institutions - i.e. the welfare state.

These two polarised views have recently been aired in public in the aftermath of the Meadow Well riots in Tyneside, when, on the one hand, state officials laid responsibility on the doorstep of 'loutish behaviour', criminals and uncaring parents, while on the other hand, leading clergy referred to the strong contribution made by 'social deprivation, poverty, poor housing and illiteracy'. Smith goes on to 'define' the 'underclass' as consisting of family units which are economically dependent on state benefits (excluding state pensioners). Smith raises the question as to whether this group exhibits a visible 'culture of dependency'. Anthony Heath (1992 in Smith 1992, pp. 32-8), in his survey concluded that 'the data available to us fail to confirm the notion of a culture of dependency.' Heath also found that there was no sound basis for arguing that there is a distinct culture associated with the 'underclass': 'the members of the underclass simply illustrate tendencies that are widespread in mainstream society as well.' For example, levels of participation in the political process and structures among the employed groups vary according to educational standards and achievements and it is down to the substandard education prevalent among the 'underclass' that explains their low participation in this sphere.

Cottingham (1982, p. 3) usefully catalogues the life experiences faced by many members of the 'underclass' and these correspond with the theoretical arguments of both left and right perspectives:

-   severe income deprivation - poverty and dependency on welfare;
-   unstable employment (or unemployment, unemployability);
-   low skills;
-   limited access to, or involvement with, education, social services etc;
-   persistent poverty: 'not just temporarily poor; they are enmeshed in inter-generational poverty'
-   spatial concentration; the underclass is typically ghettoised;
-   high incidence of health problems, physical and mental.

There has been no greater proponent of the concept of the 'underclass' than the American political scientist, Charles Murray (1984 & 1990) who claims to have intellectualised this notion in his books. The 'underclass' are not just the poor, but are a group who have refused to integrate with mainstream society. The term does not relate to a measurement of poverty, but rather to a 'type of poverty' Murray differentiates:

> One class of poor people was never even called "poor". I came to understand that they simply lived with low incomes... Then there was another set of poor people, just a handful of them. These poor people didn't lack just money. They were defined by their behaviour. Their homes were littered and unkempt. The men in the family were unable to hold a job for more than a few weeks at a time. Drunkenness was contributed a disproportionate share of the local juvenile delinquents. (Nov. 1989, pp. 26-46)

Murray argues that, historically and currently, the poor are not a homogenous group, who are simply different from the rest of society because they have less money. The notion of the poor which identifies an 'undeserving' or 'feckless' element steeped in a culture of poverty, is, Murray suggests, regarded by most intellectuals as 'the figment of the prejudices of a parochial middle class'. Similarly, the term, the 'underclass' is understood as 'just another refuted concept periodically resurrected by conservatives who wish to constrain the redistributive potential of state welfare'. (p. 26). In arguing that Britain, like the US, has an underclass, Murray explains:

I am not talking here about an unemployment problem that can be solved by more jobs, nor about a poverty problem that can be solved by higher benefits. Britain has a growing population of working-aged, healthy people who live in a different world from other Britons, who are raising their children to live in it, and whose values are now contaminating the life of entire neighbourhoods - which is one of the most insidious aspects of the phenomenon, for neighbours who don't share those values cannot isolate themselves. (p. 27)

An editorial in the Sunday Times (1990, p. 4) at the same time adopted Murray's sentiments in its own words:

The underclass spawns illegitimate children without a care for tomorrow and feeds on a crime rate which rivals the United States in property offenses. Its able-bodied youths see no point in working and feel no compulsion either. They reject society while feeding off it; they are becoming a lost generation giving the cycle of deprivation a new spin ... No amount of income redistribution or social engineering can solve their problem. Their sub-lifestyles are beyond welfare benefit rises and job creation schemes. They exist as active social outcasts, wedded to an anti social system.

Unsurprisingly, Murray's theories were extensively employed to justify policies aimed at reducing social welfare spending and to consolidate even further, the isolation of the poor who were regarded as 'politically disposable and fiscally extravagant' (Bridges & Finegold 1982, p. 30). Here, Murray endorses the orthodox economic theory of poverty causation, as discussed in Chapter One, by arguing that the inferior lifestyles of these denizens of the ghettos are the result of individual, rational choice. Rather than being passive recipients of social and economic policies, members of the 'underclass' are actively engaged in the pursuit of their own interests. What differentiates them from 'normal' society is that they act out the 'rational contest' in a vacuum, lacking in any moral constraints or community regulations. Their values are 'now contaminating the life of entire neighbourhoods'. (Murray 1990, p. 4)

Murray listed three 'early-warning signals' of the development of an 'underclass': illegitimacy ('which in my view, is the best predictor of an underclass in the making'); violent crime; and drop-out from the labour force. These three factors tempted Mann (1992, p. 106) to interpret Murray's perception of the 'underclass' as 'criminally violent bastards who refuse to work'. Illegitimacy is an indication of an attitudinal differential between those who do not see marriage as an essential element of reproduction and those who do. But, Murray reminds us, the relatively significant rise in illegitimacy is visibly clustered among the lowest social class. Because the lower class has traditionally been perceived by their proneness to immediate gratification, 'Single young women get pregnant because sex is fun and babies are endearing.' (p. 43). He attempts to justify illegitimacy as an indication of an 'underclass' by refuting any morality or sanctity of marriage: 'Communities need families. Communities need fathers.' (p. 28). The welfare of families, the health of the economy are dependent upon consolidating the family as the bone and sinew of society and the economy. And worse still, long term welfare dependency is prevalent among young women who have children without husbands, such children achieve far less at school then others from 'normal' families and they do not have a paternal role model to imitate. Murray conveniently overlooks the fact that, although single parent families run a very high risk of living in poverty, four times as many married couples with children live on or below the Income Support poverty line.

In the US - the New Jersey area of Camden for example (the 'Essex of America') - policies for single parent families are enacted which are clearly underpinned by the assumptions of Murray. For those existing single mums who are 'irrational' enough to have a second child, there is no additional welfare payments. But if she is 'rational' enough to marry a man other than the father of her child - who, presumably, is deemed unfit and unstable - she can obtain a 'dowry' of $21,000. Director of the local government ministry, Carol Kasabach, pleads: 'Please, please, don't copy it in England.' (cited in Hugill 1993)

As Murray and other Right wing analysts have proposed the breakdown of the traditional family as a major arena for many of the social and economic ills related to the 'underclass' - e.g. low educational attainment, juvenile delinquency, violence, law breaking, sexual abuse - it is worth observing that, again, Murray has conveniently overlooked data which show that these phenomena are certainly not idiosyncratic to one parent families. Anna Coote et al (1990, p. 25) show that: 'Most domestic violence and child sexual abuse is perpetrated by married men against their own wives and children ... The great majority (84 per cent) of adults convicted of criminal offence are male; and men account for an even higher proportion (91 per cent) of those convicted of violent crimes. Many of these male convicted criminals are married men and it is undoubtedly the case that many boys learn to be violent and/or criminal by following the example of their fathers.' Thus critics suggest that the family can be and often is an oppressive structure that imposes dependency upon women and generated the main arena for the perpetration of male violence against women and children. It is apparent that problems in youth can be the result of inadequate parenting, but many parents are not as well equipped as others to offer the protection, emotional support and discipline which children require. In other words, a deprived lifestyle with

158

adequate incomes and/or appropriate child care arrangements make a success of their children's upbringing and their family's welfare. The Hobson's Choice then for the single mother is to: (a) remain at home, spend the days only caring for her children, risk a life of poverty and deprivation and relegate her family into the 'underclass' or; (b) obtain a paid job, leave her children to go out to work and fail to fulfil her 'natural' role as mother and sole carer - 'natural' as defined by society. (An interesting small scale study of the 'home alone' phenomenon on Merseyside suggested that economic necessity, male partner generated debt, social isolation and the lack of adequate, affordable child care facilities were the dominant influences on women who leave their children at home alone while they went out to work. Stitt S. & & & Doherty S. 1994). The development and emergence of an 'underclass' is thus the resultant consequence, not of immorality or deviance, but of social and economic arrangements. The only reason that this 'underclass' lives in a different world is that they have no choice; many lone parent families are 'dumped' in run down, 'sink' housing estates by local authority housing management in collaboration and cooperation with social work services.

Alan Walker (1990, p. 54) illustratively points out a few facts in the illegitimacy debate which Murray overlooked. 'The illegitimacy ratio i   n Denmark is more than double Britain's and ... that society is not on the brink of disaster. Moreover, in Britain, the data show that marriage breakdown is the main cause of lone parenthood, not illegitimacy.' And Nicholas Deakin (1990 in Walker 1990, p. 60) also presents facts which Murray has sought to ignore: ' ... half those born illegitimate has their two parents living together at the time of birth; and many of these relationships will in due course result in the marriage of the natural parents. Alternatively, the mother may either marry or cohabit with another man, thereby providing a surrogate male parent for her children. Why step parents to not feature in Murray's account is a mystery, given the exceptionally rapid growth over the last decade of families that are thus "reconstituted".' Single parenthood thus cannot be regarded as either a static condition or an immoral one. It is rather a point in the life cycle, leading in various directions with potentially, a multitude of destinations. Increased levels of illegitimacy can also be explained within the concept of the decline in the popularity of marriage, bringing Britain more into line, not with the USA, but with the like of progressive states such as Denmark and Sweden.

Rosie Waterhouse (1993) also offered statistics which portrayed a very different profile of the single parent family then the image encouraged by government sentiments. The number of lone parents increased from 840,000 in 1979 to 1.3 million in 1991; the respective numbers of such households receiving Income Support were, 320,000 and 1 million. Official predictions suggest that there will be about 1.7 million single parents by the year 2000 and 1.4 million of these will be in receipt of Income Support. Between 1981 and

1991, the breakdown of single parent families was:
   divorced and separated: 660,000 or 52 per cent (1991), N/A (1981);
   single, never-partnered: 430,000 or 35 per cent (1991), 160,000 (1981);
   ex-cohabiters: 100,000 or 8 per cent (1991), 75,000 (1981);
   widowed: 78,000 or 6 per cent (1991), 135,000 (1981).
Thus the fastest growing group has been the single, never-partnered. Although they make up 35 per cent of all lone parents, more than 80 per cent of that group are under 30 years of age. The number of teenage lone parents is **just five per cent** - about 65,000. The widowed group were the only category which actually decreased in numbers. More than half (51 per cent) of all Afro-Caribbean mothers are lone parents, compared to 14 per cent of all mothers. Only 9 per cent of Asian mothers are lone parents. But among the Afro-Caribbean population, 59 per cent of lone mothers have an earned income, as have 38 per cent of all ethnic minority single mums, suggesting that the 'burden on the state' thesis is not as extensive as government ministers would portray, at l;east among black single mums. And the thesis is further challenged by the statistics which show that 45 per cent of Income Support claims by single parents last less than a year, and 65 per cent last less than two years, suggesting that a substantial proportion, if not a majority, of lone parents seek and obtain independent, earned income sources (or decide to cease claiming welfare benefits). The highest concentrations of single parenthood are in Merseyside and Tyne & Wear (26 per cent), followed by Scotland (20 per cent), and Greater Manchester (16 per cent). The lowest incidences are in the South west and East Anglia. A geo-economic direct correlation is apparent between single parenthood and material advantage/disadvantage. (Brindle 1993, p. 2)

   In the 1970s, Keith Joseph initiated a massive research programme designed to empirically and scientifically reinforce his theoretical fetish at the time, the 'cycle of deprivation'. Joseph had argued: 'Perhaps there is at work here, a process, apparent in many situations but imperfectly understood, by which problems reproduced themselves from generation to generation.' Because of an excess of births which was apparently occurring in mothers of social class V, 'the balance of our population, our human stock, is threatened.' He suggested birth control as a method of avoiding the excessive pro-creation of 'problem children, the future unmarried mothers, delinquents, denizens of our borstals, subnormal educational establishments, prisons, hostels for drifters'. (Joseph, 1972). The result was a £1 million investment in research, 37 different studies writing 20 books, all of which concluded that there is no evidence of a direct continuity of social problems between generations. Rutter & Madge (1976, pp. 143 & 304) commented that, 'At least half of the children born into a disadvantaged home do not repeat the pattern of disadvantage in the next generation. Over half of all forms of disadvantage arise anew each generation ... continuities are by no means inevitable and there is no general sense in which "like begets like"'.

But it was 1993/94 in which a mountain of evidence emerged on single parenthood and poverty/the 'underclass', provoked entirely by the government's attempts to lay much of the responsibility for the breakdown of the social fabric on, particularly, young mums with illegitimate children. After the tragic murder of James Bulger in Tyneside in 1993, Social Security Secretary, Peter Lilley, stated: 'We have produced a generation of fatherless children. No father to support them, discipline them and set an example.' (it is not quite clear whether the 'we' in Lilley's statement referred to society in general, or to Tory Ministers and MPs. One wonders to what extent Lilley's sentiments extend to the contribution made by the numerous Tory MPs who, in 1993 and 1994 admitted to fathering, in some cases one, in other cases numerous, illegitimate children to the development of an 'underclass' - sic.) His arguments was that James' murder and the post war increase in violent crime was mainly the product of the increasing numbers of fatherless families. And Home Secretary, Michael Howard, at the Tory Party Conference in October 1993 stated: 'So called "progressive" theories in the 60s and 70s made excuses for crime ... Part of this story has been the decline of the traditional two parent family. The children, instead of learning the difference between right and wrong, may instead concentrate on how not to get caught.' All the research which exists suggests that no such correlation exists.

children from such families do, evidence seems to suggest, become more aggressive in later life than those from two parent families - but not as a result of illegitimacy or the absence of a father. Research suggests that the main reason is that most single parents are separated or divorced and are much more vulnerable to poverty. Single parenting in itself does not cause violence. The most significant increase in crimes against the person have occurred, not since 1950, but since 1979 - when the Conservatives came to power. Oliver James (1993), a clinical psychologist, produced statistics which showed that, between 1979 to 1986, there were 4,000 more crimes of violence against the person each year than the previous year. But since 1987, the rate of increase has tripled to an unprecedented 13,000 per year. The government has offered no rational explanation for this explosion. It has preferred to avoid pointing out that the increase in children raised in lower income families was from 19 per cent in 1979 to 30 per cent in 1981 and has remained at this rate ever since. As James concludes,

Just when the children of the new poverty begin to grow up, the unprecedented rise in violence against the person begins ... Why, then, has there been such a focus in recent years on illegitimacy and single mothering? The answer is that it detracts from the true cause of increasing violence: poverty.

The Home Secretary, Michael Howard, at the Tory annual conference in 1993 went, at least, halfway in agreeing with the underpinning theme concerning the single parent and crime debate when he was forced, by academic and pressure group research, to concede that:

> It does not appear, therefore, that the fact of lone parenthood is in itself associated with crime; it is the quality of care within the family which counts, not whether it is given by one parent or two. But the children of lone parents are more likely to be brought up in poor families, and this appears to be associated with low educational attainment and delinquency.

In June 1993, the moral onslaught on the young single mums and their illegitimate children reached fever pitch. A caricature of the typical single mother as a 'feckless' teenager sponging off the nanny state hit the headlines of the tabloids. She is an unmarried girl, living in a council flat, is dependent on welfare payments, and fails to teach her child or children the difference between right and wrong. The father, of course, is long gone. The Secretary of State for Wales, John Redwood, argued in Cardiff in July 1993: 'hat is worrying is the trend in some places for young women to have babies with no apparent intention of even trying a marriage or stable relationship with the father of the child.' It was left to academic and pressure group research, reported in the quality press, to launch the data-based counter attack. For example, Ghazi and Gerard reported in the *Observer* on 11 July 1993 that:

- nine in ten single parents are women and the vast majority (952,000) do depend on Income Support;
- only 45,000 of these are teenagers;
- b ut Britain has the fourth highest teenage birth rate in Europe;
- around 33 of every 1,000 births are to mothers aged between 15 and 19 years old, 83 per cent of these to unmarried girls;
- 70 per cent of Britain's single mothers are mature women who are either widowed, separated or divorced;
- the rest - around 4000,000 - are young single mothers;
- the fastest growing group of single parents, contrary to popular myth, is not teenage single parents, but 20 to 24 year olds;
- 90 per cent of single parents stated to a DSS survey that they wanted to work in future and 55 per cent would work immediately if they had child care support.

Single parenthood, like marital breakdown, transcends class divisions (and even the vast gulf between unemployed households and government ministers). But the consequences are much worse for the poor. Lower income single parent families are much more likely to concentrate in urban estates and the worst of the private rented sector - or in temporary accommodation, such as Bed and Breakfast hotels or hostels for the homeless (see Stitt, Griffiths & Grant, 1993). It is clear that, on aggregate, the financial costs to the state of the growing number of single parent families, is increasing at a rapid rate. Between 1981 and 1991, the social security bill for these families trebled in real terms and in 1993 stood at an annual figure of £5 billion (excluding maternity and child benefit). But, as to the claim by Adrian Rogers, Director of the Conservative Family Institute, that these benefits are 'pretty lavish', on an individual family basis, there is little luxury involved in daily standards of living. Just over half of all single parent families had an income of less than £100 a week in 1993. A single parent with one child would have received £67.55 Income Support, plus child allowance (£15 to £34 per week) in 1993. (Ghazi & Gerard 1993, p. 19).

One of the central planks in the Conservative government's attacks upon single parent families in 1993/94 has been that, particularly, teenage girls deliberately become pregnant to obtain council housing and that deterrents to such practices should be built into the benefit system. Health Minister, Tom Sackville, who himself spent £20,000 on adopting a son and a daughter, stated in 1993: 'A comprehensive housing and benefit system has reinforced the illusion that anyone can have a baby, regardless of their means.' The Secretary of State for Social Security, Peter Lilley, at the Tory Party Conference on October 7th 1992 stated: 'I've got a little list of benefit offenders who I'll be rooting out ... young ladies who get pregnant just to jump the housing list, and dads who won't support the kids of ladies who they have ... kissed.' (One is left to ponder whether that list should include some of Lilley's Westminster colleagues). And Housing Minister, Sir George Young, told the same conference that: 'How do we explain to the young couples who wait for a home before they start a family that they cannot be rehoused ahead of the unmarried teenager expecting her first, probably, unplanned child?' The idea that homeless single parents get priority access to council housing has been labelled a 'common myth' by the Institute of Housing. Its study (cited in Simmons 1993) emphasised that the correlation between having a child and seeking council housing is 'at best tenuous'. Directors of housing in 30 local councils provided statistics which showed that, for nine authorities out of ten, 'it is rare for unmarried teenage mothers or pregnant girls to present themselves for rehousing.' And statistics show that, although about 50 per cent of all one parent families live in council housing, over 33 per cent are owner occupiers. And among single mothers aged sixteen and seventeen years of age, nine out of ten **live with their parents**. Statistics speak louder than moral prejudice and economic/fiscal desperation.

Of course, it has been observed that government plans to reduce the growth of single parent families finds a comfortable niche in the Tories 'back to basics' objectives. In November 1993, Peter Lilley, the Social Security Secretary, in a review of welfare benefits, catalogued three main suggestions to achieve a reduction in the burden on the state of the growth of single parents:

1   tackle incentives to become or remain a lone parent;

2   offer incentives for single parents to support themselves through work and child maintenance;

3   increase the responsibility of a young lone parent's own parents to provide support.

This third objective is clearly an attempt to engineer a return to the extended family and to the Poor Law concept of the 'liable relative'. One suggestion considered is the withdrawal of one parent benefit, paid to all lone parents and worth £6.05 a week and an extra £4.90 a week for those lone parents on income related benefits up to April 1994. Another consideration is to remove from local authorities the obligation to rehouse single parents (and others) under the age of twenty one.

And if central government perceives unmarried motherhood as a 'disease eating away at our civilization', the statutory education authorities appear unconcerned about helping, via schools' teenagers to avoid unwanted pregnancies. A 1993 amendment to the Education Bill will enable schools to meet their requirements to offer sex education through merely one optional single session for pupils between eleven and sixteen. It will be non-compulsory for children whose parents raise objections. Yet data exists which proves that countries with the most expensive sex education have the lowest teenage pregnancy rates and that the better the sex education, the higher the age at which teenagers first have sex. According to Annabel Ferriman (1993), 'Contrary to what people such as Mary Whitehouse and Victoria Gillick might believe, sex education appears to postpone sexual activity rather than encourage it.'

John Ashton of the Mersey Regional Health Authority referred to a 1986 study of 37 nations which showed that those countries with lower rates of pregnancy were those with a high degree of acceptance of teenage sexuality, good quality sex education and user friendly clinical services for younger people, such as the Brook Advisory Centres. Conversely, those countries with limited sex education are more likely to have high rates of teenage pregnancy. For example, in the Netherlands and Sweden, where sex education is extensive and uncontroversial, where contraceptives are cheap and easily available, where confidentiality binds doctors who prescribe the pill for young girls, where an extensive network of family planning centres guarantee anonymity, teenage pregnancy rates are far lower than in Britain: 9 per 1,000 in Holland; 30 per 1,000 in Sweden; 69 per 1,000 in Britain, which is the highest rate in Europe. (The rate in the US, another country where sex education is ambiguous, is 100 per 1,000) (cited in Ferriman 1993). In Holland, sexual intercourse is 'officially tolerated', if not formally legal, at the age of twelve, yet teenage pregnancies in this country are the lowest in the Western world, and teenage abortion rates are ten times lower than in Britain. In 1991, only eighteen Dutch girls under the age of fifteen had babies and 4,145 girls between fifteen and nineteen. This was about half all teenage pregnancies in the whole country. The other half were terminated. In Britain, 8,000 girls under 16 become pregnant each year. A third have abortions, 'leaving about 5,000 babies to be born to mothers who are themselves little more than children' (Belleman, 1993). The 'underclass' thesis has not yet entered the political or academic debate in the Netherlands. The sex education programmes and the absence of the morality approach to teenage sexuality and pregnancy goes a long way towards explaining why.

As for crime, 'First and most obvious, the habitual criminal is the classic member of the underclass.' And like his illegitimacy argument, Murray offers not the slightest hint of statistical reinforcement that crime is more prevalent in the lower social classes than others. He uses subjective observation and one or two case studies, confident that 'Reality will force theory to its knees.' (Murray 1990, p. 35). One is left wondering how those members of the Royal Family who have regularly been convicted of drinking and driving, or illegal drug possession would react to Murray labelling them as 'classic members of the underclass'. The Criminology Department of the University of Edinburgh published major research findings in October 1992 which indicate that middle class children are as likely to be involved in criminal activity as those from working class areas, providing an empirical demolition of this particular aspect of Murray's thesis. (Campbell, D., Jan 1993).

Lastly, 'The definitive proof that an underclass has arrived is that large numbers of young, healthy, low-income males choose not to take jobs.' He adds cautiously, but anecdotally, 'The young idle rich are a separate problem' (p.35), but does not offer any explanations as to how they differ. And if that were not bad enough, according to Murray, the 'black economy' is rampant in Britain among those who are officially registered as unemployed and are in receipt of welfare benefits, but who are clandestinely working for money, and failing to declare it.

These three key groups mentioned by Murray have also been adopted by Wilson (1987) as the basis for defining an 'underclass'. He goes on to link these three - unemployment among young males; the upsurge in the numbers of young single mothers; and the rising criminal activity among some young men - through the introduction of the concept of the 'marriageable pool'. This pool of marriageable men - i.e., the source of potential husbands or long term partners for young women - has been decreasing in size, at least in American cities. Notwithstanding the decisions women might make about their choice of working or not, and notwithstanding whether many women might or might not want to acquire a 'traditional' husband or partner, such marriageable men are becoming more and more scarce. Increasing numbers from the ghettos are unemployed or casually employed, or are frequently imprisoned because of their careers of crime. The marriageable pool is getting smaller among the 'underclass', resulting in an increase in lone mothers.

Predictably, Murray's solutions to the three main elements of an 'underclass' are steeped in orthodox economic and social theory: punish the unemployed through withdrawal of all benefits; punish the criminals through more use of prisons; and even punish the young single mums through 'social stigma' and reducing the financial incentives (benefits) to getting pregnant. 'Social stigma is an essential ingredient of social order and must, slowly and cumulatively, be restored.' (Murray, 1990). Implicit in these measures and explicitly stated by Murray, the 'underclass' is the pathological manifestation of a tradition of dependency generated by state welfare provision. By proposing economic measures as a response to what Murray believes is an economic phenomenon, he overlooks the fact that, although welfare benefit levels afford a lifestyle of bare subsistence, it can hardly be argued that they function as a financial incentive to pursue the life of a single parent. For Murray, fundamentally, his 'underclass' thesis was not an attempt to reinforce the culture of poverty model: on the contrary, in line with orthodox economic theory, he consciously swerved towards an explanatory model based on financial decisions. If his 'underclass' could be defined in relation to long term dependency on welfare handouts, then such dependency was the result, not of cultural traits, but of a rational decision taken by some poor families that, all things considered, they were better off in receipt of benefits than making the effort to avail of the opportunities which society offered to all citizens. Providing social security benefits at a level which allowed this situation to occur is tantamount to an expression of disrespect for the 'respectable' poor who work hard to make ends meet on low wages. The answer, of course, for Murray and his cohorts, does not lie in setting a minimum wage level which would keep those in employment on incomes above the state-determined welfare benefit levels: this would be unacceptable interference in the free market economy. The policy response is to radically reduce or, for many on the Right, abandon social security provision for the unemployed. However, it is apparently much more probable that such policy measures as Murray proposes, which are clearly intended to discourage irrational behaviour and decisions, will actually result in a deterioration of the phenomenon they are planned (ostensibly) to tackle - i.e. the consolidation of the marginalisation and exclusion of the poor from the general community.

This has been apparent, Cornford (1992, p. 60) argues in the social security system of the 1980s. In encouraging division rather than integration, the ethos of the scheme has been to provide benefits as a right to the 'deserving' cases who have worked for and earned them and to deter the 'undeserving' from claiming other than as a last resort: 'Hence that other demon of welfare, "the scrounger", the individual version of the underclass'. The stated objective of social security throughout the Thatcher years has been to target benefits on those most in need, practically to make the most efficient use of scarce resources, and morally distinguishing between those who really need help and those who can be blamed for their own difficulties. This leads to a two-tier system, with a sympathetic scheme for the 'respectable' needy and begrudged provision for the 'underclass', reinforcing their isolation and perpetuating their 'threatening' behaviour.

In relation to this, both proponents and critics of the concept of the 'underclass' agree that the emergence and expansion of such a group is closely linked to the increase in persistent and long term unemployment. But the bulk of research findings suggest that persistent unemployment is the product of structural and institutional factors and not of the aspirations and attitudes of those most vulnerable to it. And also proven is the obvious fact that the unemployed become isolated from contact with those in employment, further alienating them from the work society. Data from the Social Change and Economic Life Initiative 1986/7 survey showed that the unemployed were less likely than the employed to engage in leisure activities with non-family members. As the period of unemployment lengthens, the pattern of sociability declines. The unemployed also have different social networks from the employed. The latter consisting mainly of others in employment, whereas among the unemployed, contact with people with jobs gradually declines. Unemployed people, in the words of one of the researchers:

> found themselves increasingly cut off from an effective support system that could help them meet financial difficulties, that could give psychological support and that could provide information about jobs that was needed if people were to escape from the condition of unemployment. Changes in the pattern of sociability therefore increasingly helped to reinforce their exclusion from the labour market. (cited in Smith, D. 1992, p. 91)

As regards crime being a significant explanatory indicator of an 'underclass', it is retorted by authors such as Bill Jordan (1989, p. 104) that a highly individualistic society, as envisaged by the Right, would generate irresistible incentives to employ illegal methods to attain what society has held up to the population as achievable. In order to obtain the incentives and rewards available to the majority in the labour market, those excluded must 'do the double'. In order to acquire property, they must steal. In order to bring about a more equitable distribution of power in society, they must use violence. The fact that a disproportionately large number of the 'underclass' engage in criminal activity, makes it very difficult for the police to apprehend more than a token few examples. It is thus in the collective interests (the 'common good') of such an 'underclass' to have as many members as possible engaged in lawlessness. When such individuals come to the attention

167

of the statutory social services, usually via the courts system, Rodger (1988) argues that 'correctional' rather than 'appreciative' approaches of social work intervention reinforces their awareness of isolation, difference, exclusion.

Paul Spicker (1993) has more general, fundamental criticisms to make of Murray's 'underclass' thesis, particularly t he fact that Murray's arguments are based almost entirely on observed material, with a virtual total absence of any evidence or data to reinforce his views. For example, long term unemployed households develop a dependency upon welfare handouts. There are central assumptions in such arguments: (a) incentives and disincentives are successful operatives; (b) individuals avoid work and practice immorality. Thus if people are provided by the state with an income for simply being idle, that is the option that they will naturally choose. But they must accept the responsibility for such choices. Conservative philosophy has traditionally adhered closely to the notion of original sin and the imperfectability of human beings. Spicker has three central problems with these assumptions:

1 responses are proportionate to financial incentives - the bigger the incentive, the greater the response - but it may require a considerably substantial incentive to alter preferences and choices - wherewithal to finance such idleness, then financial incentives would need to be proportionately massive. Are these idle rich then to be labelled as belonging to an 'underclass'?;

2 incentives are influenced by costs and benefits and the financial costs of being poor, unemployed or a single parent are substantial;

3 Murray concentrates upon economic incentives and thus ignores moral, social and psychological elements. Recent Tory philosophy appears to have concentrated too strongly on the inherent weaknesses of human nature, rather than on human worth and dignity.

There is thus strongly convincing evidence which is in direct conflict with theories which explain the 'underclass' as a product of either a shift or a decline in cultural values, or a reaction to the nature of welfare benefits. The available data suggest that a more feasible account centres on persistent high unemployment as a result of the inherent inability of the labour market to absorb economic recession. This weakness arises from the nature of and relations within the institutions of the labour market and from the conflictual arrangements between employers and trade unions. Certain families and groups are hardest hit by long term unemployment and gradually become detached from the employed sphere. This, in turn, leads to the development of different lifestyles and radical restructuring of their cultural values as a result of their unemployment. Dahrendorf (1992, p. 57) summarises the ethical dilemma for the powerful in British society of the existence and level of tolerance of an 'underclass':

> They could live quite happily with an underclass of 5, 10, 12, 15 per cent for a very long time and if they are rich enough and have (suitable) arrangements ... they can feed the underclass and not bother about the fact that they are not part of the labour market and indeed may not be a part of political or social life in general ... tolerating a group of people for whom this is true, while professing values like those of work and the family, means that one tolerates a not insignificant group who has no stake in the accepted general values ... (thus) one cannot be surprised if people at the margin, and many others, increasingly cast doubt on these values and the values themselves begin to become much more tenuous and precarious than is sustainable for any length of time ... many of the breaches of law and order in our cities express a disdain for prevailing values ... the underclass is not going to march on Westminster or start a new class war; but the underclass is the living doubt in the prevailing values which will eat into the texture of t he societies in which we are living. In fact, it has already done so, which is why there is a very strong moral case for doing something about it.

What remains to be held valid is the concept of the 'underclass' as a comprehensive and persuasive explanation of, not just poverty and deprivation in Britain, but most essentially, inequality. Murray and his cohorts are engrossed in the behaviour of the poor and seemingly not concerned in the least with the behaviour of the rich. Bob Holman (August 1990) explains:

> Murray has no blame for the behaviour of the rich. Cabinet ministers who beget children outside of marriage, Oxbridge students who use drugs, stockbrokers who commit fraud, the London Docklands affluent ... build security fences to make themselves a separate group do not lead Mr. Murray to write an attack on the "overclass". By just blaming the poor, he is just making them victims.

Murray's ideological stance allows the public to acknowledge that poverty exists: but we have no reason to feel guilty about it or to do any collective thing about it. What appears to have been established thus far is that the idea of the 'underclass' has provided a degree of foresight into the future shape of British social structures if current policies, debates and trends continue, whatever the causal factors., However, there is a clear dilemma for proponents of the anti-social underclass thesis in terms of the policy prescription for dealing with these 'problems'. Murray would have communities and society shame the members of the underclass into a 'normal' or 'conventional' lifestyle - i.e. integrating them rather than excluding them. The paradox is clarified by Braithwaite (1989):

> Interdependent persons are more susceptible to shaming ... societies in which individuals are subject to extensive interdependencies are more likely to be communitarian ... shaming produced by communitarianism can be either of two types - shaming that becomes stigmatisation and shaming that is followed by reintegration ... in societies where shaming does become reintegrative, low crime rates are the result ... Shaming that is stigmatising ... makes criminal subcultures more attractive. (cited in Rodger 1992, p. 612)

This chapter has referred to the arguments which suggest that social and economic policies involving the 'underclass' have had much more of a stigmatising than a reintegrative effect, thereby perpetuating the perceived deviant behaviour and the existence of this marginalised sub-people. In discussing the problem of poverty in 1913, famous social democrat, Richard Tawney, expressed sentiments which are as pertinent to understanding the 'underclass' in Britain int h e 1990s as they were in the pre-war era. Poverty is:

> the condition of the normal man (and woman) in normal circumstances, neither better nor worse off than his (or her) neighbours, not of those whose failings qualify them to be the text for moralists, and who are no more common int eh manual working classes than in other sections of the society. It is in short the question of the economic status and opportunities of those who make up seven-eighths of this community, not of any submerged residuum ... The problem of poverty with which the student is concerned is primarily an industrial one - and only secondary in its manifestations - (found) in the mill, in the mine or at the docks - not in casual wards or on the embankment. (cited in Townsend 1976, p. 171)

Conservative MP for Stratford-upon-Avon, Alan Howarth (1993, p. 15) warns that there is a crucial need for clarification about the language which we use when discussing poverty because such talk demonstrates as much about the value systems of the commentators as those of the poor. Terms which have come to replace poverty - social exclusion, dependency, underclass' - all express our own moral fear and disapprobation. The 'underclass' is a source of concern to society in general, less because of their material deprivation and more because they appear to refuse to conform to widely held norms. The 'underclass' are wilfully ignorant, sexually subversive, idle, welfare scroungers, recidivist criminals and society can and should use social policy to launch a counter attack. Instead, Howarth argues that: 'Conservatives should insist, not only that there is such a thing as society, but that human dignity can only be realised in community. Unemployment and poverty are conditions of exile from community, and their existence diminished us all.'

170

Whether through moral panic or frantic economic concern, attacks on the living standards of single mums and their children, on the long term unemployed, would simply encourage more bitterness and impoverishment and lead to a truly troublesome, destabilising and ultimately destructive 'underclass'.

Conclusion

Introduction

This conclusion will offer some statistical and anecdotal evidence of the extent, causes and nature of poverty in Britain in the 1990s. It will specifically summarise a research exercise and findings already published in 'Poverty: Rowntree Revisited' (Stitt & Grant 1993) in order to reinforce the central theme permeating the arguments in this book so far: i.e. the vast bulk of poverty in Britain is the product of structurally induced social and economic policy by, not only the Tory governments of the 1980s and 90s, but also, of successive governments in modern history. This exercise measured the extent of **'primary poverty'** in Britain, this is, poverty caused by receipt of inadequate income, earned or otherwise, no matter how wisely spent, and therefore, by definition, poverty beyond the control of individuals and households. Evidence from other research and discussions on related policy developments in the 1990s will also be presented to offer a comprehensive portrayal of a poverty, approaching Third World proportions, in one of the richest nations on earth as we approach the 21st century.

There are a number of facets to the concept of social citizenship and the levels of empowerment that this entails. Relative notions of deprivation have exposed the exclusion of low income households from 'social life'. But an

---

[1] *(This section has been researched by and jointly written with Diane Grant, researcher at the Centre for Consumer Education & Research, Liverpool John Moores University)*

etc. This concluding chapter presents the findings of research which has aimed to 'step into Seebohm Rowntree's shoes' and establish a primary/subsistence poverty line for families with children in Britain in the 1990s. This poverty line will then be applied to official data to determine the numbers living in Britain below such a standard of living and these will be compared to the findings of Rowntree in 1899, 1941 and 1950.

The central task of the research is to employ a heuristic measurement of poverty - i.e. 'primary subsistence poverty' - adopted originally for this purpose by B.S. Rowntree in 1899, and to draw such a poverty line for 1992 which will be used to measure the extent of this type of deprivation in Britain today. The task is not another phrasemongering attempt to propose a different model of measuring/defining poverty. A core premise of the exercise is to accept, as Rowntree did, the arena for analysis set by the policy making process as the terms of reference for the debate. Rowntree founded his 1899 study upon the same approach - his primary poverty line was constructed so that not even the most vehement critics of his conclusions could accuse him of including non-necessities in his weekly subsistence standards or of grinding a political axe. The poverty line drawn in this exercise will follow as closely as possible, the methodology, approach, values and decisions identified in Rowntree 1899 exercise (with the exception of fuel, which will be explained in that section). Rowntree published the results of his major studies in 1901, 1936/41 and 1951. In each, he drew a subsistence poverty line and measured the numbers of people living on or below this standard in the city of York. Each time, he found poverty was decreasing in numbers. Pilot studies carried out recently (Stitt 1992) suggests that this research will show a substantial nation wide increase in subsistence poverty - i.e. an inability to afford necessities for physical efficiency. The aim is to allow those who deny the existence of such deprivation to determine the measurement, and then to test this against official data sources and original, 'fresh' data. Thus, not only will the numbers living on or below such a standard be shown, but these calculations will be compared with those of Rowntree's findings to construct an historical comparison.

A subsistence food minimum has been drawn up using the opinions and calculations of expert nutritionists. A primary fuel poverty line has been constructed by seeking expenditure data from poor households. The clothing index is the product of gathering opinions from the same households as to their ideas of a minimum wardrobe stock. The sundries element has involved using Rowntree's judgements to draw up an informed, yet somewhat subjective calculation of the minimum sundry necessities required for a subsistence lifestyle. Then these calculations will be aggregated into a weekly income level for an adult couple with two children aged eleven or under, not as a recommendation or prescription, but simply to argue that the extent of such poverty as uncovered by Rowntree in the first half of the 20th century.

Poverty is not only about shortage of money. It is about rights and relationships; about how people are treated and how they regard themselves; about powerlessness and loss of dignity. Yet the lack of an adequate income is at its heart. (Faith in the City, Church House, 1985)

The research

A study of 'primary poverty' in families with children, based on he works of B.S. Rowntree, was conducted in 1992 by a team of researchers at the Centre for Consumer Education & Research at Liverpool John Moores University. The aims of the exercise were to: (1) establish the depth and nature of **inescapable** poverty among families with children and; (2) determine, using Rowntree's methods and rationale, whether the numbers of citizens living in primary/subsistence poverty in the UK had increased or decreased. The study took almost exactly the same form as that employed in 1899 by Rowntree and his investigators, with the use of the interview as the main contact from which information was obtained. Rowntree also used the expert opinions of nutritionists to calculate a basic dietary and he made subjective assessments of the day-to-day household sundries element of the budget. In all of Rowntree's calculations, he was careful to ensure that only a minimum budget standard was adhered to (Rowntree 1901, p. 101). He was conscious of the fact that anything over and above such a standard would have rendered his work vulnerable to attack from those whom he sought to inform - i.e. the policy making process. The expertise in the study came from community dieticians, nutritionists, home economists and clothing experts, all of whom contributed to constructing what Rowntree called in 1901, a 'primary poverty' line - a standard of subsistence and physical efficiency below which it was not possible to live a non-poor lifestyle no matter how frugally and providently the weekly budget was manipulated. He interviewed those people who resided in areas where evidence of his own theories were observed - i.e. pinched faces, ragged clothes and squalid housing.

Rowntree had determined a primary poverty line for a 'moderate family' which, at that time, consisted of mother, father and three children. Changes in family size over time have reduced the most typical family composition (with children) to one constituting a couple and two primary school children and so this model has been used for the purpose of this study. It was thought to be impractical and inappropriate to follow Rowntree's rationale for reaching a 'poor' sample - by observing traits and behaviour patterns normally associated with the poor - in 1992. The current Income Support levels were used to determine an arbitrary measure from which, it could be assumed, families fitting our moderate size and relying on such a benefit could be construed, without challenge, as poor and thus targeted. As this benefit represents the safety net income for all citizens (in theory), it has become accepted as a semi-official poverty line. After contacting the sample through various agencies and publications, it was possible to arrange informal meetings with families, enabling the nature and ethos of the work to be scrutinised before households made the decision whether or not to take part. The meetings were conducted to explain the nature of Rowntree's work and to 'break the ice' for some of the families who viewed with natural and conditioned suspicion, anyone who wanted to know personal details of their income and expenditure.

Clothing

For the clothing component, the interviewer used the question Rowntree had posed to his sample in 1899 *verbatim*:

> What in your opinion is the very lowest sum upon which a (man) family can keep him/herself in clothing for a year? The clothing should be adequate to keep the man (family) in health, and should not be so shabby as to injure his chances of obtaining respectable employment. Apart from these two conditions, the clothing to be the most economical obtainable.' (Rowntree 1901, p. 107-8)

Simple forms were completed with the help of the interviewer, denoting how much the families estimated that they required to spend on clothing and they were assisted with these by referring to clothing and footwear lists as guidelines. The respondents were asked by the interviewer to provide the cost of each particular item (the most economical price obtainable), and how long it would last. This enabled the researcher to cost the item down to a weekly sum and to construct a weekly clothing budget. As was shown in Chapter 4 on gender and poverty, in general, it is women who shoulder the task of managing the family budget and it was the women in the sample who were able to give the best estimates of the costs of clothing and how long they would last. The advisory clothing lists were drawn up by textile experts based on a minimum needs wardrobe. However, if items were considered essential by families and they had not been included in the list, the interviewer added them. Each item was then given an expected economical cost and lifespan based on the experience of the families and then reduced to a weekly replacement cost.

Many of the respondents quoted clothing replacement costs from small chain clothing stores or from markets. References were made to the quality of such items and how they did not expect to get 'too long out of them'. In addition, it was apparent that school uniform played a great part in helping the mothers to stretch their clothing budget. One parent expressed concern about the high cost of replacing 'good' trousers; she said that it was no use buying 'cheap'

175

for school, as they were worn 'day in, day out' for most of the year, so she preferred quality items as they had stood the test of time. Many families on Income Support receive help from local authorities in the form of School Clothing Grants. These grants can be a lifeline for these families, although, according to the families, the amounts allocated are insufficient to provide all the necessary school clothing. In order to reflect the monetary help given, the clothing estimates in this exercise were reduced to reflect the help afforded by these grants.

In general the women interviewed knew from hard experience how long a pair of shoes would last for their children. Some of the families interviewed stressed the difficulties they experienced when budgeting for children's footwear due to arduous wear and tear. One woman interviewed spoke of the anguish she felt every time her son needed his shoes replacing: 'approximately every six weeks, he wears away the front of his shoes.' The child's school has a policy of sending home children who turn up in training shoes, thus in the past, the mother has had to keep her son away from school until she has been able to purchase a new paid of school shoes. Another mother told of how her son came home only two days into the new term with holes in the knees of his trousers, and thus she reckoned he needed three pairs of trousers each term. As well as the durability of an article and the wear it receives, the rate of growth of children also contributes to the equation of replacement costs, with some families buying new shoes every three months as the children outgrow them. Often the only way in which families can keep up with the demand for clothing replacements is with the use of mail order catalogues (Cohen 1991). Some of the women had to use the catalogues to purchase Xmas clothing and presents resulting in further demands on their budgets.

One particular problem faced by mothers when replacing children's clothing and especially footwear, is that they are battling, on the one hand, with trying to budget for all the families needs whilst, on the other hand, the children are being coerced by the advertising industry into demanding brand names., The raising of children's awareness and expectations places added pressures on parents as well as increasing peer pressure of those children who are unable to obtain the goods due to limited parental income. The job of replacing clothing which is acceptable to the child can then become a battle of wits especially if it results in children refusing to wear certain items, as was cited in the survey. To those 'experts' who seek to criticize families for purchasing such goods, it might be worth noting that in this sample of families, those who had chosen the more expensive items of footwear generally found that they lasted longer, and that the cheaper version had to be replaced more often. On analysis, the weekly breakdown costs found the more expensive items to be more cost effective, although the initial outlay for many of the families prohibited such a choice.

176

One man spoke of how he justified his decision to spend £75 (by mail order) on a pair of Doc Marten boots. He argued that they were casual, classic boots, which were tough and waterproof, and as he walked everywhere, he needed strong footwear. He also said that if he obtained work, they would be hardwearing and serviceable. He expected them to last more than five years. In comparison, another respondent felt that he could only afford £15 for a pair of shoes but said that they would only last six to eight months, if he was lucky. The difference is that on average, the £75 pair of boots would cost 28 pence a week to eventually replace and the cheaper pair 46 pence per week, a blatant case of the poor paying more for basic necessities in life and an excellent example of the providence which characterises the financial decisions taken by many poor people, contrary to myths peddled by the orthodoxy and sections of the media. Generally men estimated more for their footwear costs than women; this was certainly the case with denim jeans, with the men quoting higher costs than women, justifying the theoretical point made on the political economy of household budgeting in the discussion on gender and poverty. It was found that essential items commonly taken for granted by the rest of society were omitted by the sample from the lists. Ladies' boots were one such item, with many of the women believing that they were not a necessity. Speaking about the boots she was wearing one woman remarked: 'One has a hole in it, the other hasn't, so I avoid puddle with this foot', symbolising the hard lessons learned by the poor in stretching their incomes.

Estimates of pricing were found to be significantly higher from one particular family in the sample. It was established that this family had only recently become dependent on Income Support, due to the closure of a local factory. The woman's personal clothing estimates, when costed, accounted for almost a quarter of the total weekly benefit allowed for the whole family. It was clear that the family had not yet come to terms with their new lowly financial status, nor had they attempted to purchase clothing from their reduced income. Feeling desperate at the level of benefit which the family had been allocated, the woman remarked that the payment they were receiving from the DSS to pay for all the family's needs and meet bills was not much above what she used to spend on food alone, when working. As in Rowntree's study, it would not have given a true picture if extreme estimates were included in the clothing budget (Rowntree 1901); therefore this family's clothing figures were omitted from the final calculations.

It was found that most of the families were adept at managing their budgets. Often faced with a changing set of priorities - e.g., a fuel bill or an urgent clothing replacement - they had found ingenious ways of stretching their meagre income: 'What you see outside is not the same as what is hidden' said one woman. 'I don't wear nighties, I would live a really nice one but I can't afford it. I usually wait and see if I get one as a gift or else I wear his (husband's) old T-shirts. No one sees them to they?' Another mother had found a way to save money on the children's nightwear by waiting for the sales of large T-shirts for £1 each and buying half a dozen. It appeared from the study that, for many men, the wearing of pyjamas is not the social custom it once was and this extended to boys, many of whom slept in their underwear. When men were asked what they would do about pyjamas if they needed to go into hospital, one man replied that he could borrow a pair or he would wear those issued by the hospital. Using the information obtained from the sample families, the research exercise was able to provide details of costings and construct of the weekly family clothing budget.

Fuel

In 1899, Rowntree constructed his own minimum fuel budget standard, basing his calculations on an assumption of needs as follows:
Summer ..... 1 bag of coal] Average 1½ bags of coal at 1s. 3d per bag:
Winter ..... 2 bags of coal] = 1s 10d per week.

The collection of fuel expenditure data in Rowntree's approach in 1936 and 1950 took the form of asking families what types of fuel they used and the estimated weekly costs. For convenience sake, this latter approach was adopted for the purposes of this study, even though, it must be acknowledged that equating actual expenditure with basic needs, particularly among fixed low income households, is fraught with methodological and practical difficulties. Some of the families, in common with other reported findings, had discovered that they were unable to budget for fuel bills and consequently found themselves in financial difficulties (Cohen, 1991). This resulted in direct deductions at source from their benefits to pay off the outstanding bills. Although this method is, superficially, convenient, it effectively pushes other necessities further down the priority list. It also takes away the freedom of choice that the majority of the working population take for granted. In one case, the mother, who was having £10 a week deducted from her benefit payments for fuel arrears, had no money left to buy food and her Child Benefit was not due until the following day, which resulted in the family going without food for over 24 hours. The payment of the (future) bill had effectively deprived the family of food.

Rowntree made the assumption in 1899 that, 'The amount of fuel used does not vary with the size of family as there is usually a fire in the living room only'. He estimated the costs of coal at 1s 3d per bag and allowed for two bags in winter and one bag in summer which averaged out at 1s 10d per week. In 1936 he simply obtained actual family fuel expenditure and averaged the amounts for the whole year. In 1950 Rowntree and Laver interviewed 30 households and obtained their estimates for coal, coke, gas and electricity in both winter and summer and averaged them down to a weekly cost of 7s 7d.

This study followed Rowntree's method of 1936 and 1950 in obtaining fuel expenditure from 18 families. Many of the households had already made arrangements with fuel suppliers to pay their bills by budget plans. The amounts quoted varied from £8.00 to £20.00 weekly for electricity, and from £2.12 to £15.00 for gas, relatively more than actual expenditure figures given in the Family Spending report for families of two adults and two children with incomes of less than £275 weekly: gas, £4.37; electricity £6.83 (1992 prices) (Central Statistics Office, 1992 p. 45). The Family Spending survey also found that the average weekly household expenditure on fuel was £11.11 for all households and £12.70 for all households with two adults and two children. The Social Trends report estimated that the average fuel expenditure for all households at current prices was 3.7% of the total income (CSO 1992, Table 1). The fuel expenditure as determined from this survey for families of two adults and two children in 1992 was £18.31, approximately 30% more than the amount cited in Family Spending, and amounts to more than 17% of total income for such families receiving their entitlements of £105 on Income Support. This could be due to a variety of factors such as price rises, housing type and insulation efficiency (Boardman, 1992 p. 15). Generally, it is the insulation of the property and the type of fuel and heating system which dictates whether a home can be made warm at an affordable cost, with insulation efficiency improving as incomes rise (Boardman 1992, p. 105). However it should be noted that families on low income tend to have the less efficient modes of heating, thereby incurring extra costs (Stitt, 1991). In addition to insulation and housing type, unemployment effectively compels families to spend long hours at home thereby incurring extra costs for heating. It would seem that higher fuel bills are endemic to unemployed and low income families.

It must also be pointed out here that no allowance has been made in the minimum fuel estimates for extra costs incurred by disability or illness. The OPCS (1988) Survey of Disability in Britain estimated that there were approximately 6.5 million children and adults with disabilities, the majority of whom are dependent upon welfare payments as their primary income source. This study suggested that more than one in three families with a disabled child needed to purchase more domestic warmth because of the disability and almost one in four disabled people could not afford to spend the extra money on fuel which their disability required.

Efforts to cut energy costs generally need capital expenditure to insulate homes (Boardman, 1992 p. 70). Certain schemes have operated in the past which attempt to help people on low income to reduce their fuel bills, but they are small scale affairs and cannot reach even a small fraction of the dwellings which require improvements. The Family Service Unit reported families turning off their heating until the children returned home from school in a desperate attempt to stave off high fuel bills, (Cohen, 1991) a practice known as 'voluntary disconnection'. In addition, fuel deductions at source from social security payments were made in 200,000 cases for gas and in 92,000 for electricity in 1992 (Lennard, 1993 p. 6). Other reports have emerged which found that four out of ten poor families were having deductions taken out of their social security to repay loans from the social fund (National Children's Homes 1992). The increased use of pre-payment meters can also be perceived as extending the opportunity for poor families to 'voluntarily' disconnect their fuel supply, effectively masking the true scale of fuel poverty because such consumers do not show up on the official disconnection statistics. In 1992, 2.3 million electricity and 780,000 gas pre-payment meters were in use in Britain (Lennard, 1993 p. 6).

For families caught up in the trap of rising bills with a static income, the results can be very stressful. One mother interviewed in this study told of how she has gone from a healthy ten stone woman, (she produced a photograph), down to a very unhealthy seven stone. Her doctor had prescribed anti-depressants and had advised her to 'stop worrying'. This family lived in a small terraced house which had one gas fire in the living room and no other forms of heating. The baby had been diagnosed as having asthma and the mother believes it is due t the dampness of the bedrooms caused by the lack of upstairs heating, a point well documented by medics (Radical Statistics Health Group, 1991). She would ideally like a mobile heater of some sort but cannot afford the initial outlay, nor does she want the added fuel costs. This catch-22 situation is not uncommon among many families who effectively are confined to one room in a dwelling due to a lack of affordable heating.

Personal and household sundries

When Rowntree calculated his budget for personal and household sundries in 1899, he gave no real explanation as to how he arrived at his figures. What was clear from his amounts was that Rowntree had not in fact allowed for any form of travelling, leisure pursuits or 'luxuries' of any kind. It was also apparent that the cost of sick clubs and burial clubs had also been jettisoned. Rowntree obtained his information on household sundries from interviews with working class women. From this data, he estimated that the sum of 1s 8d weekly would cover all the necessary household sundries expenditure of a family of two adults and three children. Basically all that Rowntree had allowed for was the costs incurred in 'washing and cleaning materials, renewals of linen, pots and pans'. In his subsequent surveys Rowntree was not so parsimonious, as he acknowledged that the poor, like others, 'could not live on fodder along'. He began to include various items which were of a minimum nature but which reflected current social practices. For example,

180

he allowed for the daily purchase of a newspaper, the use of a wireless, travelling expenses to and from work (1s.), and sick club and trade union subscriptions. In the calculation of the personal sundries element, Rowntree was forced to make certain subjective assumptions on the elements of his minimum subsistence standard. He found great variance among the expenditure quoted from the men he interviewed, ranging from 6s 11d to 20s 5d a week. Rowntree stated: 'as a result of my enquiries, I came to the conclusion that 9s a week was the lowest sum that I could include in my budget for personal sundries'. He invited readers to judge whether his allowance was liberal or otherwise.

In order to calculate a 1992 minimum sundries budget, social and economic changes that have occurred since those historical surveys had to be taken into account. Just as Rowntree had found it difficult to make judgements on what to include and exclude, so did the team engaged on the Liverpool Study. The personal care budget included a small first aid kit, items for personal cleanliness and a minimum amount of cosmetics. All of the items were scrutinised by a team of home economists and brought down to what can only be described as a minimum needs budget, exactly what Rowntree had attempted to construct. To illustrate the complexity of the task, one need only look at the list of items available today for personal care. Is it reasonable to include hair conditioner, or moisturiser, after-shave or perfume? Obvious needs such as toothbrushes and sanitary protection were included, as were hair brushes and combs. The list became more niggardly as the items were pruned down; an example of the subjectivity of the task involved is illustrated by deciding how often would a person need to get a hair-cut - is twice a year a minimum standard? The final assessment of the aggregated responses amounted to £6.49 weekly for a family personal care budget. It must be stressed here that no allowances whatsoever have been made for expenditure on alcohol or tobacco, even though many social scientists (e.g. Graham, 1984) argue that, for example, smoking is a necessity for maintaining many families' health, as it can be a means by which mothers of low income households cope with the daily stresses and strains of a poverty lifestyle. However, again in pursuit of pre-emptying predictable criticisms for including non-necessities, these two contentious items were disregarded.

Certain household items are now taken for granted and in 1992 have been deemed as essential. Items such as televisions, telephones, refrigerators and washing machines are owned by the vast majority of the population and the costs of replacing some such items have been included in the budget. The inclusion of a television thereby incurs further costs in the form of a television licence required by law. Grey areas still exist, in particular in the ownership of or access to a video recorder, inclusion of a family holiday, day trips or visits to the cinema. The team excluded certain items from the list and did not follow the rationale for inclusion solely on the grounds that a large percentage

181

of the population have access to such items. The rental of a telephone is one item the team felt could be 'done without', even though the Family Spending survey cites 87.4% of the population having a telephone (CSO, 1992) and, it could be argued, it is an essential asset for an unemployed person actively seeking a job. The list of sundries was drawn up by the home economists involved in attempting to step into Rowntree's shoes and ask themselves the question: If Rowntree had been devising a minimum standard in 1992, would he, for example, have included a video recorder? The Liverpool team established that the cost of purchasing a video recorder was cheaper than hiring one. Similar debate ensued over the inclusion of trips to the cinema and if so, how many?: would it be construed as extravagant to include day trips, or a week's holiday? Some of the home economists placed a weeks' family holiday as a priority over the use of a video, others conceded that if a family had little money to actually go out, then the video recorder may be their only source of entertainment. The question then arose, if it was included, how often would films for leisure viewing be hired? Some said once weekly, others felt that beyond the bounds of necessity. In an effort to accommodate all opinions, it was decided to aggregate the estimates of all the researchers involved. Such a debate is, of course, ongoing as the social needs and expectations of even the poorest sections of the population evolve in tandem with *vox populi* and the dominant ideology.

A Mintel 1994 survey of 'British Lifestyles' showed that the number of households in Britain with three or more televisions had doubled since 1985 and the number of dishwashers had trebled. The survey, in observing that those who had weathered the recession lead an increasing luxurious lifestyle, showed that, while in 1939 food eaten at home accounted for about 40 percent of the average household expenditure, by 1993 this had fallen to 11 per cent (cited in Erlichman, Feb. 2nd 1994). The food estimates in this poverty line accounts for almost one third of the weekly sum. Between 1985 and 1993, the national amount spent in Britain on hair and beauty treatment increased by £2.1 billion; private education fees rose from £1.4 billion to £5.4 billion; between 1988 and 1993, the numbers taking their main holidays abroad increased - those holidaying in Britain fell from 34 million to 26 million. Although, in general, the nation's standard of living increased and for the non-poor, their lifestyles have improved significantly, these 'relative' trends have not been allowed to influence the 'primary poverty' estimates of minimum needs in this survey. Hopefully, this reinforces the harsh stringency of the poverty line constructed and the desperately poor lifestyles led by those whose incomes, through no fault of their own, fall below the primary poverty line.

Household goods such a furniture, carpets, curtains and all household textiles were discussed with the aim of reducing the list to a minimum amount. Debate ensued as to whether it was reasonable to suggest that new items of furniture as opposed to second-hand should be costed. As a way of resolving this issue, both new and 'older' pieces of furniture were costed and given an approximate lifespan, with the result, as expected, being virtually no difference in the weekly cost. Reports have shown that it is no uncommon for people on low incomes to be without basic furniture and in many cases being unable to replace worn-out items (FSU 1991, CPAG 1992, p. 49). The Social Fund budgeting loan scheme was introduced to meet 'important intermittent expenses ... for which it may be difficult to budget'. The major drawback is that the loan has to be repaid out of weekly benefit, perpetuating greater difficulties, with families having to live on even less than the basic income support minimum for several months. Claimants are often refused Social Fund loans because they are deemed too poor (sic.) to be able to repay them. It is common practice for families on low incomes to obtain such items as household goods from mail order catalogues, indeed for many it is the only avenue open to them (CPAG, 1992). Without the capital to purchase outright, many families have to obtain such goods on the 'never, never', but a credit rating is often denied due to their economic status or previous bad debt.

Families interviewed in this study had in the past obtained Social Fund loans. One man spoke of how his family had been rehoused in a three bedroomed house from a one bedroomed flat. He had applied for a loan for furniture, beds, bedding and carpets; he had 'put in for more', as he was told that 'they never give you what you ask for' He was allocated £150, ' joke' he commented, 'the thing is, they are not giving it to you, you still have to pay it back'. Another woman spoke of her son, who has a rare disease which results in him vomiting regularly. Her washing machine 'packed up', and she applied for a budgeting loan for a washer-drier, her application being supported by medical letters explaining her son's problem. She was refused on the grounds that she had an immersion heater and a veranda on which to dry her clothes. ?She also had an outstanding Social Fund loan for a telephone installation which she was paying back at the rate of £10 weekly. She was told at the time that a telephone was considered a luxury item but in view of her son's medical situation they allowed her the loan. Stores such as these illustrate the difficulties families face when household items need replacing and why it is important to quantify these items in a minimum weekly sum and include them in the weekly budget. The aggregated amount estimated for household goods in this Rowntree 1992 poverty line was £16.58 a week and for household services, £2.72.

Leisure is an area which the majority of the population take for granted; its pursuit, however, is denied to many living on low incomes as the cost is prohibitive. For a family to take a weekly swimming session at a local pool would cost around £5. A trip to the cinema would cost over £10 for our moderate family of four, which is almost 10 per cent of the total Income Support rate of £105 for our family. In adhering to Rowntree's ethos of physical efficiency, it was determined that weekly trips to the local baths could not be construed as extravagant, indeed many reports have expressed concern about the health effects of lack of exercise on both adults and children. Critics could argue that the swimming trips could be substituted with a brisk walk, itself a valuable exercise, but alternatively it could be argued that, by the whole family taking part in such a social as well as healthy pastime, this is, in the longer term, more enjoyable and cost effective in terms of morale and well being. It would also help them save on their water heating bills, as a shower following a swim would help them avoid taking a bath/shower at home. In addition, most of the nation's poorest families living in 'inner cities', much removed from areas which are designed for (and indeed safe for) leisure walking. Constantly adhering to the frugality of Rowntree's minimum budget standard, it was decided that only one trip per week per person, using local public transport cheap day tickets would be included. This presupposes that all shopping or visits to relatives or the cinema or baths should be undertaken in one journey in the same day. Therefore the minimum weekly cost of transport for a family of four would cost £4.90. If we compare the cost of a family swimming session of £5 to the average expenditure on leisure services for similar family compositions of £27.67 weekly (CSO 1992), it reiterates the meagreness of the amount allowed. Visits to the cinema were not deemed by the team to be essential and **only one trip per year** was included in the list.

Rather than list the items which were included, a more illustrative perception of the minimum standard for leisure is provided if some of the major items not included were mentioned. There is no allowance for entertainment outside the home in the form of a social evening or a dance or disco; no allowance has been made for alcohol; trips to the zoo, theatres, and funfairs have all been omitted. No allowance has been made for spectator sports such as football matches, nor has membership of and subscriptions to children's groups been disallowed for - e.g. Scouts, Cubs, Brownies and Guides - as well as participatory club sports - e.g. judo, keep fit, dancing lessons etc. Rowntree allowed for the purchase of a daily newspaper, as did this study, but only for the cheaper tabloid types and no allowances were made for the purchase of magazines, records or comics. The following quotation describes poignantly the practical implications of the lack of resources available to obtain such items for one of the men interviewed:

> Do you know what hurts the most, and I can put up with most things, it's not being able to put my hand in my pocket and buy a magazine. I can be in WH Smith's and see a magazine I would really like, but I haven't got £2 in my pocket to call my own. It's the little things that really get me down.

He went on to say that he can live with the deprived state of his own life but he felt degraded for his children:

I haven't had a holiday for twelve years now, the last one I had was before I got married. Then we had the kids and money was short, then I lost my job. The kids have only been to Blackpool for two weekends with the grandparents. Sometimes she (wife) would go and stay one night for a break, but me, I haven't been anywhere'. He went on to describe the struggle involved when the school sends letters home for money for day trips: 'I know they can't do anything about it, they have to ask for kids to go to Camelot. We ended up borrowing the money from her mother. I couldn't have told the school I didn't have it, well, it would have looked awful on the kids, wouldn't it? I know of kids around here whose parents keep them off when a day trip is laid on because they can't afford it and they won't tell anyone. People have got pride.

Many children who display musical talents are given lessons by their LEA as part of their schooling. This incurs costs for the parents in the purchase of replacement parts for instruments and purchase of new music books. One parent whose daughter was taking part in a concert explained that all the family would like to go and see her perform and the daughter wanted them to attend, but at £4 a ticket only one of them could afford to go. The aggregate amount allocated by the research team for leisure goods and services amounted to £14.35 weekly.

Rowntree devised his primary poverty line without housing costs. This study has adopted the same approach, but with some important differences imposed on the calculations b y recent developments. Since the abolition of the local council rates system and the implementation of the Poll Tax in 1989, (which was replaced by the Community Charge in 1993, after the conclusion of this stage of the research) adults who previously received housing benefit due to entitlement to Income Support or Unemployment Benefit have had to contribute 20 per cent of the full rate out of their benefit. The Poll Tax bill varied between councils, as does the Community Charge levy, and in Liverpool the annual amount payable for 1992 was £398. The cost for those groups of people who have to pay 20 per cent therefore amounted to £1.53 weekly. In our moderate family, two adults would need to find £3.06 weekly for payment of the Poll Tax/Community Charge. As it is a compulsory/legal requirement, this study concludes that this amount should be included in the minimum household sundries list.

As a result of the abolition of the rating system, households who used to pay their water rates as part of their overall rates bill now receive separate notification of their water costs. In essence this bill is now deemed as important to families in terms of a necessity as gas or electricity, as non payment can result in disconnection the DSS acknowledges this fact by using the deduction at source practice such as that used for fuel debts to deduct water rates debt. The abolition of the rating system has also been responsible for the two tier system of measurement   now in practice by the private water companies.   Water rates used to be based on rateable values of properties; however dwellings completed after the abolition of rates do not have the rateable value assessed.   Some of the properties have been metered whilst some have been given an arbitrary rateable value based on similar properties and locations.   In the Merseyside area, rateable values vary due to property size and location.   A spokesperson for North West Water said that properties can have different water rates from one end of the street to the other.   One person interviewed had a rateable value of £97 p.a. whereas further up the road, the rateable value was £250 p.a.   The families interviewed in this study lived in a variety of dwellings with varying rateable values, each paying significantly varying water rates.   The water authority spokesperson determined a 'guestimate' figure of £200 p.a. as the best average of the rateable values of properties in Liverpool.   In view of the apparent differences of water rates payable by different households, it was decided to devise a water rates budget which would follow as closely as possibly Rowntree's minimum allowance.   This was achieved by using the so called 'average' rateable value of £200 as the starting point, then locating the lowest rateable value of the respondents questioned, which was £97 p.a.   The median sum was identified and thus the rateable value for a 'less than average' dwelling in Liverpool was determined at approximately £148.20.   The water rates figures has been calculated in the following way:

```
                                      £
Rateable value x .272p (Water services)  =  40.40
   "       "    x. 476p (Sewerage)        =  70.68
Plus Standing Charge                      =  25.00
                                            136.08
```

Thus a water charge of £136.08 would cost a household approximately £2.42 weekly.

Food:

It is apparent that constructing a food budget which fulfils government guidelines and conforms to present eating patterns would be paramount when constructing benefit levels.   The Department of Social Security do not appear to have undertaken such a fundamental exercise since the implementation of the standards suggested by Beveridge in 1942, which had been founded upon the Rowntree method of devising a dietary which was of a minimum nature, but adhering to current nutritional guidelines. (Stitt 1991).   Research conducted by concerned groups has found that food poverty exists on a far greater scale than was previously thought. (Milburn, Clark & Smith 1987,

Cole-Hamilton & Lang 1986). Estimates of the average weekly cost per person of the British diet taken from the Family Spending survey amount to £15.63 (at 1992 prices) among families of two adults and two children. For the same families with incomes below £275, the corresponding figure is £13.47 per person. Both of these estimates do not include sweets, alcohol or meals out. This study did not include these items in its calculations for two reasons: firstly, consumption of sweets and alcohol, whilst desirable by some and socially acceptable by many, is however not essential to health. Alcohol provides calories but little else in terms of nutrients, whereas sweets provide carbohydrates and calories and are known to contribute to the disease of dental cavities (Dept. of Health 1989); secondly, inclusion of such items would attract condemnation which would ultimately detract from the fundamental aims of the study which are to follow as closely as possible the methods of Rowntree. Rowntree did not include alcohol in his 1899 poverty line - but did so in her 1936 and 1950 studies. In stating that it would not be prudent to include them, the study acknowledges and accepts the criticism that food budgets should include items and costings that reflect social customs. By opting to leave these popular items out, the absolute frugality of the dietary is reinforced and offered only as a minimum subsistence standard for food. The social stigma and feelings of degradation for children who cannot afford to buy any sweets and for adults who avoid nights out because they cannot afford to buy a drink have, of necessity, been excluded from consideration.

One of the most flexible items in a household budget is food but to expect families to make changes which could cost them more is inconceivable. However it has been found that even though constrained by low income, poor families were able to purchase nutrients more cost effectively than their wealthier counterparts (with the exception of vitamin C). Health and nutrition education has been quite successful but it cannot solve the fundamental problem of poverty preventing families from affording a dietary which is conducive to physical efficiency, customary and likely to be eaten. Whilst on the one hand, educators in schools are informing their charges of what constitutes a healthy diet, at lunch time the practice is somewhat different. Those who stay for free school meals, as was the case for the children in this study's nutritional guidelines. The problems are then compounded at home where choice of foods in low income households is limited to what is left in the cupboard. One mother explained how distressed she felt when her children came home from school after having taken part in a healthy food lesson: 'Mum, why don't we eat healthy food? The teacher says we should have fruit every day'. This mother had previously described how she manages when money is short: 'If I need extra money for say something like clothes or a bill, it is generally the food that I have to cut back on. I buy a 56lb sack of spuds and two trays of eggs, then for tea its either egg and chips or chips and eggs. The other day I only had two eggs int he fridge so I made scrambled eggs and toast for him and the kids and I just had a cup of coffee. That is all I had until the next day when I cashed my order book.'

One of the women interviewed told of how she had explained to her family doctor that she was suffering from tiredness, bloated stomach and persistent constipation. The doctor informed her that she was not eating the correct foods, that changing her dietary to include more fruit and vegetables would help. She was also told to cut down on fat consumption. Her response was to buy low fat spread instead of her usual cheaper margarine. But what she found was that the family did not like the new spread and refused to eat it; she did not believe it was worth trying again as it had cost her more money to buy the low fat spread than her usual butter. As for the fruit and vegetables, she said she simply could not afford to buy them. Some families often found that they had run out of food before their benefit was due. This was occasionally overcome by making abundant supplies of tea and toast and going to bed early. The women's meals often consisted of eating the leftovers from their children's plates.

For many families in the sample, there was a strong dependence on the goodwill of others when it came to food. Couples told of how each set of grandparents help them out on a weekly basis. One woman's parents brings a bag of meat which includes mince and a chicken to the family home each week, whilst her husband's parents bring fresh fruit and vegetables from their local market. Accessibility to economical foodstuffs is a major factor for low income families. The latter family live on a recently built housing estate, their nearest local shop is expensive and the cheaper supermarket is a 25 minutes bus ride away. This family budget just on £20 weekly for food, (£5 per person per week) and believe that they would not manage to pay for their bills without the help they receive from their parents. As well as receiving help for food once a week, one of the grandparents comes to their home to take them to a large discount supermarket for all their weekly shopping. One family who had no one such as grandparents to turn to in a crisis were interviewed for the study. The mother had spoken about the time she had no money left from her benefit to buy baby food. She had a small stores of foods for the rest of the family but none were adequate for the seven month old baby. The DSS said they would not help her and she should try to get help from a friend or relative. In desperation she went to the local clinic and told them of her plight. They responded by giving her 24 cans of baby fisherman's pie dinners which had been poor sellers, and were coming to the end of their sell by dates. She commented wryly 'its a good job he likes them.' What if he hadn't?

Another mother did not even have a slice of bread in the house on the day her benefit was due. She had to get the children ready for school and they all had to leave the house without breakfast. She then queued at the Post Office for her benefit and rushed into the nearest cake shop and bought two pasties for the children to eat on their way into school. Before criticising this action, the first thing to be aware of is that the children received energy in a form that they would eat (giving them food which was unfamiliar may result in refusal to eat - food not eaten has no nutritional value whatsoever). The mother could have returned home with a packet of cereal and then the children would have arrived even later for school. The sad irony is that those two pasties could have provided box of healthy cereal for a week. This is not a criticism of how the situation was dealt with but an illustration of how poverty can generate poor and physically inefficient eating habits.

Some reports (mainly government commissioned) have commented that eating healthier food does not necessarily involve greater expense and in some cases can be cheaper than current average expenditure, whereas other sources have determined the opposite - that eating healthy food costs more. It is certainly borne out in the National Food Survey (1990) that those from higher income groups consume more nutritious foods and spend more money on their dietaries than socio-economic group E2. The lowest income group consumes, on average, more potatoes per person than all other income groups and more sugar, fats, cakes and biscuits than higher income groups, the foods which are, of course, cheaper to purchase, with a consequently lower nutritional value. A National Children's Home (1992) survey found that if poorer families had an extra £10 a week to spend, many stated that they would spend it on healthy foods - e.g. lean meat, vegetables, fruit etc. As well as obtaining their nutrients from their chosen foods much more cost effectively than non poor families, low income households face the inescapable dilemma of these foods also containing more fats and sugars. The poor cannot afford to make a mistake when it comes to nutrition, as food not eaten has no nutritional value. It is a perfectly sensible response by poor families to serve food which is tried and tested and which will be eaten and will satisfy, even though it is higher in fats and sugars. The concept of re-educating people into eating healthier is similarly sensible in principle, b ut the reality is that families in poverty do not have adequate funds from which to make such changes.

A study by the Food Commission and the National Children's Home charity in 1994 suggested that poor relief levels do not allow families to afford to buy the dietaries for children prescribed in Victorian workhouses, dietaries which include gruel, bread and meat only three days a week. The Chief Executive of NCH, Tom White stated: 'It is appalling as we approach the year 2000, that even an 1876 workhouse diet is too expensive for the families of one in four of our children.' (cited in Brindle, 2 February 1994). In Bethnal Green workhouse in London in 1876, a child's dietary included: breakfast of bread and gruel; lunch of bread, pea soup and suet pudding, or three days a week, meat and potatoes; supper of bread with milk, cheese of broth. At 1994 prices, such a weekly menu would have cost £5.46. The notional amount allowed for food (see Stitt 1989 for the process of arriving at such amounts) have been £4.15. A 1913 workhouse diet comprising: breakfast of bread and milk; lunch of beef, vegetables or potatoes and fresh fruit pudding; supper of seed cake and cocoa, would have cost £7.07 in 1994, 70 per cent higher than the poor relief food allowance in 1994. In an open letter to the Prime Minister, the NCH argued that such base poverty, homelessness and a crumbling welfare state are wrecking the lives of millions of British children: 'Back to basics is an ideal for these children too: the basics that so many of them lack - a home of their own, food on the table and warm clothes on their back.' (cited in Brindle, 2 February 1994).

These findings were ridiculed by Right-wing demagogue James Le Fanu, author of 'A Phantom Carnage: the Myth that Low Income Kills', written for the Conservative think-tank, the Social Affairs Unit. He mockingly derides the NCH's arguments in a dismissive manner which exposes a characteristic cruelty, or at best, nonchalance towards the poor in Britain. He asserts: 'Any modern day Oliver Twist would be snatched up by the Social Services before he could lift up his bowl to ask piteously for "More please".' Calling the findings 'barely credible', 'ludicrously inflated', 'downright nonsense', 'manipulative', 'an appalling claim', and the researchers 'poverty mongers', his **SOLE** 'evidence' which he offer to contradict the mountain of data from social scientists, pressure groups and the poor themselves, is that he visits homes in inner city areas and sees ' ... that they are not overcrowded. They **usually** have sole use of a bathroom, there is the inevitable TV and often a video is b linking away beneath it.' And that was the extent of his 'common sense' argument. Le Faum's poisonous ravings are only given space in this book to make the following points: his statements reflect the nature of widespread perceptions of poverty, the poor and poor relief in the policy making arena as we approach the 21st century; his total lack of any empirical data to substantiate his Poor Law attitudes makes research exercises like this all the more important; his assertions that, for example, if a home is not overcrowded and the family have sole use of a bathroom, a television and, perhaps, a video recorder, then they could not possibly be poor. Within this assertion lies the true views of the True Blues on the definition of poverty. Le Fanu is a general practitioner, whose weekly income would be in the region of £1,000 per week. Without an iota of research into the issues which he so wisely presents himself as an expert, it would be tempting to ignore his arguments as those of the loony-Right. This would be an extraordinarily dangerous approach to take as be belongs to and publishes for the Social Affairs Unit, an advisory think-tank of the Tories.

The study team believed that it would be virtually impossible to devise a universally acceptable dietary and so the decisions on which foods to be included in the shopping basket were determined by consulting National Food Survey (NFS) data and with reference to the National Advisory Council on Nutrition Education (NANCE 1983) report and the government's Dietary

Recommended Values (DRVs) (Committee on Medical Aspects - COMA - 1991). The reasons for choosing such a frugal diet have been to establish the austerity of the methods of Rowntree, who had used dietaries inferior to those afforded to the paupers in the workhouses of York, and to adhere to his criteria of a physical efficiency diet. Rowntree observed the diets of many families and he included their food choices in his dietary, whilst fulfilling the minimum nutritional requirements laid down by American nutritionist Atwater (Rowntree 1901, p. 94). In Formulating a 1992 Rowntree dietary, the only variable used was that of similarity to current consumer habits.

The construction of a subsistence dietary for 1992 had to take account of the enormous social and economic changes that have taken place since Rowntree's surveys. The revolution in food production, preparation and storage has been one of the major stimulus for change. Households now have a much wider choice of foods from a vast array of outlets. Ownership of refrigerators is now common and this fact influenced the first assumption made, that a moderate family would have the use of a refrigerator with a small freezing compartment. A further assumption was made that when the oven was in use, optimum utility was made of the space and energy to cook other foods. (However, a Mintel 1994 survey found that the poor may suffer from a lack of cooking facilities and fuel which may have a detrimental effect on their eating patterns - cited in@Erlichman, 2 February 1994). The dietary chosen was devised for one week only; it fulfilled the NANCE recommendations and the government's own DRVs. Rowntree's dietaries for adults were based on the nutritional requirements for a 'moderately active' lifestyle; the energy levels for the adults in this survey were based on an 'inactive lifestyle'. The dietaries in this study are thus lower in energy than those of Rowntree. In common with social custom and current practice, the protein content was constructed to provide approximately 15 per cent of the energy value of the whole diet. Rowntree calculated the energy requirement for each family member and then combined the totals to produce a total energy requirement for a family for one day. Similarly, this study determined the main nutrients for a 1992 dietary.

In common with Rowntree, there is little fresh butcher's meat; one chicken is used as the basis for two meals, liver is cooked once and a beef stew using minced beef, constitutes all the meat allowed for the week. The construction of the diet uses average portion sizes (Crawley 1988) and does not allow for fluctuations in appetite or personal preferences. Based on the assumption that maximum use is made of the oven when in use, scones and rice pudding can be made when the oven is in use. Fresh fruit is included on most days as is wholemeal b read and cereal. It was felt that in view of the vast array of convenience foods available, some token 'convenience' foods should be used. Frozen fish fingers are included, as are tins of tuna, baked beans, soup and tinned tomatoes; all these foods have been chosen primarily for the convenience factor and their nutrient content.

The costings for the foods used a nationwide community based food store which stocks brand name goods - Kwik-Save. This type of store was chosen in preference to other competitors who stock unknown branded foods, generally not of UK origin. The rationale for the decision to cost the basket of food here was based on two reasons: firstly, the customer needs to be sure that the food purchased will be eaten - unknown or strange brands may not be accepted by the family; secondly, when the other shops were visited, it was found that a large proportion of the foods did not display informative nutritional labelling. For economic reasons, most of the fresh fruit and vegetables were costed at a local street market which is easily accessible by good public transport. All households waste food but if all foodstuffs bought were consumed, it would reveal a higher energy intake per capita of the population. On average across all income groups, approximately 5 per cent to 7.5 per cent of household food ends up in the bin. (Winlock, Buss & Derry 1980). To strengthen the frugality of the dietary on offer,no allowance for wastage whatsoever has been built into the diet. In simple terms, all food purchased must be eaten, otherwise the nutrient standard specified will not be reached. A Mintel survey published in 1994 on 'British Lifestyles' revealed that families on poor relief benefits cannot afford to experiment with meals which might be rejected by their children. (cited in Erlichman, 2 February 1994)

The cost of free school meals was also a factor which served to reduce the food budget. Where parents receive Income Support, their children qualify for free school meals. The number of meals over the school year account for approximately 7 per cent of all meals. The weekly cost of the dietary was then reduced to reflect the saving for the food budget. The Association of London Authorities in 1994 carried out a survey which central government had refused to do itself and showed that over 50 per cent of children in the poorest boroughs in the capital are entitled to free school meals and 25 per cent of all London school children receive free meals. Just three years previous, in 1991, the latter figure was one in six. In the poorest areas now, free school meals are the rule rather than the exception. In Tower Hamlets in 1993, 59.1 per cent of primary and 64.9 per cent of secondary school children qualified for this poverty benefit. The respective figures for Hackney were 55.8 per cent and 56.1 per cent, followed closely by Southwark and Islington. Even in the outer London boroughs like Waltham Forest, eligibility and take up of free school meals has been increasing rapidly: in 1991, 18 per cent of children were getting free school meals; by 1993, this had risen dramatically to 49.2 per cent of primary and 35.9 per cent of secondary school children. (Brindle, 1 February 1994). The final cost of the 1992 minimum weekly dietary amounted to £35.26 for the family.

In constructing a minimum subsistence level, the study took account of the predictable criticisms which could be levelled at the research. There was concern that the calculations should not be misused and misinterpreted in similar ways to Rowntree's works. The formulation of a minimum budget standard for food has not been intended as an adequate or acceptable standard; it is meant to be a subsistence standard which conforms to government guidelines on healthy eating and below which, physical efficiency cannot be guaranteed. It has been constructed to challenge the oft-quoted excuse that primary food poverty is the result of mismanagement of an otherwise adequate income and the purchase of 'unhealthy' foodstuffs. The then Minister of Health, Edwina Currie, in 1989, stated rather frivolously and Northeners' health standards were so inferior because they consumed the wrong foodstuffs. Neither the content of the dietary or the minimum costings are meant to be prescriptive, but are presented as a heuristic device to expose the depth and nature of family poverty in Britain in the 1990s.

It should be restated that this diet does not allow for food wastage, all food bought and prepared must be eaten, otherwise all nutrients as recommended by government agencies will not be available to the family. The diet is constructed for one week only and solely for those meals specified, with no additions for extras from which a show of hospitality can be made to guests or visitors. There is nothing in stock for special occasions, neither is there sufficient quantities of food to be carried over from the previous week. The only left over items in stock would be flour and cooking oil. No money is kept back from the food budget to allow for children to purchase either the occasional bag of sweets; neither can they purchase foods from the school tuck shops. Any help received in the form of free school meals has been deducted from the weekly food budget. It is not therefore an adequate diet nor could it ever be described as a prescription for an acceptable standard. The diet cannot be criticised on the grounds of extravagance of content or price, but it can be criticised on the grounds that it is wholly inflexible and does not contain the type of meals which the vast majority of the population would like to have to consume on a regular basis.

The next part of the study involved determining how many families of this type were living below such a standard. The data available to Rowntree was more accessible than to this study which was forced to rely on government publications of low income data, which, the Introduction suggested, have been severely curtailed and made much more highly selective. Rowntree had access to information on incomes of all families in York; this type of data is not available for the city of Liverpool. However national data does exist as to the numbers of households below average income. Further information was obtained relating to the proportions of families with between one and four or more children contained within each quintile.

The 1992 primary poverty line for a family of four has been calculated at £1228.46 per week. Looking at the data, the second quintile median income is £129.00. Accepting that half of the families in this layer would be above this income and half below, it is safe to assume that **in the region of 30 per cent of all families with children are living below the minimum standard set by the Rowntree poverty line**. Although the poverty line drawn here has been constructed on the basis of subsistence needs for a family of man, woman and two children, it can be appropriately applied to all families with dependent children. Official statistics show that this type of family is the most common of all families with children. Furthermore, there are significantly more families with three or more children than there are those with only one child, with 22 per cent of one child families in the bottom quintile, as opposed to 44 per cent with three children or more. Similarly in the second quintile, there are 25 per cent of one child families, as opposed to 29 per cent of three or more children. Given that the greater the number of dependent children, the greater the risk of poverty, then the estimate of 30% of all families with children living in primary poverty is almost certainly a significant under estimated. When Rowntree established his three primary poverty lines, he found that: in 1899, 9.91 per cent of the population were living on income below this level; in 1941, this had dropped to 3.90 per cent; and by 1950, the primary poor represented a mere 1.66 per cent of the whole population. Whilst acknowledging that his findings and those of this study are not strictly comparable, a figure of 30 per cent of all families with two dependent children living in primary poverty in 1992 represents a gross increase in this type of deprivation in Britain in the 20th century.

Thew current Minister for Health, Virginia Bottomley (then a researcher for CPAG) agreed with Rowntree's message and rightfully concluded in the 1970s that: ' ... those on Supplementary Benefit have to make superhuman efforts to budget wisely in the face of increasing pressure on their incomes.' (cited in Cohen 1992, p. 3). The lifestyles of Britain's poor in the 1990s have been characterised by CPAG (Cohen 1992, pp. 11-12) in five main themes, all of which have been clarified and supported by the findings of this research exercise:

- how difficulties of budgeting on benefit often lead to material hardship -for example, people are regularly cutting back on basics like food and heating because they have inadequate income;
- ill health is prevalent and lack of money makes it difficult for people to cover health related expenses;
- despite wanting to change their situation, many people feel trapped and powerless to improve life for themselves and their families. This results in considerable emotional stress;
- lack of money often leads to exclusion from normal social activities, and this is felt to be particularly hard when it affects children;
- other factors apart from money affect the overall quality of life experienced by poor families - for example, inadequate housing and a lack

of social services also have an impact.

This book opened with a quotation relation the experiences of Scousers leaving their families in Merseyside to do'London's dirty work' and although the regionalist flavour of this story might have diminished somewhat as the recession bites deeper into the hear of affluent England, the skewing of the British economy in favour of the better-offs has continued to produce a widening gulf between earners in the prosperous South and those in the North of England, Scotland, Wales and the North of Ireland. The dual, parallel trends of the expansion of service industries in and around London and the de-industrialisation in the manufacturing heartlands have contributed to the traditional North-South divide and 'helped make Britain the most unequal society since records began more than a century ago'. (Hencke, Elliott & Kelly 1994). In the past 15 years, the income of the richest one per cent of earners in London and the South east has increased by three times the amount of similar high earners in Tyne & Wear. B ut the gap between the North and South was also reflected in the earnings of the bottom 50 per cent of the working population. The incomes in the South east doubled from £3,778 to £7,944, an increase of £4,166 whilst those in the North witnessed a rise from £3,243 to £6,866. The richest 20 per cent enjoyed 37 per cent of post tax income in 1979, rising to 44 per cent by 1992. The poorest 20 per cent took 9.5 per cent of the total in 1979, buy by 1992, that had fallen to 6.5 per cent. A major source of the widening of the gap between the rich and poor can be largely identified in the government's conscious attempts to increase the income differentials through the tax system. The more affluent have, predictably, been the main beneficiaries of income tax cuts with the top marginal rate of earned income reduced by 83 per cent in 1979 to 40 per cent in the mid 1990s.

In 1973, Jan Pen, an economist presented a simile which depicted income distribution in Britain. An individual's earned income was presented in height and he assumed that they would all walk past a fixed point in one hour, headed by the smallest and ending with the tallest. Pen carried out a study based on this model for the Institute for Fiscal Studies in 1988-89 and assumed that the average sized person would be five feet five inches tall and this would represent a weekly income level of £236. The IFS found that almost everyone who passed the post in the hour were 'shorties'. The smallest passed first and within two minutes, people are about two feet tall. At the half way stage - 30 minutes - they are 4 feet 8 inches and it is a full 37 minutes into the walk that a person of average height walks by. At only three minutes before the hour, those passing by would be eleven feet tall. Only in the last few seconds to the 'giants' appear. The most affluent person in Britain would probably be much higher than ten miles tall. (Hencke et al 1994)

Poverty is corrosive of citizenship. To be poor is to endure conditional citizenship. It appears a cruel irony that, whilst national concerns are directed

195

towards the issue of European citizenship, Britain holds millions of families whose social citizenship rights are grossly infringed upon the bare facts of a life of grinding poverty. The classic definition of the concept of social citizenship was laid open by T.H. Marshall (1952):

> Citizenship is a status bestowed on those who are full members of a community. All who possess the status are equal with respect to the rights and duties with which the status is endowed ... societies in which citizenship is a developing institution create an image of an ideal citizenship against which achievement can be measured and towards which aspirations can be directed ... By the social element I mean the whole range, from the right to a modicum of economic welfare and security to the right to share to the full in the social heritage and it live the life of a civilised being, according to the standard prevailing in society.

The emphasis on needs, as well as rights, acknowledges that everyone has basic needs and a requirement for 'a modicum of economic welfare and security' which, if not fulfilled, will disentitle them from their rights. These needs present at two fundamental levels: (a) to participate fully in social life with self respect and the respect of others; (b) the satisfaction of basic needs such as an adequate diet, proper clothing, a warm home, and various sundry necessities. It is this latter definition which #has been addressed and exposed as lacking by this research. It is however acknowledged that the former is, by far, a much more justice - and citizenship-based arena for discussion of the rights of the poor. But, in order to attempt to expose the gross depth of poverty and the extent of the denial of citizenship rights to the poor in Britain in the 1990s, the failure of society to provide even a bare, subsistence lifestyle for the poor is the kernel of this discussion. Poor people lack the resources to fulfil what is expected of them, not just as national citizens, in the community, at the workplace; but also in meeting the basic needs of subsistence.

The European Union (EU) recommends that member states establish minimum income levels:

> (a) to recognise the basic right of a person to sufficient resources and social assistance to live in a manner compatible with human dignity as part of a comprehensive and consistent drive to combat social exclusion, and to adapt their social protection systems, as necessary ... ;

> (b) to organise the implementation of this right according to the following practical guidelines:
> - fixing the amount of resources considered sufficient to cover essential needs with regard to respect for human dignity ... (cited in Veit Wilson 1994, pp. 4-7)

Elsewhere, the EU employs terms such as a standard of living 'worthy of a human being' the opportunity to 'appear in public without shame', the ability to 'take part in the life of the community'. The poor are 'persons whose resources (material, social and cultural) are so limited as to exclude them from the minimum acceptable way of life in the Member State in which they live'. Veit Wilson (1994, p. 7) sums up the EUs approach to a minimum, acceptable or decent lifestyle as: ' ... one which respects human worth and dignity and does not lead to people being ashamed or excluded'. The research findings in this exercise expose how far behind the EUs decency threshold the poor in Britain in the 1990s exist when it is considered that the minimum income estimates employed here took account of basic material requirements only. Little wonder that the Tory administration of the 1980s and 90s has rejected the concept of defining an adequate income at whatever level. And little wonder that, during the 1980s, Britain acquired one of the highest poverty levels in countries in the EU and was exceeded in comparative prosperity, not only by Germany, France, Denmark and the Benelux countries, but by Italy and some regions of Spain. m The European Commission issued figures on 24 February 1994 which showed that, in 1991

- on the one hand, wealth per capita in Britain was 98 per cent of the European average;
- on the other hand, 30 per cent of Britons lived in regions with only 90 per cent of the average. (Palmer, 25 January 1994)

The study showed that, in comparing per capita production in 1991 with 1980, for the very first time, three regions in Spain - Madrid, Navarre and the Balearic islands - were more prosperous than Britain. , Only four countries were poorer **OVERALL** - Greece, Portugal, Ireland and Spain. , Regionally, South Yorkshire and Merseyside, with only 77 per cent of the EU average, are, again, for the very first time, entitled to substantial regional assistance, with other poorest regions in the EU including the North east, Wales, the Scottish Highlands (78 per cent) and the North of Ireland (74 per cent). These data expose the validity of the late 1980s Italian claim of 'il sorpasso ' - that their economy had overtaken the UKs, a suggestion derided with indignant guffaws in Whitehall at the time. Palmer points out that the statistics might have presented an even more grim scenario for poverty in Britain had it not been for German reunification and the subsequent pulling down of the German indicators from 119 per cent in 1980 to 106 per cent in 1991. The most prosperous regions in the EU were: Hamburg (209 per cent); Isle de France (172 per cent); Lombardy (139 per cent); Brussels (170 per cent).

If an important element of social citizenship if the 'opportunities to make choices', (Dahrendorf 1976) these choices for the poor are absent when it comes to deciding what is for dinner, whether to turn the heating on or not, whether or not to buy a new pair of shoes for children etc. If freedom of choice is an important element of citizenship, then this research has demonstrated that poverty curtails such freedom. The freedom to eat as one wishes, to go where and when one likes, to pursue the leisure activities which others expect, all are denied to those without the money to afford them. According to Tyneside CPAG:

> The picture which emerges from this detailed study of family lives is one of constant restriction in almost every aspect of people's activities ... The lives of these families, and perhaps most seriously, the lives of the children in them, are marked by the unrelieved struggle to manage, with dreary diets and drab clothing. They also suffer what amounts to cultural imprisonment in their home in our society in which getting out with money to spend on recreation and leisure is normal at every other income level ... Clearly (their income) is not enough to allow ordinary families to share in conventional living standards. (Bradshaw & Holmes, 1990)

The decision of the government in 1993 to impose VAT on domestic fuel will undoubtedly have a greater impact on poor families because of the differential burdens which fuel bills represent. Ten per cent of the total weekly spending of the poorest quintile in the population is devoted to fuel, whilst for the richest fifth, it represents only three per cent. Hutton and Hardman (cited in Lennard, 1993 p. 6) predict that the poorest fifth of the population will use over 13 per cent of their total weekly spending on fuel by 1995, whilst the richest 20 per cent will increase the proportion of their weekly expenditure on fuel to less than five percent. The compensation package which the government announced in 1993 included the provision of the princely sums of 50p a week for a single retired person and 70p for a couple. However, in a Parliamentary answer on February 28th 1994, a Social Security Minister stated that: 'The rate of pension is reduced where basic pension entitlement is less than 100 per cent. This will have the effect of reducing the extra help in proportion to the percentage rate of basic pension entitlement.' (cited in Campaign Against Poverty Action Sheet 60, March 1994, p. 1). It is thus clear that this compensation package will only go to pensioners who receive the full basic retirement pension or who are on Income Support. There are over one million pensioners (11 per cent) who do not receive the full basic retirement pension whose average weekly pension is only 62 per cent of the full pension. Women who have pensions payable on their own contributions are particularly badly affected, with 29 per cent of them getting less than the full pension, and their average pension is only 58 per cent of the full pension. Figures were not given for the numbers of people on Income Support who are not in receipt of the full pension, but it is clear that there are many pensioners who will not receive the full 50p. to cover VAT on fuel (in itself, insultingly inadequate).

The scientific results of this research reinforce this picture and argue that poverty is even deeper than the anecdotal image offered by most poverty studies and give substance to the claim of Rowntree that scientific knowledge can be used to expose the 'inescapable' nature of poverty in Britain for many millions of families. It is concluded that poverty means the exclusion from the standards of living and the lifestyles, not just of one's fellow citizens, but also that deemed as the lowest upon which citizens in a civilised society should be expected to subsist. 'Properly understood, a poor citizen is a contradiction in terms.' (Vincent, 1991, p. 205)

Such poverty as exposed by the research findings in this chapter defies esoteric and official semantics and is best described as 'old-fashioned' and 'miserable' poverty. This chapter and this book has banished the myth that such a lifestyle is the result of mismanagement of household income which is, in every other respect, adequate. Yes, the poor in this sample smoked cigarettes, drank endless cups of tea and coffee and ate biscuits and cakes in order to dull their hunger pangs. Yes, the poor in this sample drank alcohol (occasionally) as a means of releasing tension, holding on to some semblance of social contact and escapism. Suffering from poor nutrition and wearing sub-standard clothing, yes they tried to keep warm by using wasteful heating appliances like electric bar fires. But are these practices vulnerable to change via lessons from well meaning domestic scientists? Lecturing the poor on the errors of their lifestyle in the 1990s is as ineffective and futile as it was in Victorian Britain when middle class philanthropists extolled the virtues of porridge and cod's head soup. The poor need, first and foremost, more money, a lot more money. George Orwell claimed in 'The Road to Wigan Pier' that 'If the unemployed learned to be better managers ... I fancy it would not be long before the dole was docked correspondingly.' (cited in Campbell, 1984, p. 9). Orwell demonstrated his belief here that poor relief's major function is not to relieve poverty; it is to perpetuate it, by punishing the poor and ensuring their readiness to accept employment at wage levels conducive to maximum profit for employers.

The lack of three meals a day, living in a cold, damp slum, not having shoes to put on children's feet, going to bed early in order to save fuel and to sleep off hunger pangs, being ashamed of one's clothing; all of these would be damning indictments of many 'Third World' countries or of Victorian/Edwardian Britain. That they are the day to day experiences of anything up to one third of families with children in Britain in the 1990s is a facet of the societal and economic arrangements which every citizen should be outraged at. The study of poverty in Britain has become 'feminised' and 'racialised' (as Chapter Four argued) - but it has also become 'Third Worldised' and 'Victorianised'. The term poverty cannot be, as central government would wish, dissolved into a semantic acid bath, nor diluted into a more precise, clinical, sterile form, as many academics would wish. Terms such as the lower class, the manual class, even the 'underclass', all overlap with this evil of poverty; but they relate to structures of classification or stratification and are thus not interchangeable with 'the poor'. More significantly, these terms lack the emotional appeal inherent in the use of the term poverty, which is perceived as being synonymous with the 'needy' who can morally and justifiably make a plea for help to the non-poor. Poverty demands assistance/support/action, it sets alight a flame of commiseration, it provokes a basic instinct to care for and protect and it makes a valid claim for the conversion of idealistic justice and altruism into progress aimed at its eradication. For these reasons, politicians and academics should not be allowed to render the term poverty extinct. Not that such an eventuality has any possibility of coming to bear, as long as millions of people in Britain confront the experience of grinding, humiliating, hopeless poverty every day of their lives. The following experiences (reproduced at length, with the kind permission of the *Guardian*) will not allow the 'human experience', as opposed to the academic or political concept, of poverty to disappear from the public debate:

> It is quiet in the graveyard ... The young undertaker steps out and pulls on his black leather gloves, the two officers from the Salvation Army slip their caps under their arms and look down at their feet, the nice woman from social services tuck her handbag into her side and all of them glance at the tiny wooden coffin, no bigger than a shoe box ... (they) go down the hill ... down to a little rectangle of lawn behind a hedge, the public plot for babies whose parents cannot afford their funeral ... There are very few mourners for the funeral of the unknown baby.

The body of a 7 pounds, 8 ounces, 22 inch long baby girl had been found by Salvation Army workers in a plastic bag in one of their charity bins just before Christmas 1993 in the West Midlands. Nick Davies (March 10th 1994) asks:

> Was it simply ignorance and fear, a young girl who concealed her pregnancy from everyone, even herself, and finally gave birth with nothing but confusion for company? Or had she encountered some overwhelming worry which had persuaded her to decide deliberately that she must let her baby go?

The death of the baby, named 'Sally-Ann', generated a whole quagmire of unanswered, unpleasant questions about:

> Mothers who have no money for their children; children who beg food from door to door; mothers who have no partners, no home that's worth the name, no help, no possible escape. And all of these different glimpses form part of one escapable image, of impoverished mothers shovelled over the brink by the pressure of daily life ... Sally-Ann has become a symbol for all the unknown children who have become victims of the new poverty.

While trying to picture the brief life history of Sally-Ann, Davies imagines that she might have been born in one of Birmingham's tower blocks 'where scores of young families are trapped 24 hours a day and where the only playground for the children is a corridor decorated with urine and graffiti'. (One in every 25 children in Britain today lives in a home officially condemned as unfit for human habitation). She might have been born in one of the estates where:

> Almost everyone is in debt. Some borrow from loan sharks who charge interest at 140 per cent and then come round and threaten to torch the house if they fall behind with their payments. Some steal, some smoke dope or drink, and a few dive off the tower blocks to escape. There was a man in Nechells who did that recently, who put a bag over his head before he jumped, as if he was so ashamed of everything that he wanted to die unrecognised.

Had Sally-Ann's mother been born and lived among Britain's poor:

> she would have known that one certain simple way to make life even worse would be to have a baby. There was a time when the great fat safety net of the welfare state used to reach out and catch women with babies, but the net has been cut to pieces. Free milk, free vitamins, free meals have been snatched from the hands of most children. Maternity grants and maternity allowances have been abolished.

Had Sally-Ann's mother been one of the employed population:

> she would have faced a financial disaster. At best she would have been given only £52.50 a week in Statutory Maternity Pay; at worst, she would have joined the thousands of working women who are now pushed through loopholes in the law because they have not held the same job for at least two years or because they do not earn enough to qualify. Where once the law protected her, she might well also have lost her job forever.

More probably, the unfortunate mother would not have been employed, in which case:

> she might have been able to beg a £100 maternity payment from the ruins of the welfare state - nowhere near enough for clothing and a cot and bedding and buggy and bottle and all the other props of motherhood ....
> It is there only for those who are poor and broke.

Five years ago, that accounted for one in five of all the children who were born in Britain. Now it accounts for one in three.

201

Wherever she lived:

> If she had trouble heating her home, she would simply have gone cold. Electricity and gas companies now routinely install meters in the homes of poor families: if they have no cash, they have no heat. In Birmingham alone, some 600 people die each year from winter hardship.

If Sally-Ann had lived, what quality of life might she have expected?

> On these estates, children die at twice the rate of their counterparts in the middle classes. Their diets are worse, they are shorter and lighter, their teeth are more rotten, they are more anaemic. The industrial economy which was built on the backs of their ancestors is being pulled down on top of them and there is little that the local authorities can do to protect them. Maybe Sally-Ann's mother looked at the wasteland around her and decided that, if all life was as meaningless as this, then there was no meaning to her child's life either ... It is as if she cared about the child enough to be sure that she wanted to save her from the life that oppressed her, and if she did feel like that, she would not be alone.

As Sally-Ann is being buried in the paupers' plot:

> all Birmingham is afloat on commerce. All the trades of dire necessity run through the streets like waste water, beggars selling smiles, old women working shifts in litter bins, men slaving over cider bottles, and single mothers who tried to buy a dream and could not afford it.

Experiences like this defy attempts to measure and define poverty away or to conceptualise into a clinical, paradigmatic matrix. Sally-Ann's mother would have an answer for John Major when he asked in Glasgow recently: 'Poverty! What Poverty?' or for the academics who argue that life on welfare benefits is too comfortable and that the economy requires cuts in poor relief payments to ensure a steady supply of workers who will labour for profit-maximising wages.

In order to eradicate the life experience of poverty it requires a major re-evaluation of society's values and perceptions. It is the wish of many citizens to believe that poverty can be tackled and eliminated in the absence of any substantial alterations to or diminution in their standard of living. As Donnison (1992) concludes:

> It took half a century for the idea of subsistence to replace earlier concepts of pauperism and destitution on which Victorian policies were founded. This time however, we may not be permitted so leisurely a learning period. The growth of disorder and violence in our poorer neighbourhoods may compel us to think harder and learn faster. (*The Guardian*, September 30th 1992)

Bibliography

Abbott, P. & Wallace, C. (1990), *An Introduction to Sociology: Feminist Perspectives*, Routledge, London.

Abel-Smith, B. & Townsend, P. (1965), 'The Poor and the Poorest', *Occasional Paper in Social Administration*, No.17, G. Bell & Son Ltd., London.

Alcock, P. (1987), *Poverty and State Support*, Longman, Harlow.

Admin, K. & Leech, K. (1988), 'A New "underclass": Race and Poverty in the Inner City' in *Poverty*, No.70, CPAG, London.

Amsden, A. (ed.), (1980), *The Economics of Women and Work*, Penguin, Harmondsworth.

Ashton, P. (1984), 'Poverty and its Beholders', *New Society* (18 October), London.

Baran, P. & Sweezy, P. (1966), 'Monopoly Capitalism', *Monthly Review Press*, New York.

Becker, S. (ed.), (1992), *Windows of Opportunity: Public Policy and the Poor*, CPAG, London.

Belleman, S. (1993), 'Let's Talk About Sex', *The Guardian*, 19 November.

Beveridge, W. (1942), 'Social Insurance and Allied Services', Cmnd. 6404, HMSO, London.

Blackburn, C. (1991), *Poverty and Health* Oxford Univ. Press.

Boardman, B. (1992), *Fuel Poverty*, Belhaven Press.

Booth, C. (1897), *Life and Labour of the People of London*, McMillan, London.

Bradshaw, J. (1986), 'Back to Budget Standards', *Paper to the Social Administration Conference*, University of York.

Bradshaw J. et al., (1987) 'Evaluating Adequacy: The Potential for Budget Standards' *Journal of Social Policy* Vol.16, No.2, pp.165-181.

Bradshaw, J. & Holmes, H. (1990), *Living on the Edge*, CPAG, London.
Bradshaw, J. & Millar, J. (1991), 'Lone Parent Families in the UK', *DSS Research Report*, No.6, HMSO, London.
Bridges, A. & Finegold, K. (1982), 'Paradigms, Politics and Policies' in Cottingham, C., *Race, Poverty and the Urban Underclass*, D.C. Heath, Lexington.
Brindle, D. (1994), 'Basic Benefits "Will Not Buy Children A Workhouse Diet"' *The Guardian*, 2 February.
Brindle, D. (1994), 'Poverty Highlighted by School Meals Survey', *The Guardian*, 1 February.
Brindle, D. (1993), 'Curb on Lone Parents Falls Foul of Facts', *The Guardian*, 9 November.
Briggs, A. (1961), Social Thought and Social Action, Greenwood, London.
Brown, C . (1984 *Black and White Britain: the Third PSI Study*, Gower, Aldershot.
Bruce, M. (1961), *The Coming of the Welfare State*, Batsford, London.
Bryson, L. (1992), *Welfare and the State*, MacMillan, London.
Buck, N. (1992), 'Labour Market Inactivity and Polarisation: A Household Perspective on the Idea of an Underclass' in Smith, D. (ed.), *Understanding the Underclass* PSI, London.
Campaign Against Poverty (1992-93-94), *Action Sheets*, No.45,54 & 60, Manchester.
Campbell, B. (1984), *Wigan Pier Revisited*, Virago Press, London.
Campbell, D. (2 January 1993), 'Criminal Age', *The Observer Magazine*, London.
Central Statistics Office (1992), 'Family Spending: A Report on the 1990 Family Expenditure Survey', *Government Statistical Service*, London.
Central Statistics Office (1992), *Social Trends*, No.22, HMSO, London.
Charles, N. & Kerr, M. (1988), *Women, Food and Families*, Manchester University Press.
Child Poverty Action Group 1993), Annual Report 1992-3, London.
Church of England (1985), 'Faith in the City', *Church House*.
Clark, K.D. (1965), *Dark Ghetto: Dilemmas of Social Power*, Harper & Row, New York.
Close, P. (1989), *Family Divisions and Inequalities in Modern Society*, Macmillan, London.
Coates, K. & Silburn, R. (1970), *Poverty: The Forgotten Englishman*, Penquin, Harmondsworth.
Cohen, R. (1991), *Just About Surviving: Debt and the Social Fund*, Family Service Units, Bradford.
Cohen, R. (1992), *Hardship Britain: Being Poor in the 1990s*, CPAG, London.

Cole-Hamilton, I. & Lang, T. (1986), 'Tightening Belts: A Report on the Impact of Poverty on Food', *London Food Commission*

Cooper, S. (1985), 'Observations in Supplementary Benefit Offices: The Reform of Supplementary Benefit Working Paper C', PSI, London.

Coote, A., Hardman, H. & Hewitt, P. (1990), *The Family Way*, Institute for Public Policy Research, London.

Cornford, J. (1992), 'Policy Issues and the Underclass Debate' in Smith, D *Understanding the Underclass*, PSI, London.

Cormack, R., Osborne, R., & Miller, R. (1983), *Religion, Education and Employment*, Appletree Press, Belfast.

Corrigan, P. (1980), *Capitalism, State Formation and Marxist Theory*, Quartet Books, Canada.

Cottingham, C. (1982), *Race, Poverty and the Urban Underclass*, D.C. Heath, Lexington.

Crawley, H. (1988), *Food Portion Sizes*, HMSO, London.

Cross, M. (1993), 'Generating the "New Poverty": A European Comparison', in Simpson, R. & Walker, R. (eds.), (1993), *Europe: For Richer, For Poorer*, CPAG, London.

Dahrendorf, R. (1976), *Inequality, Hope and Progress*, University of Liverpool Press

Dahrendorf, R. (1987), 'The Erosion of Citizenship and its Consequences for Us All', *in New Statesman*, 12 June, London.

Dahrendorf, R. (1992), 'Footnotes to the Discussion' in Smith, D. (ed.), *Understanding the Underclass*, PSI, London.

Daly, M. (1989), *Women and Poverty*, Attic Press, Dublin.

Davies, N. (1994), 'A Psalm for Sally-Ann', *The Guardian*, 10 March.

Dean, H. (1991), *Social Security and Social Control*, Routledge, London.

Delphy, C. (1984), *Close to Home: A Materialist Analysis of Women's Oppression*, Hutchinson, London.

Department of Employment (1990), *New Earnings Survey*, HMSO, London.

Department of Employment (April 1990), *Employment Gazette: Labour Force Survey*, HMSO, London.

Department of Health (1989), 'Dietary Sugars and Human Diseases', *Report on Health and Social Subjects No. 37*, HMSO, London.

Department of Health, Committee on Medical Aspects (COMA) (1991), 'Dietary Reference Values for Food, Energy and Nutrients for the UK', *Report on Health & Social Subjects No. 41*, HMSO, London.

Department of Health & Social Security (1975), *A Synopsis of Research Relevant to Determining the Adequacy of Supplementary Benefit Scale Rates*, Economic Advisors Office, HMS0, London.

Department of Health & Social Security, Committee on Medical Aspects (COMA) (1984), 'Diet and Cardiovascular Disease', *Report on Health & Social Subjects No. 28*, HMSO, London.

Department of Health & Social Security (1985), *Reform of Social Security, Vols 1 & 2*, Cmnd. 9512 & 9517, HMSO, London.

Department of Health & Social Security (1988), *Low Income Families 1985*, HMSO, London.

Department of Social Security (1990 & 1993), *Households Below Average Income 1988/9 and 1991/2: A Statistical Analysis*, HMSO, London.

Desai, M. (1986) 'Drawing the Poverty Line: On Defining the Poverty Threshold, in Golding P. (ed) *Excluding the Poor*, CPAG, London.

de Schweinitz, K. (1943) *England's Road to Social Security*, University of Pennsylvania, USA

Doeringer, P.B., (1980), 'Segmented Labour Markets' in Amsden, A. (ed) *Women and Work, pp. 211/231*, Penguin, Harmondsworth.

Doeringer, P.B. & Piore, M.J., (1971) *Internal Labour Markets and Manpower Analysis*, Lexington Books, USA

Donnison, D. (1980), 'For Whose Benefit? A Discussion with Ruth Lister' in *Community Care*.

Donnison, D. (1982), *The Politics of Poverty*, Martin Robertson, Oxford.

Ennals, S. (1991), 'The Social Fund' in *British Medical Journal*, vol. 302, 12 January.

Erlichman, J. (1994) 'Live in the 90s: TV Dinners & Servants for Some', *The Guardian*, 2 February.

Erlichman, J. (1994) 'Poor "Are the Least Likely to Worry about Nutrition"', *The Guardian*, February knead.

Fainstein, N. (1986), 'The Underclass Mismatch Hypothesis as an Explanation for Black Economic Exploitation', *Politics & Society*, Vol. 15 No. 4 pp. 403-451.

Family Budget Unit (1990), *Working Papers 1-13*, University of York.

Ferriman, A. (1993) 'More Sex in the Class, Please', *The Observer*, November knead.

Field, F (1988), in *The Guardian*, August knead, London.

Field, F (1989), *Losing Out: The Emergence of Britain's Underclass*, Grawel, Oxford.

Field, F. (1990), 'Britain's Underclass: Countering the Growth' in *Institute of Economic Affairs*, 'The Emerging British Underclass', London.

Fitzgerald, E. (1981), 'The Extent of Poverty in Ireland' in Kennedy, S., *One Million Poor*, Turoe Press, Dublin.

Freedman, R. (1961), *Marx on Economics*, Penguin, Harmondsworth.

Fuchs, V. (1967), 'Redefining Poverty and Redistributing Income', *Public Interest No. 8*.

Galbraith, J.K. (1958), *The Affluent Society,* Penguin, Harmondsworth.

Gans, H. (1990) 'Deconstructing the Underclass: The Term's Dangers as a Planning Concept', *American Planning Association Journal,* Summer, pp. 271/277.

George, V. (1968) *Social Security: Beveridge and After,* RKP, London.

George, V. & Howards, I. (1991) *Poverty Amidst Affluence,* Edward Elgar, Aldershot.

George, V. & Wilding, P. (1985), *Ideology and Social Welfare,* RKP, London.

Gifford, Lord QC., Brown, W. & Bundey, R. (1989) *Loosening the Shackles: First Report of the Liverpool 8 Inquiry into Race Relations in Liverpool,* Karia Press, London.

Gilbert, B.B. (1968) *British Social Policy 1914-1939,* Batsford, London.

Glendinning, C. (1987), 'Impoverishing Women' in Walker, A. & Walker, C. (eds) *The Growing Divide: A Social Audit 1979-1987,* CPAG, London.

Glendinning, C & Millar, J (1987 & 1922), *Women and Poverty in Britain,* London.

Glendinning, C. & Millar, J. (1989), *New Directions for Research on Women and Poverty: Exploring the Research and Policy Agenda,* Thomas Coram Research Unit, University of Warwick

Glendinning, C. & Millar, J (1991) 'Poverty: The Forgotten Englishwoman' in MacLean, M. & Groves, D. (eds), *Women's Issues in Social Policy,* Routledge, London.

Gordon, D. (1972), *Theories of Poverty and Underemployment,* Lexington Books, USA.

Gordon, P. & Newnham, A. (1985), *Passport to Benefits? Racism and Social Security,* CPAG, London.

Gordon, P. & Newnham, A (1986), *Different Worlds: Racism and Discrimination in Britain,* Runnymede Trust, London.

Gough, I. (1979), *The Political Economy of the Welfare State,* MacMillan, London.

Graham, H. (1984) *Women, Health and Family,* Wheatsheaf, Brighton.

Graham, H. (1987) 'Women's Poverty and Caring' in Glendinning, C & Millar, J., *Women and Poverty in Britain,* Wheatsheaf, London.

Graham, H. (1987) 'Being Poor: Perceptions and Coping Strategies of Lone Mothers' in Brannen, J. & Wilson, C. (eds), Give and Take in Families: Studies in Resource Distribution, Longman, London.

Green, D. (1992), 'Liberty, Poverty and the Underclass' in Smith, D. (ed), *Understanding the Underclass,* PSI, London.

Guardian (1993), 8 September, London.

Ghazi, P. & Gerard, L. (1993) 'Separation: Fiction and the Facts', *The Observer,* 11 July.

Haines, H. (1979) 'Cognitive Claims-making, Enclosure and the Depoliticisation of Social Problems' in *Sociological Quarterly*, Vol. 20, No. 1.

Hall, S., Critcher, C., Jefferson, T., Clark, T., & Roberts, B. (1978), *Policing the Crisis*, Macmillan, London.

Harrington, M (1962), *The Other America: Poverty in the US*, MacMillan, London.

Harrison, P. (1984), *Inside the Inner City*, Penguin, Harmondsworth.

Heath, A. (1992) 'The Attitudes of the Underclass' in Smith, D. (ed), *Understanding the Underclass*, PSI, London.

Hencke, D., Elliott, L & Kelly, R. (1994), 'Rich-Poor Divide Leads to Wide North-South Gap, *The Guardian*, 6 March.

Holman, P. (1978), *Poverty: Explanations of Social Deprivation*, Martin Robertson, London.

Holman, B. (1990), 'in Social Work Today', 16 August, Birmingham.

Holman, B. (1994), 'Shaken, Not Heard', *in the Guardian*, 12 January, London.

House of Commons (1979), Hansard, 6 November, HMSO, London.

House of Lords (1991), Hansard, 21 March, HMSO, London.

Howard, A. (1993), 'The Conservative Case for Compassion', *the Observer* 14 November.

Hugill, B. (1993), 'Hard Brits Geared Up for Tough Love',*the Observer*, 21 November.

James, O. (1993), 'Vicious Outcome of the Poverty Trap', *the Observer*, 23 May.

Johnson, P. & Webb, S. (1990), 'Poverty in Official Statistics: Two Reports', *Institute of Fiscal Studies*, London.

Jordan, B. (1989), *The Common Good: Citizenship, Morality and Self-Interest*, Blackwell, Oxford.

Joseph, K. (1972), 'The Cycle of Deprivation', speech given at conference organised by the Pre-School Playgroup Association, 29 June.

Joseph, K. & Sumption, J. (1979), *Equality*, John Murray, London.

Joshi, H. (1987), 'The Cost of Caring', in Glendinning, C. & Millar, J. *Women and Poverty in Britain*, Wheatsheaf, London.

Kincaid, J.C. (1973), *Poverty and Equality in Britain*, Penguin, Harmondsworth.

Kosa, J. & Zola, I.K. (1975), *Poverty and Health*, Harvard University Press, Mass.

Kumar, V. (1993), 'Poverty & Inequality in the UK: Effects on Children', *National Children's Bureau*, London.

Land, H. (1983), 'Poverty and Gender: the Distribution of Resources Within Families' in Brown, M. (ed.), *The Structure of Disadvantage*, Heinemann, London.

Land, H. & Rose, H. (1985), 'Compulsory Altruism for All or an Altruistic Society' in Bean, P., Ferris, J. & Whynes, D. (eds.), *In Defence of Welfare*, Tavistock, London.

Leather, S. (1992), 'By Bread Alone? Poverty and Diet in Britain Today' *MAFF Consumer Panel Secretariat*, January, London.

Leather, S. (1992), 'The politics of the Right and the wrong food', Paper given to LAYN Network *Day Food and Low Income Initiatives*, 2 October, London.

Le Fanu, J. (1994), 'A Phantom Carnage: The Myth That Low Income Kills', *Social Affairs Unit*, London.

Leifbried, S. & Ostner, I. (1991), 'The Particularism of West German Welfare Capitalism: the Case of Women's Social Security' in Adler, M., Bell, C., Clasen, J. & Sinfield, A., *The Sociology of Social Security*, Edinburgh University Press.

Lenin V.I. (1963), 'Collected Works' Vol.2, *Progress*, Moscow.

Lennard, L. (1993), 'Fuelling Poverty' in *Poverty 86*, Winter, CPAG.

Lewis, J. & Piachaud, D. (1987), 'Women and Poverty in the 20th Century' in Glendinning, C. & Millar, J., *Women and Poverty in Britain*, Wheatsheaf, London.

Lewis, O. (1965), *The Children of Sanchez*, Penguin, Harmondsworth.

Lister, R. (1979), 'The No Cost, No Benefit Review'. *Poverty Pamphlet*

Liverpool City Council, Corporate Policy & Information Unit (1989), 'The Liverpool Audit of Life Survey', Liverpool C.C.

Low Pay Unit (1988), 'The Poor Decade: Wage Inequalities in the 1980s', London.

Lynes, T. (1985), *Maintaining the Value of Benefits*, PSI, London.

McEvaddy, S. & Oppenheim, C. (1987), *Christmas on the Breadline*, CPAG, London.

Mack, J. & Lansley, S. (1985 & 1991), *Poor Britain*, Allen & Unwin, London.

MacGregor, S. (1988), 'The Pool tax and the Enterprise Culture', Centre for Local Economic Strategies, Manchester.

MacGregor, S. (1990), *Tackling the Inner Cities*, Clarendon Press, Oxford.

MacNicol, J. (1988), 'The Pursuit of the Underclass' in *Journal of Social Policy*, Vol.16, No.3, pp.293-318.

Mann, K. (1992), *The Making of the English 'Underclass'? The Social Divisions of Welfare and Labour*, OUP.

Marshall, T.H. (1952), *Citizenship and Social Class*, Cambridge University Press.

209

Marx, K. (1946), 'Wage-Labour and Capital' in *Selected Works*, Vol.1, Lawrence & Wishart, London.

Marx, K. (1967), 'Capital', Vol.1, 2nd edition, New World Publications, Moscow.

Marx, K. (1970), 'Capital', Vol.1, Lawrence & Wishart, London.

Marx, K. (1976), 'Capital' New Left Books/Penguin, London/ Harmondsworth.

Marx, K. & Engels, F. (1962), 'Selected Works', Vol.1, *Progress*, Moscow.

Matza, D. (1966), 'The Disreputable Poor' in Bendix, R. & Lipset S.M., *Class, Status and Power*, The Free Press, New York.

Mencher, S. (1967), *Poor Law to Poverty Programme*, University of Ppittsb urgh Press, USA.

Middleton, M. (1971), *When the Family Failed*, Gollancz, London.

Milburn, J., Clark, A. & Smith, F. (1987), 'Nae Bread', Health Education Department, Argyll & Clyde Health Board, Glasgow.

Millar, J. (1992), 'Lone Mothers and Poverty' in Glendinning, C. & Millar, J., *Women and Poverty In Britain*, Wheatsheaf, London.

Millar, J. & Glendinning, C. (1989) 'Gender and Poverty' in *Journal of Social Policy*, Vol.18, No.3, pp. 363-381.

Ministry of Agriculture, Food & Fisheries (1992), 'The Cost of Alternative Diets', in National Consumer Council, *Your Food: Whose choice?*, HMSO, London.

Morley, B. (1988), 'Women, Poverty and Social Work', in Becker, S. &

MacPerson, S., *Public Issues, Private Pain: Poverty, Social Work and Social Policy*, Social Services Insight Books, Nottingham.

Morris, L. (1994), *Dangerous Classes: The Underclass & Social Citizenship*, Routledge, London.

Mowart, C.L. (1961), *The Charity Organisation Society*, Methuen, London.

Murray, C. (1984), *Losing Ground: American Social Policy 1950-1980*, Basic Books, New York.

Murray, C. (1989), 'The Underclass: A Disaster in the Making', *the Sunday Times Magazine*. 26 November.

Murray, C. (1990), 'The Emerging Underclass', INT institute of Economic Affairs, London.

National Advisory Council on Nutritional Education (NANCE) (1983), 'A discussion Paper on Proposals for Nutritional Guidelines for Health Education in Britain', Health Education Council, London.

National Assistance Board (1965), 'An Examination of the Adult Scale Rates', HMSO, London.

National Association of Citizens Advice Bureaux (1984), 'Supplementary Benefit Review' *Evidence Paper*, London.

National Children's Home (1992), 'Deep in Debt', London.

National Food Survey Committee (1990), 'Household Food Consumption and Expenditure', Annual Report, HMSO, London.

Nevin, C. (1987), 'Scousers: Doing the South's Dirty Work' cited in Oppenheim (1990), *Poverty: the Facts*, CPAG, London.

Novak, T. (1984), *Poverty and Social Security*, Pluto Press, London.

Observer (1993), 23 May, 3 October, 14 November, London.

OECD (1976), 'Public Expenditure on Income Maintenance Programmes', Paris.

Oppenheim, C. (1990), *Poverty; the Facts*, CPAG, London.

Orshansky, M. (1969), 'How Poverty is Measured', *Monthly Labor Review*, Vol.92, No.2, New York.

Palmer, J. (1994), 'Britain Joins the Poor of the European Union', *the Guardian*, 25 January.

Radical Statistics Health Group (1991), 'Missing: A Strategy for Health', Vol.33, 3 August.

Reich, M. (1980), 'A Theory of Labour Market Segmentation' in Amsden, A. (ed.), *The Economics of Women and Work*, Penguin, Harmondsworth.

Rex, J. (1988), *The Ghetto and the Underclass: Essays on Race and Social Policy*, Avebury Press, Aldershot.

Robinson, F. & Gregson, N. (1992) 'The "Underclass": A Class Apart?' in *Critical Social Policy*, No.34, Summer.

Rodger, J. (1988), 'Social Work as Social Control Re-examined: Beyond the Dispersal of Discipline Thesis' *in Sociology*, Vol.22, No.4.

Rodger, J. (1992), 'The Welfare State and Social Closure: Social Division and the Underclass' *in Critical Social Policy*, No.35, Autumn.

Rose, M. (1972), *The Relief of Poverty*, MacMillan, London.

Rowntree, B.S. (1901), *Poverty: A Study of Town Life*, Thomas Nelson & Son Ltd., London.

Rowntree, B.S. (1937), *Human Needs of Labour*, Longman, Green & Co., London.

Rowntree, B.S. (1941), *Poverty and Progress*, Longman, London.

Rowntree, B.S. & Laver, R. (1951), *Poverty and the Welfare State*, Longman, London.

Runciman, W.G. (1990), 'How Many Classes are there in Contemporary British Society?', *in Sociology*, Vol.24, No.3, August.

Rushdie, S. (1982), 'The New Empire Within Britain', *New Society*, 9 December.

Rutter, M. & Madge, N. (1976), *Cycles of Deprivation*, Heinemann, London.

Seabrook, J. (1985), *Landscapes of Poverty*, Blackwell, Oxford.

Sen, A. (1979), 'Issues in the Measurement of Poverty', *in Scandinavian Journal of Economics*, Vol.2, pp.285-307.

Silburn, R. (1988), 'Definitions, Meanings and Experiences of Poverty: A Framework', in Becker, S. & MacPherson, S., *Public Issues, Private Pain*, Social Services Insight Books, Nottingham.

Simmons, M. (1993), 'Howard Targets Lone Mothers', *the Guardian*, 6 October.

Simpson, R. & Walker, R. (1993), *Europe: For Richer, For Poorer*, CPAG, London.

Skellington, R., Morris, P. & Gordon, P. (1992), *'Race' in Britain Today*, Sage, London.

Smith, D. (ed.), (1992), *Understanding the Underclass*, PSI, London.

Social Security Committee (1991), 'Low Income Statistics: Households Below Average Incomes: tables 1988', HMSO, London.

Spicker, P. (1993), *Poverty & Social Security: Concepts & Principles*, Routledge, London.

Spicker, P. (1993), 'The Underclass: Some Notes on Poverty & Exclusion', *paper to the Social Policy Association Annual Conference*, July, University of Liverpool.

Stitt, S. (1989), 'Supplementary Benefit: A Test of Adequacy by Disaggregation', *PhD. thesis, Department of Social Studies*, Queen's University, Belfast.

Stitt, S. (1991), 'Of Little Benefit', *Campaign Against Poverty*, Manchester.

Stitt, S. & Doherty, S. (1994), 'The 'Home Alone' Phenomenon: Mothers, Work & Poverty', *paper to the Social Policy Association Annual Conference*, July, University of Liverpool.

Stitt, S. & Grant, D. (1993), *Poverty: Rowntree Revisited*, Avebury, Aldershot.

Stitt, S., Griffiths, G. & Grant, D. (1994), 'Homeless & Hungry: the Evidence from Liverpool', *Nutrition & Health*, Spring.

Stitt, S. & McWilliams, M. (1986), 'A Life of Poverty: N. Ireland', *N.I. Poverty Lobby*, Belfast

Summer, W.G. (1883), *What Social Classes Owe to Each Other*, Harper & Bros., New York.

Supplementary Benefit Commission (1977), 'Low Incomes - Evidence from the SBC to the Royal Commission on the Distribution of Income and Wealth', *SBA paper 6*, HMSO, London.

Taylor-Gooby, P. & Dale, J. (1981), *Social Theory and Social Welfare*, Edward Arnold, London.

Thompson, E.P. (1968), *The Makings of the English Working Class*, Penguin, Harmondsworth.

Townsend, P. (1954), 'Measuring Poverty' *in British Journal of Sociology*, London.

Townsend, P. (1970), *The Concept of Poverty*, Heinemann, London.

Townsend, P. (1976), 'Areas Deprivation Policies', *New Statesman*, 6 August.

Townsend, P. (1979), *Poverty in the UK*, Penguin, Harmondsworth.

Townsend, P. (1985), 'Review of Poor Britain', *Poverty*, Vol.61, CPAG, London.

Townsend, P., Corrigan, P. & Kowarzik, U. (1987), 'Poverty and Labour in London', *Low Pay Unit*, London.

Townsend, P. (1987a), 'Poor Health', in Walker, A. & Walker, C. (eds.), *The Growing Divide A Social Audit 1979-87*, CPAG, London.

Townsend, P. (1987b) 'Paradigms of Poverty: A Comment', *in Journal of Social Policy*, Vol.15, No.4, pp.497-8.

Vaux, G. & Divine, D. (1988), 'Race & Poverty' in Becker, S. & MacPherson, S., *Public Issues, Private Pain*, Social Services Insight Books, Nottingham.

Veit Wilson, J. (1981), *New Society*, Vol.58, No.986, London.

Veit Wilson, J. (1985), *Supplementary Benefit: What is to be Done?* Monograph, Newcastle upon Tyne.

Veit Wilson, J. (1986), 'Paradigms of Poverty: A Rehabilitation of B.S. Rowntree' *in Journal of Social Policy*, Vol.15, No.1.

Veit Wilson, J. (1989a), 'The Concept of Minimum Income and the Basis of Social Security Scales' *ESRC Research Workshop on Social Security*, 14 July.

Veit Wilson, J. (1989), 'Minimum Income: Memorandum laid before the social Services Committee', *HOC paper 509*.

Veit Wilson, J. (1992), 'Condemned to Deprivation? Beveridge's Responsibility for the Invisibility of Poverty ', paper for the International Conference on *Social Security 50 Years After Beveridge*, University of York, September.

Veit Wilson, J. (1992), 'Muddle or Mendacity The Beveridge Committee & the Poverty Line', *Journal of Social Policy*, Vol.21, No.3, July, pp.269-301.

Veit Wilson, J. (1994), 'Drawing the Poverty Line: Social Justice, Poverty & Minimum Income Standards', *Submission to the Commission on Social Justice*.

Vincent, D. (1991) *Poor Citizens: The State & the Poor in the 20th Century*, Longman, London.

Walker, A. (1983), 'The Reform of the Supplementary Benefit Scheme' in Jones, C. & Stevenson, J., *Yearbook of Social Policy in Britain 1982*, RKP, London.

Walker, A., Winyard, S. & Pond, C. (1983), 'Conservative Economic Policy: The Social Consequences' in Bull, D. & Wilding, P. (eds/), *Thatcherism and the Poor*, CPAG, London.

213

Walker, R. (1990), 'Blaming the Victims' in Murray, C., *The Emerging Underclass*, IEA, London.

Walker, R. (1987), 'Consensual Approaches to the Definition of Poverty: Towards an Alternative Methodology' in *Journal of Social Policy*, Vol.16, No.2, pp.213-226.

Ward, S.(1977), *How Children Learn*, Sage, London.

Waterhouse, R. (1993) 'Cabinet File quashes Lone-Parent Stereotype', *the Independent*, 20 November.

Watts, H. (1987), 'New American Budget Standards: Report by the Expert Committee on Family Budget Revisions', *Institute for Research on Poverty*, University of Winsconsin, USA.

Wenlock, R.W., Buss, D.H. & Derry, B.J. (1986), 'Household Food Wastage in Britain' in *British Journal of Nutrition*, No.43, London.

Wilson, J.W. (1987), *The Truly Disadvantaged: The Inner City, the Underclass and Public Policy*, University of Chicago Press, USA.

Worsley, P. (1984), *The Three Worlds*, Wedenfeld & Nicholson, London.